Testing Deaf Students in an Age of Accountability

Testing Deaf Students in an Age of Accountability

Robert C. Johnson and Ross E. Mitchell, Editors

Gallaudet University Press Washington, DC

Gallaudet University Press
Washington, DC 20002

http://gupress.gallaudet.edu

Printed in the United States of America

Library of Congress Cataloging-in-Publication Data

Testing deaf students in an age of accountability /
Robert C. Johnson and Ross E. Mitchell, editors.
p. cm.
Includes bibliographical references and index.
ISBN 978-1-56368-392-3 (alk. paper)
1. Deaf children—Education—United States. 2. Deaf students—United States. 3. Educational tests and measurements—United States. 4. Educational equalization—United States. I. Johnson, Robert Clover. II. Mitchell, Ross E.
HV2545.T47 2008
371.91′2—dc22 2008028531

The paper used in this publication meets the minimum requirements of American National Standard for Information Sciences—Permanence of Paper for Printed Library Materials, ANSI Z39.48-1984.

To David S. Martin, Judith L. Mounty, and Michael A. Karchmer for their many contributions and leadership, without which the 2002 national conference on high-stakes testing at Gallaudet University, the foundation for this volume, would not have been possible.

Contents

Part Two: Case Studies from Selected States

Foreword

Joseph "Jay" Innes

The chapters in this book address one of the education profession's most complicated issues—how to conduct fair and equitable assessments of deaf students, particularly during the era of increased accountability mandated by the No Child Left Behind Act (NCLB). While the focus of the book is the assessment of deaf students, the issues raised and discussed are also applicable to other special populations. In essence, this is a book about achieving social justice by addressing educational policies, practices, and problems that have increasingly complicated the profession's ability to ensure fairness in testing and equality of opportunity—the latter a fundamental principle of the U.S. Constitution and a right afforded to every citizen.

Though the complications are longstanding and often intertwined with issues of language and communication access, NCLB has greatly increased the urgency of finding valid and reliable solutions. Several chapters in this volume note that the 1975 passage of what we now call the Individuals with Disabilities Education Act resulted in a historical shift from what was primarily a centralized delivery model, based in special, separate schools where expertise was clustered and organized, to a regional model in which services and expertise are dispersed across local jurisdictions, often in the hands of individuals with little or no experience working with deaf students. Provoked by the special demands placed on teachers of deaf students by statewide, standards-based assessment programs and the requirements of NCLB, a growing number of educators, assessment experts, and policymakers have become increasingly aware of the complex issues surrounding the assessment of these students. This volume includes a range of perspectives by a select group of such professionals. The chapters describe the many inherent difficulties associated with assessing deaf students' proficiency on a general curriculum, but they also suggest numerous possible solutions to those challenges.

It is easy enough to understand that assessment of an individual's ability must be consistent with his or her learning experiences and opportunities to master a curriculum. However, real and meaningful access for deaf students (and other students who have language and communication access issues) requires much more than placement in classrooms where the curriculum is being presented. If access to the curriculum, instruction, and classroom discourse is reduced because of language or communication issues—as is the case with many deaf children due to the provision of well-meaning but often inadequate accommodations—one must automatically ask if any related assessments are truly fair.

For years, a number of national organizations and prominent individuals, both within and outside the field of deaf education, have expressed concern, and even alarm, at the increased use of assessments—especially a single exit exam—in high-stakes decision making. The authors in this volume discuss these concerns and respond to them by emphasizing the importance of using appropriate and fair assessments based first on equitable access to the curriculum, and then by addressing the myriad issues encompassing high-stakes implications for the students. Tests and assessments conducted for such purposes often result in high-stakes consequences and have life-defining potential for the individual.

As a lifelong educator who believes that deaf children are fully capable of becoming productive citizens, if given an equal opportunity to succeed, I am elated to learn of the efforts underway and suggested in this volume to address the serious issues and obstacles described herein. High-stakes assessment programs will certainly continue to be controversial. However, as a number of the following chapter authors suggest and sometimes even state quite frankly, answers to many problems are available and waiting to be implemented. Other solutions, which may require more research and exploration, are suggested or hinted at. I thank these writers immensely for bringing these ideas and possibilities to the attention of those, like me, who are concerned with providing a fully accessible education to all deaf students.

Acknowledgments

We wish first to acknowledge the labor of Gallaudet Research Institute (GRI) personnel who, over a 40-year period, have analyzed achievement patterns of the deaf student population on various editions of the Stanford Achievement Test. Investigators in this work have included Peter Ries, Raymond Trybus, Michael Karchmer, Thomas Allen, Judith Holt, Carol Traxler, Brenda Rawlings, Ross Mitchell, Kevin Cole, Sue Hotto, Sen Qi, and others. We also wish to thank Scott Brown and Lisa Holden-Pitt of the Office of Special Education Programs and Jose Blackorby of SRI International for their support and encouragement that allowed Ross Mitchell to perform independent analyses of Woodcock-Johnson III assessment results in his chapter.

Deborah Witsken, a graduate of Gallaudet's school psychology program and the 2000–2001 recipient of the Walter Ross Graduate Fellowship at Gallaudet, gets credit for first directing GRI research editor Robert C. Johnson's attention to the unprecedented challenges posed to deaf students and their teachers by the growing accountability movement. We wish also to thank many individuals who subsequently helped during a period of orientation to the issues: Michael Karchmer, Donald Moores, and Carol LaSasso at Gallaudet University for sharing their concerns about potential threats to advancement, graduation, and postsecondary or employment options among deaf students; Jana Lollis, a teacher at the North Carolina School for the Deaf, Morganton, for providing her dissertation's review of literature on the history of the accountability movement; Oscar Cohen, Kevin Keane, and Adrianne Robins of the Lexington School for the Deaf in New York and Michael Bello, Patrick Costello, and Suzanne Recane of The Learning Center for Deaf Children in Massachusetts who provided tours of their schools and explained the school administrators' reasons for working with rather than fighting the rigorous demands being placed on deaf students and their teachers; and David Martin, Judith Mounty, and Carol Traxler for their leadership in fostering discussion and action on behalf of deaf children and deaf adults as leaders of the National Task Force on Equity in Testing Deaf and Hard of Hearing Individuals, headquartered for many years at Gallaudet University.

Special thanks are due to the many individuals who contacted us in response to an article by Johnson, "High Stakes Testing and Deaf Students: Some Research Perspectives," that appeared in the Spring/Summer 2001 issue of the newsletter *Research at Gallaudet*. One of those respondents, Jon Levy, principal of a regional deaf and hard of hearing program at University High School, Orange County, California (who is quoted in the afterword of this volume), later gave a joint presentation at Gallaudet's 2002 conference on high stakes testing and deaf students with Pat Moore (introduced to us by Levy), director of instruction at the California School for the Deaf, Fremont. Moore more recently provided the final chapter in this book. Another respondent, Stephanie Cawthon, informed us that she was conducting research on the impact of federal and state educational reform on schools serving deaf students. She has since visited Gallaudet, published in the *American Annals of the Deaf*, and is now the author of a chapter in this volume.

Although this book is not by any means the proceedings of a conference, the editors benefited in many ways from the national conference held at Gallaudet's Kellogg Conference Hotel on November 15–16, 2002, called "High Stakes Testing: Are Deaf and Hard of Hearing Children Being Left Behind?" Credit is due to David Martin and Judith Mounty for initiating and tirelessly pursuing the idea of organizing such a conference. Early planning meetings included Martin, Mounty, Robert C. Johnson, Robert Weinstock, Marilyn Farmer, Thomas Baldridge, Joseph "Jay" Innes, Nan Truitt (the 2001–2002 Walter Ross Graduate Fellowship holder), and Susan Medina. Once a date for the conference was established, a final organizing committee was developed with Michael Karchmer, director of the GRI, and Judith Mounty, director of Gallaudet's Center for ASL Literacy, acting as co-chairs. Of most relevance to this book was the work of the conference committee in identifying such presenters as Barbara Raimondo, Ross Mitchell, Betsy Case, Martha Thurlow, Jana Lollis, Michael Jones, Ed Bosso, Michael Bello, Patrick Costello, Suzanne Recane, and Pat Moore—all of whom later became authors or co-authors of chapters in this volume. We wish to thank Sera Stanis, the 2003 recipient of the Walter Ross Graduate Fellowship, for painstakingly transcribing all of the presentations from videotapes, creating files that later were sent to the above-named authors to use as needed in developing chapters for this volume.

After the conference, Karchmer, Johnson, and GRI research scientist Ross Mitchell decided that a planned, edited volume focused on problems associated with standards-based assessments of K–12 students was needed to fill in blanks and communicate needed content to a large readership. Once authors for the missing pieces were identified, the editors started working in earnest to encourage and help these authors complete their tasks. As work got underway on this project, David Martin and Judith Mounty edited and published through Gallaudet University Press a volume called *Assessing Deaf Adults: Critical Issues in Testing and Evaluation* (2005) on the related topic of certification testing of deaf professionals.

We want to thank the leaders and teachers in schools and programs for deaf students who expressed ongoing enthusiasm and encouragement to persist in this project, as well as sharing many insights that helped inform our efforts. These include Jamie Tucker and Chad Baker of the Maryland School for the Deaf, Ron Stern of the New Mexico School for the Deaf, and Claire Bugen at the Texas School for the Deaf.

Ross Mitchell wishes to acknowledge Neil Kingston, Marlon Kuntz, Ed Bosso, Joe Fischgrund, Jay Innes, Gerald Tindal, Michael Jones, Connie Nagy, Travas Young, Julie Hochgesang, and Sen Qi for many stimulating discussions about the benefits and challenges associated with the development of ASL-based assessments of academic achievement. Johnson and Mitchell together wish to thank

Suzanne Swaffield of the South Carolina Office of Assessment for directing our attention to Courtney Foster, with whom we discussed ASL and other visually accessible translations of assessments used to make testing fairer for deaf students in South Carolina. We are very grateful for Foster's contribution to this book.

Special thanks are due to Barbara Raimondo for her contributions to our introduction as well as the first chapter of the book. Her work as a liaison between the U.S. Department of Education and a special committee of GRI personnel and superintendents of schools for the deaf has helped us feel part of a much-needed ongoing dialogue between policymakers and educators of deaf students.

In addition to thanking all of our contributors for their enthusiasm, effort, and intellectual exchanges that made the project a pleasure, we wish to thank Joan Herman at UCLA and CRESST and Jamal Abedi at UC-Davis and CRESST for their collegial encouragement and confidence in the value of our project. We wish to thank Rachel Quenemoen, Sheryl Lazarus, Martha Thurlow, and Christopher Johnstone of The National Center on Educational Outcomes (NCEO) for their early and strong encouragement to develop this volume. We wish to thank Ken Olsen of Mid-South Regional Resource Center and the University of Kentucky for directing our attention to Elizabeth Towles-Reeves who later became one of our volume contributors.

Of course, we would not have completed this book without the talents and patience of our publisher, Gallaudet University Press. To John Van Cleve, Ivey Pittle Wallace, Deirdre Mullervy, and everyone else at the Press who helped to transform our manuscript into this volume, we offer our gratitude.

Finally, we wish to thank our spouses and others in our families for their tolerance of this long enterprise, which has included interference with an unencumbered retirement for Johnson and intrusions on the challenges of having a new baby in the family for Mitchell.

Introduction

Robert C. Johnson and Ross E. Mitchell

In the years since passage of the Elementary and Secondary Education Act in 1965 and the Education for All Handicapped Children Act in 1975, U.S. federal law has increasingly promoted the view that all children, including those in poverty, from minority populations, or with disabilities, have an inherent right to equal educational opportunity, as much as possible in regular school and classroom settings. Shortly after the beginning of the 21st century, those who were dissatisfied with the uneven results of this egalitarian effort prompted a reauthorization of the Elementary and Secondary Education Act, demanding that schools do everything possible to enable *all* children in every state—especially those who have historically been educated separately or in other ways marginalized—to attain "academic proficiency." The reauthorized law, known as the No Child Left Behind Act of 2001, which provides a narrow mandate and little funding, requires that states hold their public schools accountable for ensuring that all students either demonstrate proficiency on statewide assessments or make steady progress toward reaching that goal by 2014.

Although some students with disabilities are surely benefiting from this new inclusiveness and experiencing little difficulty proving their knowledge of a general curriculum on standardized tests, the overwhelming majority continue to have problems that have long presented serious challenges to educators. Teaching deaf students, for example, requires that teachers know how to communicate the curriculum through one or more of the following face-to-face modalities: American Sign Language (a complete language conveyed through movements of arms, fingers, facial expressions, and the body that has a grammar and syntax unrelated to English), some form of signing intended to represent English (Signed English, Signing Exact English, Seeing Essential English, etc.), or orally through spoken English (produced in a way intended to make words visually decipherable). Teachers must find ways to explain the vocabulary and grammar of written English to students who may never have heard a human voice speak the language. With students who use sign language, teachers must be able to understand the students' signed statements or questions. Many teachers in mainstream settings, of course, rely on interpreters to facilitate these interactions when deaf students are placed in their classes, but the resulting communication with these students, even with a highly qualified educational interpreter, is indirect and can be otherwise problematic.

Because the abilities to hear and produce spoken English remain elusive to varying degrees for many deaf individuals throughout their lives, finding the best way to teach deaf students to read and write printed English—usually learned as a phonological code of familiar speech patterns—is a subject of endless debate. The fact that most standardized assessments are presented in printed English, a code of *un*familiar speech patterns for most deaf students, helps explain the difficulties facing deaf students and their teachers in an age of accountability.

The challenges of deaf education, alien to the vast majority of students and teachers, used to occur exclusively in special schools for deaf students. In these schools, teachers and school administrators often measured academic success according to standards they believed to be fair and reasonable for this special population. Because most deaf students had (and still have) serious difficulties mastering reading and writing English, schools emphasized vocational training for all but a few academically successful students. Today, most American deaf students are learning in regular, local schools—more and more often in classrooms with hearing children, but frequently in special classes for deaf students as well. The academic proficiency of deaf students, whether in mainstream or special education settings, is increasingly measured by standards established by state departments of education for the general student population. Even in schools that exclusively serve deaf students, teachers are obliged to do their utmost to help these students learn the state's general curriculum well enough to demonstrate proficiency on standards-based assessments. In several states, deaf students who are not able to perform at this level are being denied a high school diploma upon graduation, jeopardizing their ability to get jobs or attend post-secondary programs (see Lollis, and Moore, this volume).

This book is the result of an effort to bring attention to the overwhelming challenge the accountability movement—now codified in federal law—has set before all schools serving deaf students. In light of the fact that students who are deaf, historically and on average, have performed far below grade level on standardized tests, the editors and contributors to this volume have been concerned for some time about an apparent mismatch between the idealism of the recent laws and the complex realities involved in teaching and testing this population. Our goal in this volume, therefore, has been to assemble a range of perspectives on the intent and flexibility (or inflexibility) of federal law, on achievement data regarding deaf students, on accommodations and universal design as ways of making tests more accessible, on alternate assessments for deaf students deemed unready for regular assessments, on the varying degrees of cooperation or conflict between schools for deaf students and state departments of education, and on the day-to-day efforts of teachers and school administrators to help these students measure up—one way or another—to the new standards. Our hope is that by putting these varying discussions into one book, it will be easier for all concerned to contemplate how a constructive synthesis of worthy ideals, hard realities, and pragmatic solutions can be achieved.

Apart from assessment issues, we are also concerned that as federal legislation seeks to emphasize the importance of uniform academic standards for all students in every state, some experiences important to young deaf people that have historically been linked with deaf education—such as mastering sign language, forming ties with other deaf people, and developing an identity as a culturally deaf person—may be increasingly treated as unimportant. In our view, this would be a serious loss. It is our belief, in fact, that before the daunting scale of today's inclusion-oriented challenges for deaf students can be properly understood, the extraordinary history of deaf education in America—a history resulting from the unique communication challenges presented by deaf students combined with the determination of thousands of pioneers in finding ways to educate those students—must be better appreciated.

DEAF EDUCATION IN AMERICA

Imagine having a child and not knowing how to communicate with her. Imagine that, as far as you know, no education system in which she can be effectively taught exists anywhere in your country. Imagine your child not having any way of conversing with other children or of sharing a normal childhood with them. This was the situation that Alice Cogswell's family in Hartford, Connecticut, faced in the early part of the 19th century.[1]

Alice was deafened by meningitis at age 2, and her family struggled with how to reach her and help her learn. When she was 9, her father, Dr. Mason Fitch Cogswell, a pioneering surgeon and a man of means and determination, convinced their neighbor Thomas Hopkins Gallaudet, a Yale graduate who had trained to become a Congregational minister, to travel to Europe in search of a well-developed, proven way to communicate with and teach deaf children. Americans were most aware of two European approaches at the time—the oral Braidwood method used in an exclusive private school for deaf students in England and the methodized signing used at the *Institution des Sourds et Muets* in Paris (henceforth the Paris Institute), which freely served deaf children of poor parents in France. Gallaudet, who visited both schools, ultimately chose the public-domain French option over the proprietary Braidwood method.

Gallaudet returned to the United States in the spring of 1816, accompanied by Laurent Clerc, a brilliant deaf graduate of the Paris Institute. Cogswell, Gallaudet, and Clerc worked with others to obtain a charter from the state of Connecticut to open a school for deaf children in Hartford. As a result, the first publicly sponsored school for deaf children in the United States, now known as the American School for the Deaf, opened in 1817. There, with Alice Cogswell among its first pupils, Clerc and Gallaudet worked together to develop a program and practices based on the signing or "manual" method that became the first enduring model of deaf education in America.

During the remainder of the 19th century and well into the 20th, residential and day schools that exclusively served deaf students—many patterned after the American School for the Deaf—proliferated across the United States. Because the incidence of deafness is relatively rare (affecting roughly 1 out of 1,000 children), deaf children across an entire state were often brought together at a single institu-

1. The editors wish to thank Barbara Raimondo for contributing much of this section.

tion. Trained teachers, house parents, and other staff members could be efficiently assembled at such schools, thus creating a visually accessible learning environment that could not be provided by most of the children's families or local schools throughout the states. In *A Place of Their Own: Creating the Deaf Community in America,* Van Cleve and Crouch (1989) suggest that such "tax-supported special educational institutions freed families from the terrible dilemmas that had confronted the Cogswells and [other parents]. Now, the bewildered parents of deaf children could be assured that their offspring would receive skilled instruction on this side of the Atlantic, and at relatively low cost" (p. 47).

Although education in the United States has always been, and continues to be, primarily the responsibility of states, the federal government has on many occasions played a significant role in determining how education is provided. Passage of the Morrill Land-Grant Colleges Act in 1862 was one such development. This law allocated federal funds for purchasing land on which colleges could be built in every state that was still part of the union. These land grant colleges promised to make college educations available to a much broader range of students. This spirit of creating more inclusive educational opportunities may well have played a role in the federal funding, beginning in 1857, of the Columbia Institution for the Deaf and Dumb (henceforth, the Columbia Institution for the Deaf) and approval in 1864 of the establishment and funding of a college-level program for granting bachelor degrees to deaf students (Gallaudet, 1983). When Lincoln signed the charter approving the development of a federally supported college serving deaf undergraduates in Washington, D.C., America became the first nation in the world that offered elementary, secondary, and college-level educational programs exclusively for deaf students.

Communication Issues

Until the mid-1970s, residential and day schools for deaf children were widely accepted as an excellent solution to the instructional challenges that these students presented. Schools for the deaf trained teachers in the communication method considered most effective or valuable within their program to compensate for the lack of formal instruction and experience in deaf education among applicants. To this day, it is rare for a subject-area specialist certified to teach the general student population to also have the special capabilities required to teach deaf children. Consequently, when deaf students are placed in mainstream settings, skilled educational interpreters play a critical role. Unfortunately, there is no consensus among schools and programs on how best to handle the communication issues presented by students who cannot hear. Given that effective communication plays such a vital role in education, an overview of the history of communication practices and disputes in the years since Gallaudet brought Laurent Clerc to America deserves attention here.

Although the manual communication method and philosophy that Gallaudet and Clerc imported to the United States from France[2] led to practices that were

2. The imported method and philosophy were first developed in the 18th century by the Abbé de l'Epée, founder of the Paris Institute.

widely adopted nationwide, disagreements about aspects of those practices have existed ever since. As early as the 1830s, some argued that teachers of deaf students should present signs in English word order as they spoke, thus at least referencing the language of common discourse. Others, more concerned with imparting information engagingly and efficiently, favored a more natural form of signing that followed its own rules and did not overburden itself with visual references to spoken English. Some believed that fingerspelling should be used as much as possible to create a direct connection between face-to-face communication and reading and writing, whereas others argued about the wearying concentration required and the slowness that resulted from excessive use of fingerspelling.

Those debates, however, were mild compared with disputes between educators who favored some form of manual communication and advocates of a pure oral approach. For much of the 19th century in America (roughly from 1817 to the 1880s), students who were taught in manual communication programs were learning the basics of reading, writing, and arithmetic, plus practical knowledge helpful for obtaining jobs with employers willing to learn signs, demonstrate skills visually, or write on slates to communicate with workers who could not hear or speak (Buchanan, 1999).[3] But as early as the 1840s, educational reformer Horace Mann and others, influenced by German oralists, expressed the view that it was wrong to assume that speech and effective speechreading were beyond the reach of deaf children. Mann felt that American educators of deaf students were depriving these students of skills that would help them find a wider range of jobs and fit in better with the rest of society.

In the 1860s, oralists succeeded in establishing the Clarke School for the Deaf in Massachusetts and the New York Institution for the Improved Instruction of Deaf Mutes (which later became the Lexington School for the Deaf), both of which were in competition with existing schools that used the manual method. In 1868, Edward Miner Gallaudet, son of Thomas Hopkins Gallaudet and president of the Columbia Institution for the Deaf (which later became Gallaudet College), presented a paper to superintendents of schools for the deaf, advocating a "combined method" in which students would continue to be taught in sign language but would also be given a substantial amount of instruction in articulation and speechreading. Having visited oral programs in Europe where he discovered that the approach was often successful, Gallaudet made this concession partly to head off inevitable oralist criticisms of American schools for the deaf, thereby, he hoped, preserving the use of sign language in those schools (Van Cleve, 1987).

In 1880, at the Congress of Milan, an international meeting of mostly hearing European and American educators, there was a public exhibition of deaf Italians who presumably had learned to read lips (speechread) and speak. Their demonstrations were accepted by most in attendance as evidence that deaf people can learn to understand and produce spoken language. All but one of the European

---

3. A widely circulated periodical produced by deaf people, which began in 1888 and continues to this day, is called *The Silent Worker.*

attendees voted in favor of a resolution to the effect that deaf education programs in the represented countries (seven European countries plus the United States) should henceforth concentrate on training deaf students to read lips and to speak the national languages of their respective countries. American attendees, including Edward Miner Gallaudet and one deaf delegate, opposed the resolution and voted in favor of the combined method. In spite of their dissent, the destiny of the majority of American deaf students for the next 90 years was largely determined by the influence of oralists.

As a consequence of this major international political victory, between the 1880s and the early 20th century, Alexander Graham Bell and other like-minded individuals successfully transformed deaf education in America, converting most schools for the deaf into oral schools and eliminating deaf teachers, who were seen as inadequate models of speech. Edward Miner Gallaudet retained the combined method at the Columbia Institution for the Deaf, as did the superintendents at some other schools for deaf students. Nevertheless, oralism became the dominant teaching philosophy nationwide at least until the late 1960s. During that time, deaf students were taught to concentrate on and recognize English words in the lip movements of hearing speakers. But so many aspects of pronunciation *look* virtually the same—even though hearing people can easily *hear* the differences—that speechreading of ordinary speakers in casual circumstances has always required a large amount of guesswork. Cued Speech, invented by Dr. Orin Cornett at Gallaudet College in 1966, is a method that helps resolve the ambiguity of lip movements but requires a trained cuer to be effective (Henegar & Cornett, 1971).

Deaf students in oral programs devoted much of their class time to speech instruction, with very uneven results. Although students were often punished for signing to one another, the decades in which sign language was forbidden provoked an underground devotion to its use among deaf students in residential schools. Typically, older deaf children or the deaf children who had deaf parents taught sign language to other children in dormitories, on playgrounds, and during weekends. The resulting friendships developed into lifelong social networks, known collectively as the "deaf community."

Nevertheless, an undeterred oralist philosophy dominated deaf education programs nationwide until the late 1960s when widespread dissatisfaction with the educational results of this approach and a feeling that the elimination of sign language from deaf education had been too severe prompted the birth of a new philosophy called "Total Communication." At first, fingerspelling was allowed into some programs; then school after school began to allow signs to be presented as a visual augmentation of speechreading, a practice now described by linguists as "Sign Supported Speech" (Johnson, Liddell, & Erting, 1989).

As Total Communication took hold, various groups of educators, including deaf and hearing individuals, decided to find ways to alter sign language in an effort to make it represent English visually. In addition to efforts such as Signed English, intended primarily to help hearing parents learn and use simple signs as they spoke or read to their deaf children, Linguistics of Visual English (LOVE), Seeing

Essential English (SEE I), and Signing Exact English (SEE II) were developed as serious efforts to represent through signing all aspects of spoken English, including signs invented to represent articles, prefixes, suffixes, and verbs such as *to be* that had no signing counterpart. Many signs were "initialized" with fingerspelled first letters to link the sign more clearly to an English word.

Beginning in the late 1950s, a full decade before Total Communication was born, William C. Stokoe, an English professor at Gallaudet University, began to film and analyze sign language as members of the American deaf community naturally produced it among themselves. Stokoe's groundbreaking *Sign Language Structure* in 1960 and *A Dictionary of American Sign Language on Linguistic Principles* (with Casterline and Croneberg) in 1965 challenged the prevailing view that sign language was a crude form of communication, arguing that it should be seen as an independent language—American Sign Language (ASL)—with a sophisticated structure capable of transmitting complex ideas.

Efforts by linguists, sociolinguists, and Gallaudet's National Center for Law and the Deaf began as early as 1978 to have ASL accepted as a first language for deaf students (Woodward, 1978). These advocates argued that ASL could be used in deaf education programs with the support of the Bilingual Education Act of 1978. Although the U.S. Department of Education did not accept this view, then or subsequently, several programs in various states began to use ASL in the 1990s on their own initiative, justifying this use on the grounds that ASL functions as an efficient, easily grasped medium for teaching deaf students in through-the-air instruction and discussion. Many linguists and educators continue to argue that ASL ideally serves as a first language for deaf students through which English as a second language to be used for reading and writing may be taught visually.

Today, deaf education is conducted in all of the ways just described. Oralism is still the governing philosophy of many programs, sometimes more or less by accident in mainstream programs and sometimes with the augmentation of cues in programs using Cued Speech[4] or a more recent innovation called Visual Phonics (Friedman Narr, 2006). Some bilingual programs use ASL for most instruction and discussion but use blackboards, computers, workbooks, and associated techniques such as "chaining" (signs and words with like meanings presented in rapid succession) to increase deaf students' grasp of English. A few bilingual programs use ASL for teaching some subjects and Cued English for others—a fascinating variation on Edward Miner Gallaudet's combined method. Many programs continue to use Signed English or SEE II or some less formalized system of Total Communication.

As a result, controversy still exists concerning optimal communication methods for teaching deaf children. The search for solutions to these issues has been complicated by the fact that the majority of American deaf children are no longer taught in separate, special schools where communication practices can be ex-

---

4. The method is often called Cued English when referring specifically to its use in association with that language, as is generally the case when used in schools serving deaf children in the United States.

pected to be somewhat consistent from class to class. Today, parents, teachers, and school administrators must seriously consider a deaf child's communication needs and background when making placement and accommodation decisions. The same needs and background must be carefully considered when the child is required to take a statewide test. A deaf child's access to both the curriculum and test materials cannot be taken for granted until—at a bare minimum—the communication needs of the individual child are satisfactorily met.

Joining the Mainstream

In 1975, Congress passed the Education for All Handicapped Children Act, later reauthorized as the Individuals With Disabilities Education Act in 1990. This law, in all its reauthorizations, has endeavored to find workable ways to allow children with disabilities, including deaf children, to attend regular local schools. The last three reauthorizations have made explicit the expectation that students with disabilities learn the general curriculum of their state to the extent possible. This legislation was largely a result of a successful effort by parent advocates for children with cognitive disabilities—especially those labeled as "educable mentally retarded"—who argued in district court cases (see Raimondo, this volume) that these children, often institutionalized and deprived of appropriate intellectual challenges, deserved to benefit from a general curriculum and should be admitted as much as seemed beneficial into mainstream settings (Moores, 2001, p. 19). For reasons related to communication issues already discussed in this introduction, there is much less evidence that parents of deaf children felt similar discontent with separate, special programs for children who are deaf. Nevertheless, various factors seemed to conspire to make the mainstreaming of most deaf children inevitable.

For one thing, the Civil Rights movement in America had raised questions about discrimination, disparate resources, low expectations, and benevolent paternalism associated with so-called "separate but equal" educational systems for minority populations. Although teaching deaf children required communication skills unknown by most teachers in regular schools, it was difficult to dispute that an unknown number of bright deaf students, frustrated by the pace of education in schools for the deaf, might be able to succeed in mainstream settings with the help of appropriate accommodations. Placing deaf students in special schools, in other words, was not necessarily the best solution for *all* deaf children. A range of placement options needed to be available, and Individualized Education Programs (IEPs), developed with the input of key people in a child's life, needed to be the basis for deciding where in this range a deaf child should be positioned.

The emphasis of the Individuals With Disabilities Education Act has historically been less on guaranteeing that disabled children meet the same achievement goals as other students than on ensuring that they are included and taught in whatever placement seems most likely to help children advance from grade to grade with their nondisabled peers (see Raimondo, this volume). Recent reauthorizations of this law, however, have increasingly emphasized the importance of achievement testing as a means of assessing the success of these placements. This change became strikingly clear in the 1997 reauthorization of the Individuals With Disabilities Education Act, which required that all disabled children must participate in statewide assessments. The 2004 reauthorization included many provisions related to the assessment of children with disabilities, largely to conform with the No Child Left Behind Act of 2001, which itself was a reauthorization of the Elementary and Secondary Education Act of 1965.

The Elementary and Secondary Education Act was the first federal act designed to provide financial support and guidelines directed at ensuring that "all" American children would get satisfactory elementary and high school educations. Part of President Lyndon Johnson's "War on Poverty," the law was particularly focused on enabling children with low socioeconomic backgrounds to get the help they needed to get good educations. Naturally, the emphasis on the word *all* also carried implications for children with other disadvantages.

The No Child Left Behind Act was so named to emphasize that schools not only were being *urged* to provide quality education to all students (including deaf students) but also were, in fact, being held *accountable* for doing so. Because the two federal laws (Individuals With Disabilities Education Act and No Child Left Behind) have deliberately extended their reach to embrace all children in the United States, deaf education—previously the exclusive province of state-run or privately operated, separate, special schools—has become part of a system in which the academic achievement levels of deaf students are increasingly measured by the same tests and standards applied to all other children. The rigorousness of what are considered acceptable achievement levels varies considerably from state to state, but in recent years, it has generally gotten higher nationwide.

Opportunity to Learn

The concept of *opportunity to learn,* as the term is used in No Child Left Behind, refers to the obligation of schools and teachers to make every reasonable effort to provide whatever form of instruction is needed to ensure that all students learn the material in which they are expected to become proficient. Teachers must determine the optimal mode of communication, pace of instruction, and method of demonstration needed by each child to learn the required material. To ensure that all students in a class will be ready for end-of-year assessments, teachers should do more than simply present the concepts and information contained in the state curriculum for the students' grade level. Ideally, they would also devote as much time as necessary to reviewing material and developing learning exercises that can deepen the students' grasp of the concepts being taught.

Because the emphasis in No Child Left Behind is on providing *equitable* opportunities to learn, the school should not give up on a child who is disadvantaged, difficult to motivate, or disabled. If an accommodation is needed to boost a child's achievement level and—importantly—if the child's achievement level is not yet proficient, then reasonable efforts should be made to provide the accommodation. Partly as a legacy of the Supreme Court decision in *Hendrick Hudson School District v. Rowley* in 1982, these "shoulds" do not amount to actual requirements in No Child Left Behind. With that ruling, a majority of Supreme Court justices decided that the federal government must not overstep a state's decisions concerning what must be done to provide educational opportunities for students who, in spite of a disability, are academically proficient. Nevertheless, the law does state that failure to enable students either to achieve proficiency or to make "adequate yearly progress" toward that goal can result in "serious adverse consequences" for teachers or school administrators. Jay Heubert and other experts in educational law have gone so far as to describe the high stakes assessment of students who have *not* had adequate opportunity to learn as "immoral" (Heubert, 2001).

As will become clear from reading the many chapters in this volume by specialists in deaf education, those who are familiar with the day-to-day challenges involved in preparing deaf students for statewide assessments tend to be doubtful that even "*equitable* opportunities to learn" required by No Child Left Behind will necessarily result in an *equal* opportunity to learn a state curriculum. For instance, when it comes to educational interpreting as a means for achieving equitable learning opportunities, the capabilities of interpreters vary and the information received is not necessarily equivalent to what the teacher is saying. An interpreter may not always be present or may not know the form of signing that is most familiar to the deaf student (Winston, 1994, pp. 55–62). For a variety of reasons, deaf students in mainstream settings are often reluctant to interrupt the teacher if they have difficulty understanding. Also, if there is no follow-up linking the signed information with material in the English text, then the student may have difficulty associating what was learned by means of an interpreter with a printed question on a state assessment form.

Because test designers generally assume that students taking statewide assessments already have a substantial English vocabulary by the third grade and are quite familiar with common English usage, teachers of deaf students must work extra hard not only to provide information about subject matter (social studies, mathematics, etc.) in a visually accessible modality but also to take steps to fill the gaps in deaf students' grasp of written English. Teachers in bilingual ASL–English programs use various strategies to create links between sign language and written English presentations of the same information, sometimes conducting face-to-face class discussions in ASL and then continuing the discussions in English on connected computers. During discussion of a subject or concept in ASL, teachers may write English words on the blackboard, present an ASL sign that has similar meaning, and fingerspell the English word, thus building awareness of English vocabulary. Teachers may help students analyze the structure of an ASL sentence, then show the students on the blackboard how the same sentence could be translated into English, thereby building metalinguistic awareness.

This monumental but necessary effort may require more time than is realistically available in a normal school year. The desire to unify visual and English communication, using Signed English, SEE I or II, Cued Speech, or a pure oral approach, is understandable in the context of current pressures. It must be kept in mind, however, that a history of unresolved disagreement exists concerning the effectiveness or ineffectiveness, advantages and disadvantages of each of these approaches. Given the fact that communication continues to present problems for deaf students, even in this age of accountability, it is understandable that many parents today choose to have cochlear implants surgically placed in their deaf children in the hope that this technology will provide a viable level of hearing. Some children, if the surgery and follow-up are successful, may indeed escape many of the difficulties just described, though they may face other difficulties outside the scope of this book. Whatever approach is used, of course, needs to be well-researched and chosen with great care.

It should be added that although many parents of deaf children go to great lengths to learn about the options they should explore, and though these parents often strive to learn and use some form of sign language with their preschool-aged deaf children, many others, for a variety of reasons, fail to learn how to communicate effectively with their deaf children. As a result, some children enter first grade or are transferred to a special program at a later age with too little language capability to be ready for anything approaching grade-level instruction (see Bosso, this volume). The consequences of such language delays are usually difficult for an individual teacher to overcome during the time such a child is in his or her class. Moore (this volume) goes so far as to say that parents of newly diagnosed deaf children should be required by law to learn and use sign language with their children. Her point, of course, is that a deaf child's preschool years should be seen as among the child's most important opportunities to learn. Parents must be among the child's first teachers, and in fairness to the child and to the child's teachers in school, parents should share in the accountability for these children's educations.

However discouraging the process sometimes may be, honest efforts to create equitable opportunities for deaf students to learn must be pursued not only because they are required by current federal law but also because these efforts collectively may indeed raise the level of deaf students' knowledge of a general curriculum.

KNOWING WHAT DEAF STUDENTS KNOW

Over November 15–16, 2002, a national conference called "High Stakes Testing: Are Deaf and Hard of Hearing Students Being Left Behind?" was held in Gallaudet University's Kellogg Conference Center. I. King Jordan, who had become Gallaudet's first deaf president in 1988, acknowledged in his welcoming remarks that many deaf students were indeed being "left behind" as a result of statewide testing. This answer to the conference title's rhetorical question was reinforced later in the conference by Pat Moore (this volume), who discussed the difficulties deaf students will have seeking employment as more and more states begin to withhold diplomas from students who do not pass high school exit exams.

The information imparted at the conference that seemed to support a pessimistic view of deaf students' prospects on statewide assessments consisted of Stanford Achievement Test data on the academic capabilities of deaf students analyzed over a four-decade period by researchers in the Gallaudet Research Institute (see Mitchell, this volume). In essence, the data showed that deaf 18-year-olds, historically and on average, perform at slightly below a fourth-grade level in reading comprehension and roughly at a sixth-grade level in mathematics. These areas of learning involve skills so fundamental to academic performance that No Child Left Behind and most states emphasize the importance of reading and math proficiency in statewide assessments. Betsy Case (this volume), who at the time of the conference worked for Harcourt Assessment, which continues to develop and market the Stanford tests, described the deaf student population as facing *"extra, extra* challenges passing high stakes tests."

What fascinates us is that, in spite of Stanford achievement data, No Child Left Behind does not exclude deaf students from the requirement that schools raise the test scores of *all* students to proficient levels by 2014. Even teachers of deaf students who complain that it is unreasonable to expect these students to perform so well so soon, if at all, must acknowledge that the insistent optimism of No Child Left Behind with respect to the potential proficiency of deaf students and other students with disabilities is, from one point of view, a refreshing contrast to the prejudices and stereotypes of the past. It must also be admitted that by not backing away from the requirements mandated in No Child Left Behind for "Adequate Yearly Progress," the federal government is forcing teachers of deaf students and state departments of education to consider every possible approach that might realistically be pursued to meet the law's goals. Even if 100% proficiency on state tests by 2014 is an unrealistic goal for all deaf children, any breakthrough in research or educational practice that might significantly improve this population's typical academic achievement patterns by that date would be encouraging.

Most American academic achievement tests, including math word problems, are developed in written English. The simplest explanation for deaf students' difficulties with the tests in their printed form is that deafness diminishes or precludes a person's ability to associate words on the page with well-known speech patterns (Kelly & Barac-Cikoja, 2007). This very specific problem is generally not correlated with basic intelligence. Some profoundly deaf people have to a significant degree managed to overcome this difficulty, and researchers at Gallaudet University and elsewhere are working now, in a Science of Learning Center on Visual Language and Visual Learning (VL^2), recently funded by the National Science Foundation, to determine how an individual can become a proficient reader without relying on hearing. It is hoped that if this research can shed light on the methods used by skilled deaf readers, some of that skill can be taught to other deaf people. In the long run, this research could lead to improved results for larger numbers of deaf students on statewide assessments.

One solution to deaf students' testing difficulties that may yield positive results would be for states to adopt more liberal and generous policies with respect to the accommodations used during testing. In some states (South Carolina perhaps setting the most striking example), students who are deaf may take a range of possible forms of a standard grade-level test (see Foster, this volume). For one thing, items deemed by specialists in deaf education to be biased against deaf students are routinely replaced with items measuring the same intellectual construct that do not have that bias. Also, they are given additional time, if needed, to compare difficult-to-understand items on the printed forms with the same items carefully translated into ASL or a form of Signed English on DVDs before choosing responses on the printed form. The exact accommodation used depends entirely on the accommodation the student typically receives during instruction. A student accustomed to Cued Speech, for example, may be administered the test in that way according to the requirements of a carefully prepared script for a test administrator trained in Cued Speech. Such accommodations have the effect of removing from the deaf student much of the stigma attached to this disability. They enable deaf students to demonstrate what they know in a way that is not obstructed by the manner in which they are asked to demonstrate their knowledge.

Although we will speculate in this book's Afterword on some initiatives that might make statewide, standards-based testing more accessible and fairer for deaf students, our goal as editors is not to dictate how the current age of accountability must be managed. We have attempted, rather, to assemble information we hope will be helpful to policymakers, teachers, school administrators, parents, and others concerned about the education, welfare, and future of deaf students.

A NOTE CONCERNING THE TERM *DEAF STUDENTS* AS USED IN THIS BOOK

Many readers of this volume will be surprised by the rarity of the adjectival phrase "deaf and hard of hearing" in these pages. We, the editors, chose to use the single word *deaf*, largely because it is less wordy, making the book easier to read (we hope). But there were also other, more substantive reasons for simplifying this descriptive term.

Moores (2001) defines a "deaf person" as "one whose hearing is disabled to an extent that precludes the understanding of speech through the ear alone, with or without the use of a hearing aid" (p. 11). He defines a "hard of hearing person" as "one whose hearing is disabled to an extent that makes difficult, but does not preclude, the understanding of speech through the ear alone, with or without a hearing aid" (p. 11). By those definitions, both deaf and hard of hearing students could be, and in fact are, included under our umbrella term *deaf students.* Our use of the term *deaf students,* however, can be taken to refer to both categories only to the extent that hearing loss has made the understanding of speech so difficult that an IEP has been required to help find placements and accommodations to overcome barriers to learning that might result from the hearing loss. Before the late 1980s, the term *hearing-impaired* was used to capture the same group of students who were educationally challenged as a result of hearing loss. That term fell into disfavor, however, because of its emphasis on deafness as an impairment.

We assume that an unknown number of hard of hearing students may be managing to hear their teachers and internalize spoken English well enough to have escaped the reporting system that brings data with respect to these particular students to the attention of research scientists at the Gallaudet Research Institute. For example, the data on deaf students taking Stanford Achievement Tests, discussed in Chapter 2 (Mitchell) of this volume, are based on test results for students whose hearing loss was severe enough to prompt school personnel to request information on norms for deaf students as a way of interpreting the test results. This population, which we refer to as "deaf students," is the group we are discussing throughout this book.

Chapter 13 of this volume, by Pat Moore, includes charts that contrast test results for "deaf" and "hard of hearing" students attending the California School for the Deaf. By our definition, both groups would fit under the general term used in the title of this book. Those charts show that these hard of hearing students, though performing on average at levels higher than those of the deaf students, are nevertheless experiencing significant educational difficulties that may be largely attributable to their hearing loss. (Some may have additional cognitive difficulties.) The placement of such students at schools for the deaf nationwide underscores our view that it is reasonable to include such students in the overall scope of this book's concern and to include them in the general category of "deaf students."

REFERENCES

Buchanan, R. M. (1999). *Illusions of equality: Deaf Americans in school and factory 1850–1950.* Washington, DC: Gallaudet University Press.

Friedman Narr, R. A. (2006). Teaching phonological awareness with deaf/hard of hearing students. *Teaching Exceptional Children, 38,* 53–58.

Gallaudet, E. M. (1983) (written 1895–1907). *History of the College for the Deaf, 1857–1907.* Washington, DC: Gallaudet College Press.

Henegar, M. E., & Cornett, R. O. (1971). *Cued Speech handbook for parents.* Washington, DC: Cued Speech Program, Gallaudet College.

Heubert, J. P. (2001). High stakes testing and civil rights: Standards of appropriate test use and a strategy for enforcing them. In G. Orfield & M. Kornhaber (Eds.), *Raising standards or raising barriers? Inequality and high stakes testing in public education* (pp. 179–194). New York: Century Foundation Press.

Johnson, R. E., Liddell, S. K., & Erting, C. J. (1989). *Unlocking the curriculum: Principles for achieving access in deaf education* (Gallaudet Research Institute Working Paper No. 89–3). Washington, DC: Gallaudet Research Institute.

Kelly, L. P., & Barac-Cikoja, D. (2007). The comprehension of skilled deaf readers: The roles of word recognition and other potentially critical aspects of competence. In K. Cain & J. Oakhill (Eds.), *Children's comprehension problems in oral and written language: A cognitive perspective* (pp. 244–280). New York: Guilford Press.

Moores, D. F. (2001). *Educating the deaf: Psychology, principles, and practices* (5th ed.). Boston: Houghton Mifflin.

Stokoe, W. C. (1960, rev. 1978). *Sign language structure: An outline of visual communication systems of the American deaf.* Silver Spring, MD: Linstok Press.

Stokoe, W. C., Casterline, D. C., & Croneberg, C. G. (1965, rev. 1976). *A dictionary of American Sign Language on linguistic principles.* Silver Spring, MD: Linstok Press.

Van Cleve, J. (1987). Sign language controversy. In J. Van Cleve (Ed.), *Gallaudet encyclopedia of deaf people and deafness* (Vol. 2, pp. 52–61). New York: McGraw-Hill.

Van Cleve, J. V., & Crouch, B. A. (1989). *A place of their own: Creating the deaf community in America.* Washington, DC: Gallaudet University Press.

Winston, E. A. (1994). An interpreted education: Inclusion or exclusion? In R. C. Johnson & O. P. Cohen (Eds.), *Implications and complications for deaf students of the full inclusion movement* (Gallaudet Research Institute Occasional Paper No. 94-2, pp. 55–62). Washington, DC: Gallaudet Research Institute.

Woodward, J. (1978). Some sociolinguistic problems in the implementation of bilingual education for deaf students. In F. Caccamise & D. Hicks (Eds.), *American Sign Language in a bilingual, bicultural context: Proceedings of the Second National Symposium on Sign Language Research and Teaching, Coronado, CA, October 15–19, 1978* (pp. 183–203). Silver Spring, MD: National Association of the Deaf.

Part One: *Testing and Accountability Issues*

1

Accountability in the Education of Deaf Students Under the Individuals with Disabilities Education Act and No Child Left Behind

Barbara Raimondo

It is a Wednesday afternoon in spring, and the Individualized Education Program (IEP) meeting for Jerome Kelly has begun. Jerome is age 8 years, deaf, and in second grade. Seated around the table of an elementary school classroom are Jerome's classroom teacher, his itinerant teacher of the deaf, the school principal, and his mother Shana. They are developing the IEP for the next school year. Everyone wants Jerome to do well, and everyone agrees that the school is responsible for Jerome's learning and should do everything it can to promote it. The IEP team agrees on a lot, but not everything. The subject turns to the third-grade reading assessment.

"I don't feel Jerome should take the regular assessment. His language delays are too great. He should take an alternate assessment."

"I think the only way we know whether the school is doing its job is if we give Jerome the same assessment everyone else gets."

"I think he will do fine on the regular assessment if he has accommodations."

"I think we should modify the assessment to fit his needs."

"The law doesn't allow us to modify the assessment anymore. Only certain types of assessments legally can be given."

"But IDEA says we have to treat him as an individual."

"But No Child Left Behind says he has to pass the state assessment."

"But which assessment is going to give us the right information about Jerome and what we need to do for him?"

Across this great country, educators and parents are taking stock of the new landscape in special education. The traditional emphasis on the "Individual" in the Individuals with Disabilities Education Act (IDEA 2004) now is expanding to include the accountability measures of the No Child Left Behind Act (NCLB) of 2001. Some believe that these two laws, which were written for different purposes at different times, conflict with each other. Others believe children with disabilities will never rise to the same level of achievement as nondisabled children. Still others believe that the methods required to measure academic performance are wrong or, at least, insufficient. However, over the last several years Congress and the U.S. Department of Education (USDE) have been promoting policies designed to ensure that the laws complement each other.

INDIVIDUALS WITH DISABILITIES EDUCATION ACT

Since 1975, the Individuals With Disabilities Education Act (IDEA), originally known as the Education for All Handicapped Children Act, or Public Law 94-142, has guided the provision of special education and related services to students with disabilities. IDEA was passed as the federal response to two district court cases brought on behalf of students with disabilities: *Pennsylvania Association for Retarded Children v. Commonwealth of Pennsylvania* (1971) and *Mills v. Board of Education* (1972). These cases, decided on equal protection and due process grounds, established, among other things, that children with disabilities were entitled to a free public program of education appropriate to their learning needs. To extend these rulings to the entire country, thereby creating a statutory right, Congress passed the Education for All Handicapped Children Act, which included these key tenets:

- Children with disabilities will be evaluated to determine their educational needs.
- Schools will provide eligible children with a Free Appropriate Public Education (FAPE).
- Education and placement will be based on an IEP, developed by an IEP team, which includes teachers, related service providers, and parents.
- Children with disabilities will be placed in the Least Restrictive Environment (LRE) based on their IEP needs.
- Children with disabilities and their parents will have access to procedural safeguards to protect their rights.

As stated by the USDE,

> Public Law 94-142 was a response to Congressional concern for two groups of children: the more than 1 million children with disabilities who were excluded entirely from the education system and the children with disabilities who had only limited access to the education system and were therefore denied an appropriate education. This latter group comprised more than half of all children with disabilities who were living in the United States at that time. (USDE, 2008)

IDEA historically has focused on the specific child in question. IEP teams have had latitude to determine what goals were appropriate for the child and how those goals would be measured. The IEP team could have decided whether the child should be expected to meet the same curricular objectives as nondisabled children. Early on, IDEA simply required access to an education that, in the judgment of the IEP team and based on the IEP team's standards, fit the child.

Over the years and after several reauthorizations, IDEA has shifted its focus. Although it still requires the education of children with disabilities to be individualized. IDEA today attempts to bring the quality of the education of children with disabilities in line with that of nondisabled children and measures the performance of the child in that curriculum. Influenced by the education reform movements of the 1990s, the 1997 and 2004 reauthorizations of IDEA included, among other things, the requirements that students with disabilities

- Have access to the general education curriculum–614 (d)(1)(A)(i)(II)(aa), 614(d)(1)(A)(i)(IV)(bb);
- Participate in statewide and districtwide assessments–612 (a)(16)(A), 614 (d)(1)(A)(i)(VI)(aa);
- Receive accommodations if needed to take assessments–612 (a)(16)(A), 614 (d)(1)(A)(i)(VI)(aa); and
- Be permitted to take alternate assessments if unable to take the regular assessment–612 (a)(16)(A), 614 (d)(1)(A)(i)(VI)(bb).

The judgment of the IEP team still is important in determining how to provide access to the general education curriculum, what accommodations are needed for assessments, and whether the child is able to take the regular assessment or should take an alternate assessment. However, IDEA has taken key decisions out of the IEP team's hands: the decision whether the child should participate in the general education curriculum and the decision whether the child should participate in state- and districtwide assessments. The child *must* have access to the general education curriculum and *must* participate in assessments. Further, the 2004 reauthorization also created an explicit link between IDEA and NCLB. The evolution of NCLB is important to consider first, before exploring that link.

ACCOUNTABILITY PROVISIONS OF NCLB

The NCLB is the current reauthorization of the Elementary and Secondary Education Act (ESEA), Public Law 89-10, which was originally passed in 1965 as part of President Lyndon Johnson's War on Poverty. The ESEA was intended to lift poor families out of poverty through education and was part of a series of public programs designed to assist disadvantaged families, including Head Start, food stamps, work study, Medicare, and Medicaid (Siegel, 2004). The ESEA underwent a series of reauthorizations that expanded its scope and, in the late 1980s and 1990s, called for the development of accountability measures for schools receiving funds under this law. Although the current version of this law, NCLB, signed by President George W. Bush in 2002, necessitates sanctions only for schools receiving Title I funds, its monitoring and reporting provisions apply to *all public schools* in the United States. As a consequence, sufficient information should be available to the public and policymakers so there will be "no child left behind."

NCLB requires State Education Agencies (SEAs), Local Education Agencies (LEAs), and schools to ensure that all students are "proficient" in reading, math, and science by 2014. In contrast to the individualized approach to teaching and learning in IDEA, it could be said that NCLB takes a group approach. It does so by mandating that

- All three entities (SEA, LEA, and school) make Adequate Yearly Progress (AYP);
- Classroom teachers be highly qualified;
- Scientifically based research is used to make educational decisions; and
- Parents of children in schools that receive NCLB Title I funds and that do not make AYP have the choice to transfer their child to another school. (If the school continues not to make AYP, then parents whose children remain in the school can choose to have their child receive supplemental educational services such as after-school tutoring from a private tutoring services provider.

Although each SEA has latitude as to how it defines AYP for itself, NCLB outlines certain requirements. States must define AYP in a manner that applies the same high standards of proficiency to all public elementary school students. The definition of AYP must be statistically valid and reliable, and it must result in continuous and substantial academic improvement for all students. The focus of AYP must be on academic assessments, and proficiency objectives must be outlined for students overall and for students in certain subgroups:

- Economically disadvantaged students
- Students from major racial and ethnic groups
- Students with disabilities
- Students with limited English proficiency

This subgroup disaggregation is critical. Its purpose is to highlight and make schools, districts, and states accountable for these students' performance. Traditionally, these groups often have not met school benchmarks. Publishing their scores separately allows parents, policymakers, and the public to know how well school entities are teaching these disadvantaged groups.

The AYP definition must include high school graduation rates and at least one other academic indicator, typically attendance. Both elementary and high school AYP determinations may also include other academic indicators such as achievement on additional state or locally administered assessments and decreases in grade-to-grade retention rates.[1]

If schools do not make AYP based on the criteria outlined above, they may be able to make AYP based on the "safe harbor" provision, which gives schools credit for incremental improvement that nonetheless falls short of the annual measurable objective (AMO) set for making AYP.

In 2005, in response to criticisms that the AYP criteria were too stringent, the USDE initiated a 10 state pilot program allowing "growth models" to be used. Growth models measure individual student growth over time and allow states

1. 20 U.S.C.A. § 1111 (b)(2)(C).

another way to make AYP. States applying to use growth models had to meet established NCLB principles such as working to ensure that all students attained proficiency by 2014, setting expectations for annual achievement based on meeting grade level proficiency, including all students and subgroups in the accountability system, and other requirements. In December 2007, the USDE opened growth model participation to all states meeting eligibility criteria.

Initially, when NCLB was passed, all children were expected to meet the same benchmark. At that time, there were three ways of taking the state assessment, all of which were *aligned with grade level achievement standards*. Those three ways are listed here:

1) Regular assessment with no accommodations
2) Regular assessment with accommodations (such as a sign language interpreter, extra time to take the test, assistive technology, other state-approved testing accommodations, or some combination)
3) An alternate assessment for children for whom the regular assessment, regardless of any accommodations, was not appropriate

Subsequently, the USDE issued rules with respect to the provision of alternate assessments. The first rule recognizes that students with severe cognitive disabilities require different standards. Regulations allow for alternate assessments that are aligned with alternate achievement standards.[2] Alternate achievement standards must be aligned with the state's academic content standards, must promote access to the general curriculum, and must reflect sound professional judgment concerning the highest achievement standards possible.[3] Up to 1% of the scores of the students taking these assessments can be counted as proficient for AYP determination.[4]

The second rule recognizes that a large share of students in special education do not master the same depth and breadth of the general curriculum at the same rate as the general student population but is otherwise capable of meeting many of the regular state achievement standards. These recent regulations allow for alternate assessments that are based on modified achievement standards.[5] Modified achievement standards are aligned with grade-level curriculum and with the state's academic content standards for the grade in which the student is enrolled. However, the modified achievement standards reflect reduced breadth or depth of grade-level content. Importantly, students taking an alternate assessment that is aligned with modified achievement standards must not be precluded from earning a regular high-school diploma. Special education students taking the alternate assessment must meet certain criteria, for example, that the student's disability

2. *Federal Register, 68,* 68697–68708 (December 9, 2003).

3. 34 C.F.R. § 200.1(d).

4. This numerical threshold is based on the presumption that roughly 10% of students in special education have severe cognitive disabilities. Because roughly 10% of the total student population is eligible for federal special education, 10% of special education students translates into 1% of all students.

5. *Federal Register, 70,* 74623–74638 (December 15, 2005).

has precluded him or her from otherwise achieving grade-level proficiency. These students are not the same as those identified as having severe cognitive disabilities. Up to 2% of students who score proficient on alternate assessments that are aligned with modified achievement standards may have their scores counted for AYP determination.[6]

With the addition of these latter two ways in which to take assessments, the number of assessment options has grown to five:

4) For children with severe cognitive disabilities (up to 1% of all students), alternate assessments aligned with alternate achievement standards
5) For children who meet certain criteria (up to 2% of all students), alternate assessments aligned with modified achievement standards

AT THE CROSSROADS OF IDEA AND NCLB

Conceptually, there is a lot of common ground between IDEA and NCLB (see Table 1.1). Both reinforce the idea that schools should have high expectations for their students. NCLB reinforces this idea through the AYP structure. IDEA reinforces this concept through empowering the IEP team, which includes the child's parents and others who know the child well, to design an instructional and related services program that will lead to an appropriate education for the child.

Both laws are intended to help school systems close the achievement gap. NCLB approaches this objective through making school systems accountable for the assessment scores of students in the four subgroups. IDEA approaches this objective through ensuring access to the general education curriculum in a manner appropriately suited to the child.

Both laws require the provision of qualified personnel. NCLB ensures qualified personnel through its Highly Qualified Teacher requirements.[7] IDEA ensures qualified personnel through its Highly Qualified Special Education Teacher requirements and through its related services provider requirements.[8]

---

6. This numerical threshold is based on the presumption that roughly 20% of students in special education have disabilities that interfere with demonstrating proficiency on one or more specific grade-level standards and, thereby, would fail to achieve a proficient score if required to meet the full depth and breadth of the regular state achievement standards. Twenty percent of special education students translates into 2% of all students.

7. NCLB requires teachers to be "Highly Qualified." For all teachers, this means that the teacher has received full state certification as a teacher or passed the state teacher licensing exam, and holds a license to teach. New elementary school teachers must have at least a bachelor's degree and have passed a state curriculum test. New middle and secondary school teachers teaching in core academic areas—such as reading, math, science, civics, and history—must have a bachelor's degree and have either passed a rigorous state academic subject test in each subject the teacher teaches, or have completed a major, degree, or its equivalent in each subject the teacher teaches.

8. Generally, special education teachers teaching core academic subjects must meet the requirements outlined above. In addition, highly qualified special education teachers must have obtained full State certification as a special education teacher or passed the State special education teacher licensing examination, and hold a license to teach in the State as a special education teacher.

Both laws emphasize parent involvement. NCLB promotes parent involvement through allowing parents of children in Title I schools to choose another school for their child if the child's present school does not make AYP. IDEA promotes parent involvement through its inclusion of parents on the IEP team and on the team that decides the child's placement.

So the two laws can and do work together. The fact that the IEP team needs to view each child uniquely does not preclude a child from participating in and passing a grade-level assessment. Having a highly qualified teacher providing subject matter instruction would seem to be superior to having a generic special educator teaching that material. And looking at children with disabilities as a group is probably a good way to get some measure of how well schools are teaching them. However, when considering some ways that assessment under these two laws plays out, the differences become apparent.

ASSESSMENT OF DISABLED CHILDREN UNDER IDEA AND NCLB

As previously mentioned, there are many assessment requirements in both IDEA and NCLB. Children with disabilities must take state and local assessments.[9] Alternate assessments were to be developed and conducted by July 2000[10] for students for whom the regular assessment was not appropriate.[11] Universal design principles must be used in the development of state and local assessments.[12] Assessments must be "designed from the beginning to be accessible and valid with respect to the widest possible range of students, including students with disabilities and students with limited English proficiency."[13]

Since the amendments to IDEA in 1997, IDEA has mandated that children with disabilities be included in general state and districtwide assessment programs, with appropriate accommodations where necessary. A recent GAO study revealed "at least 95% of students with disabilities participated in statewide reading assessments in 41 of the 49 states that provided data" (GAO, 2005, p. 2). However, there are barriers to carrying out the mandate to offer alternate assessments, for example, the lack of states' experience in designing these assessments (GAO, 2005, p. 19). Many states did not begin to design alternate assessments until the Individuals With Disabilities Education Act Amendments (IDEA 1997) required them to do so for the 2000–01 school year (GAO, 2005, p. 19). Cost and need for teacher training are also cited as barriers (GAO, 2005, p. 22). The GAO study

9. IDEA 2004 § 612 (a)(16)(A).

10. IDEA 1997 § 612 (a)(17)(A)(ii).

11. IDEA 1997 § 612 (a)(17)(A)(i).

12. IDEA 2004 § 612 (a)(16)(E). "Universal design" refers to a "concept or philosophy for designing and delivering products and services that are usable by people with the widest possible range of functional capabilities." This concept includes "products and services that are directly usable (without requiring assistive technologies) and products and services that are made usable with assistive technologies" (29 U.S.C. § 3002 (a)(17)).

13. 34 C.F.R. § 200.2(b)(2).

Table 1.1. Comparison of IDEA with NCLB

Topic	IDEA	NCLB
Individual/group	Based on the individual	Based on all children as a group
Individual/group	Focuses on the uniqueness of each child	All children in each grade must reach one standard
Guiding document	IEP and State plan that is designed to support the IEP	AYP definition
Evaluation	The child is evaluated based on factors unique to the child	No individual evaluation, but the labeling of the child as belonging in one or more of the subgroups
Goals	Individual goals are written for the child	Main goal is passing the annual assessment
Professional services	Services to be provided to the child or on behalf of the child determined	Services not spelled out, but core academic subjects must be taught by a Highly Qualified Teacher
Placement	Placement decided by a team that includes the parents	Placement in the neighborhood school unless it is a Title I school that does not meet NCLB measures in which case the parent can choose to move the child to a school that is making AYP (if one is available)
Qualifications	Parents and professionals who know the child and work with the child involved in this process	Professionals to be involved considered in terms of whether or not they are Highly Qualified
Goal	To provide services and placement so the child can access and progress in the general curriculum	To meet AYP

Guarantee of outcome	No guarantee that a child will meet his or her IEP goals	See Placement; also, no recourse for parents if teachers not Highly Qualified
Year-to-year progress	No guarantee that the child will progress in the general education curriculum at the same rate as his or her nondisabled peers; child may move ahead from grade to grade with his or her age peers regardless of the modifications to the curriculum made on his or her behalf; child may take more than the usual 13 years to complete a kindergarten through twelfth-grade course of study; student may continue receiving services through age 21	One of the accountability measures—the percentage of students who graduate from secondary school with a regular diploma in the standard number of years[a]
Scientifically based research	Special education and related services and supplementary aids and services outlined on the IEP should be based on peer-reviewed research to the extent practicable	To be used in reform strategies, targeted assistance programs to help schools improve, and technical assistance to schools

a. But see Notice of Proposed rulemaking—proposing to allow states to use an alternate definition for “standard number of years” for purposes of allowing students in some categories, such as students with disabilities, and under certain conditions, more time in high school before graduation. 73 Fed. Reg. 22020-22044 (April 23, 2008).

reported that only nine states are using alternate reading assessments held to grade-level standards (GAO, 2005, p. 11).[14] Therefore, the requirement that alternate assessments be available has yet to be realized. Further, students with disabilities have been excluded from assessments under the National Assessment of Educational Progress, also known as "the nation's report card."

States have begun to consider universal design principles in their assessment systems. Forty-five states (90%) report that they address universal design, with 31 (62%) addressing it at the item development stage, 30 (60%) addressing it at the item review stage, and 27 (54%) including requirements for universal design in requests for proposals for test development (National Center on Education Outcomes, 2005). However, this development is relatively new, and it is not clear that, by addressing the issue, states have actually developed truly universally designed assessments. As a result, children with disabilities, including deaf children, have taken and are taking tests that were not designed for their use. These tests have not been shown to be valid and reliable for this population. Given the consequences that can occur to the school as a result of children's poor performance on these tests, the use of these tests may be unwarranted. In addition, sometimes results on these tests are used to make high-stakes decisions such as passing a student from one grade to the next or allowing a student to graduate, although the law does not require this action. Even though discussion of this issue is outside the scope of this chapter, readers should be aware that this situation is problematic.

APPLYING IDEA/NCLB TO SCHOOLS FOR THE DEAF

The NCLB requirements that schools report and be held accountable for the performance of specific groups of students, while well-intended and laudable, may not give schools for the deaf an optimum opportunity to demonstrate how well they have taught their students as compared to how well hearing schools have taught deaf students. Let's examine four related aspects of the law: reporting performance for children with disabilities as a group; setting a minimum number of students to determine group performance (a minimum *N*); setting a minimum assessment participation rate; and determining the number of years a student is enrolled before the school is held accountable for that child's performance. Depending on how these parts of the law interact, the information value of student performance reporting and the intended accountability effects may be substantially compromised.

Number of Children With a Disability as Compared to Number of Deaf Children

The number of children with hearing loss in any school is typically very small relative to the general population. Mitchell and Karchmer (2006) estimate that at

14. These states are Hawaii, Kansas, Massachusetts, New York, North Carolina, Oregon, Utah, Vermont, and West Virginia (GAO, 2005, Appendix I, p. 30). (Please see the chapter in this volume by Pat Moore.)

least 80% of public schools with at least one deaf student have no more than three. Fifty-three percent of schools with any deaf or hard of hearing students have only one. And "nearly one of every five (19%) deaf and hard of hearing students in special education is a 'solitaire'" (Mitchell & Karchmer, 2006, p. 99). Therefore, the number of students in the school overall and the number of students with disabilities are likely to mask the score (or scores) of the deaf child (or children). Scores generally are not broken out by disability,[15] and children with learning disabilities make up 50% of the population served by IDEA (Muller 2005, p. II-20). As a consequence of the low-incidence of deafness in the general school population, it is likely that the scores for students with disabilities reflect the performance of students with learning disabilities (or other high-incidence disabilities such as speech or language impairment, mental retardation, and emotional disturbance) more than any other group. In other words, results from the students with disabilities group cannot be generalized to the deaf population.

Another factor to be considered is that schools for the deaf publish their results as they apply to disabled children as a group for the entire school, not just a subset, and as they apply to the various remaining subgroups. Although the law did not mandate explicitly for scores to be reported this way, they effectively are reported as students with a disability and limited English proficiency, with a disability and economically disadvantaged, and with a disability and of a particular racial or ethnic group. However, they are not necessarily reported that way by all schools. Although a student may fall into more than one subgroup, school score reports do not typically reflect multiple subgroup memberships for any particular students. For example, a student may be in poverty and have a disability, but the school would report that student's scores in each of those categories separately. The scores would not be reported as belonging to a child who is both economically disadvantaged and has a disability. The exception is when all students in the school fall into a particular category, for example, scores in a school in which all students are Latino effectively would be reported as Latino with a disability, Latino with limited English proficiency, and Latino and economically disadvantaged. This kind of reporting amounts to comparing apples to apples times oranges, and it seems unfair to schools for the deaf and to other similarly situated schools. After all, if a student is at academic risk by being in one of the subgroups, then that student's risk increases by being in two subgroups.

It is interesting to compare the population of deaf children in regular school settings and that in schools for the deaf along demographic categories that have different achievement profiles. According to Karchmer and Mitchell (2003), White students are clearly in the majority in regular school settings but are just barely the majority in schools for the deaf (60% and 50%, respectively). Hispanic and Black students make up nearly equal shares of the remaining special school

---

15. But a recent report studying 10 states in depth found that four of them (Arkansas, Arizona, Colorado, and Virginia) disaggregate state assessment scores at the state level, the local level, or both for students who are deaf. Of these, Colorado and Virginia described efforts to use the data to improve outcomes for students who are deaf (Muller, 2005).

population, whereas these two racial/ethnic groups constitute only slightly more than one-quarter of the deaf students in regular school settings. Profound hearing loss among deaf students in regular school settings is one-fifth the rate of that found in schools for the deaf. More than one-quarter of deaf students in regular school settings are reported to have an additional disability whereas nearly half of the students in schools for the deaf have additional disabilities. In other words, the regular school setting, which has become the more common placement for deaf students, is the setting that has the highest percentage of students from the typically better-performing groups. Overall, the scores of 75% of deaf students should be attributed to a regular public school. However, as mentioned above, those scores are dispersed among a variety of schools.

Reliability of Group Scores

Regardless of whether the percentage of students with disabilities meeting the AMO is a good indicator of the performance of deaf students in a particular school, this percentage may simply not be a reliable performance indicator at all. In cases of a small *N*, or number of students in a given subgroup taking the assessment, there are mathematical and statistical reasons for great concern. NCLB allows states to identify the smallest *N* deemed to be statistically reliable. The schools most likely to be affected by small numbers are schools in rural areas and specialized schools such as schools for the deaf. Maryland's *N* of five is the smallest (Maryland State Department of Education, 2005). From a statistical standpoint, the standard error of a percentage is quite large with an *N* of only five, which makes reliability on Maryland's reporting questionable. More important, the mathematical consequences are quite significant when *N* is small. A change of one student when calculating the percentage of students meeting the AMO is enormous for an *N* of five: There is a 20% change for each student who succeeds or fails in meeting the AMO when only five students' scores are used to make the calculation. To label a school as not making AYP or as being in need of improvement—with its concomitant potential consequences of allowing families to leave the school, requiring the school to pay for supplemental educational services,[16] having the school undergo state mandated changes through technical assistance, and ultimately restructuring if low performance persists—based on the scores of as few as five students per year seems to be a rather suspect and unstable approach to identifying schools for accountability purposes.

Setting the minimum *N* too high is also a problem, though not for mathematical or statistical reasons. When *N* is set at 50 or 100, then small schools will never have enough students per grade to have subgroup accountability. Even the more modest gains demanded by the "safe harbor" provision in NCLB do not apply when the minimum *N* for a subgroup is larger than the number of students en-

16. NCLB mandates consequences as accruing to Title I schools only, not all schools, however, there is variation among the states as to what and how consequences accrue to deaf schools. See, e.g., Cawthon, 2004.

rolled in that grade. Moreover, there is a tremendous risk that students with very specialized needs, especially when they are few in number, which is almost always the case for students who are deaf, will be overlooked or have attention to their needs delayed for lack of immediate effect on AYP status. In such cases of high minimum *N*, reliability is gained at the expense of subgroup accountability.

Assessment Participation Rules

The law requires that at least 95% of students participate in the statewide assessment as a condition of making AYP. Although this requirement was intended to ensure complete testing of all students present for testing while allowing that some small percentage of the students would have legitimate reasons for not being present, it also means that "all" does not mean "100 percent." Small numbers of students could be excluded from testing, especially where the minimum *N* for subgroups is high.

Accountability for Years of Failure

NCLB requires schools to become accountable for a new student after that student has been at the school for a year.[17] However, a deaf student often is not provided entry to a school for the deaf until the child has fallen behind his or her peers. Although a few states allow parents to apply directly to a school for the deaf for their child's admission (e.g., the Florida School for the Deaf and Blind, the Maryland School for the Deaf, and the Texas School for the Deaf), most states require parents to go through the IEP process. Often, because of a misunderstanding of IDEA's LRE provisions (Siegel, 2000) and other reasons, school district members of the IEP team are reluctant to allow a child to be placed in a school for the deaf unless that child is doing poorly in the mainstream school. Children often enter schools for the deaf with disadvantages such as severe language and academic delays. Although a school for the deaf may be able to do a lot with a child in a year—provide full access to language and communication that the child probably had not experienced until that time—if a child has not been provided full language access early and throughout life as well as access to the general education curriculum throughout school, then it is not likely that any school, no matter how outstanding, will be able to bring that child up to grade level academically in one year's time. NCLB offers neither direct consideration for misplacement of students through the IEP process nor allowance for the time necessary for special schools and programs to overcome the harm done by inappropriate or inadequate delivery of special education services. And though some states have made a distinction between the regular (sending) and special (receiving) schools when determining which school is to be held responsible for persistent low performance, this distinction neither ensures that holding regular schools accountable will cause them to improve their services nor that special schools

---

17. 20 U.S.C.A. § 1111 (b)(3)(C)(xi).

will assume full responsibility for maximizing student performance when only the regular school is held accountable.

Is One School Better Than the Other?

Because scores are not broken out by disability category, parents who consider moving their deaf child from a school that has not made AYP to a higher performing school have no way of knowing whether the deaf students in the receiving school are actually higher performing than the deaf students in the first school, assuming there are any deaf students in the receiving school in the first place. Nonetheless, NCLB implicitly assumes that because a school is not making AYP, its students, especially its lowest performing and disadvantaged students, are better off in another school.

In general, many parents are turning down the opportunity to place their child in a higher performing school. *Education Week* reported that eligible students who transferred to a higher-performing public school under NCLB averaged 1% nationwide during the 2003–2004 school year (Olson, 2005). It seems that parents are not in as much of a hurry to leave underperforming schools as policymakers predicted. Christy Foors, a mother of a second grader said, "I have no desire or plan to move him. I fully intend to keep him at [his school] through sixth grade," adding, "I'm impressed that [the school] does as well as it does." Ms. Foors, who is also a vice president of the school's PTA, said one aspect she likes is the school's ethnic diversity. "Sure there's tons of room for the school to grow, but it's such a small number of kids that failed. This school is getting better and better every year" (McNeill, 2005). A parent of five children in an Oregon school was surprised when his children's school was labeled underperforming. "They did an excellent job for my kids. I was very pleased. When we had any concerns, we just went and talked with them and they got fixed," he said (Loew, 2005). Documented stories of parents of deaf children pursuing or rejecting the opportunity to transfer their children from an underperforming school to one that has a sustained record of making AYP are difficult, if not impossible, to find.

This difference in perspective between policymakers and parents may exist in schools for the deaf that do not make AYP. An important question to consider for children in schools for the deaf that do not make AYP is: Will those children be better off in mainstream schools? As part of the team that decides placement, or in states where parents can choose to send their child to the school for the deaf without going through the LEA, parents presumably express their opinion about where their child should attend school. Some of these parents probably agree with Will's mom, who moved her child from a general education classroom to a specialized program:

Up 'til now, Will was mainstreamed with an interpreter. He was only one of three deaf kids in the whole school, and the only one who was mainstreamed, so he was rather isolated. Some of the hearing children did learn to sign (especially the girls), but Will never formed any deep relationships with the kids there, even though he did make a lot of hearing friends. The teachers were eager to teach him, since most of them had never taught a deaf student before. The main problem was the interpreter. She was an adequate signer, but not as good a voicer. And if she was absent, Will often was sent to the library, or the teachers let other kids "interpret" for Will. Or he'd have subs who were less than adequate . . .

[After moving to the bilingual school]:

This year it's amazing how effortless communication is. All our issues in the mainstream were communication access; now that is not an issue at all. Every kid in the school can sign anything to him and all his teachers can sign fluently with him. All the kids are required to sign, even the hearing ones. The people who work in the lunch room, the bus drivers, the office staff members, the principal and the board are all fluent signers and most of them are deaf. Will's math teacher is male and deaf (I think it's so important for him to see deaf role models). (Raising Deaf Kids, n.d.)

It may be that the unique qualities that draw parents and students to schools for the deaf will keep them there, regardless of the school's AYP status. However, under NCLB, these qualities carry no weight.

It seems clear that in many places, schools for the deaf serve the students that public schools traditionally have had a harder time serving—students from minority backgrounds and students with disabilities. These are the very students NCLB intends to benefit, and schools for the deaf should be doing everything they can to bring students to or above grade level. However, the current NCLB accountability system may not provide sufficient opportunity to compare the progress of students in mainstream programs to that of students in schools for the deaf.

WHAT IS NEXT?

Concerns about NCLB have been raised from many corners. From complaints about lack of funding (National Council of Teachers of English, 2004) to the perception that noncore academic subjects or recess must be sacrificed to meet NCLB goals (National School Boards Association, 2003) to the perceived overemphasis on testing, many have opposed elements of NCLB. The USDE has responded verbally and, in some cases, through action. Many schools have failed to make AYP based on the scores of students in the disability category. As previously stated, the USDE has issued regulations pertaining to students with severe cognitive disabilities. Those students can take alternate assessments that are held to alternate achievement standards. The scores of up to 1% of students statewide can be included in the state accountability system in this category.

As also mentioned, the USDE has issued regulations to be used with students with disabilities who take alternate assessments that are held to modified achievement standards. The scores of up to 2% of students statewide under this construct can be included in the state accountability system. This 3% (the 1% of students held to alternate standards and the 2% held to modified standards) amounts to a large percentage of the school-age disability population. Approximately 50 million children attend elementary and secondary school (U.S. Census Bureau, 2005), and

3% of this population is 1.5 million. Six million children ages 6 through 21 are served under IDEA (USDE, 2003, p. 21); therefore, this 1.5 million figure amounts to 25% of the school-age disability population. These two sets of regulations acknowledge the difficulty that schools, LEAs, and SEAs have experienced in meeting AYP because of the scores of some students with disabilities. Further, when it announced the 2% policy, it also announced a new "common-sense" approach to NCLB:

We are willing to show states a more workable and informed approach on other [than the 2% policy] aspects of the law. . . . Another example of such flexibility could include a request for the use of growth models; or states may have their own proposals for demonstrating progress and effective implementation; these principles will help the Department consider and help states implement those ideas. (USDE, 2005b)

When this new approach was unveiled, Secretary of Education Margaret Spellings said, "Times have changed. A spirit of reform and renewal now governs public education in America. It's a spirit that, like America, looks forward, not back. 'Education should not be static or stagnant,' Maryland State Superintendent Nancy Grasmick has said. 'It should be dynamic'" (Spellings, 2005b). Subsequent to this announcement, the USDE unveiled plans to allow up to 10 states to pilot a "growth model" accountability plan. This model allows states to develop new ways of measuring AYP (Spellings, 2005a). Today USDE allows all states to propose a growth model in their accountability plans.

The USDE has been sued by teachers' unions (National Education Association, 2005) and states, such as Connecticut, (Harrison, 2005) over funding issues.[18] The State of Utah passed a law giving priority to Utah's education standards over federal education standards (Associated Press, 2005). It allows education officials to ignore NCLB requirements that conflict with Utah state requirements. The state brands NCLB as an "unfunded mandate," although it receives $76 million under NCLB. This money could be lost if the USDE finds the state out of compliance with NCLB. Subsequent to the state law being passed, Utah applied to the USDE for waivers of some provisions of NCLB (MacFarland, 2005). Although the state plan was ultimately approved, this incident illustrates the tension between states' desire to receive NCLB money and states' objections to some NCLB provisions.

Other objections around NCLB focus on the law's emphasis on standardized testing (Gollan, 2005). At the same time, NCLB supporters comment on how it has improved student performance. Dr. Deborah Jewell-Sherman, superintendent of Richmond Public Schools, stated:

In Richmond City Public Schools, we embrace the No Child Left Behind Act as a means for refined and deepened academic focus for all students. Our district is committed to high expectations for all and has implemented a new accountability

18. The NEA case currently is in the Court of Appeals for the Sixth District. The Connecticut court ruled in favor of the secretary.

system, the Balanced Scorecard, which is an approach to strategic management that ensures clarity of vision, strategy and action. This initiative is used to ensure the accountability of our school board, central office administrators, school administrators and classroom staff. (Jewell-Sherman, 2005)

Similarly, Kati Haycock, President of The Education Trust, reported:

Almost four years ago, the [House Education and the Workforce] Committee showed great leadership in charting a new course in federal education policy. There is much more work still to do and new challenges continue to emerge. Thanks in large measure to NCLB, however, the nation is finally getting traction on correcting the deep inequities that have for so long stunted the growth of so many of our young people and dishonored our democratic ideals. Because of NCLB, achievement gaps are no longer simply tolerated; a culture of achievement is taking hold in our schools, and we are better poised to confront the new challenges. (Haycock, 2005)

WHAT SHOULD THE REAUTHORIZED NCLB INCLUDE?

In the reauthorization of NCLB, the USDE has stated that it will be seeking to improve teacher quality, enhance parent choice, and make high schools accountable (USDE, 2007). Recently, it has allowed states to report AYP based on a growth model, and many advocate for use of a growth model in the reauthorized law. Fairness would argue in favor of developing a formula that attributes an appropriate portion of a student's scores to the appropriate entity. For example, if a school does not receive a child until the child is in seventh grade and if the child is reading on a fourth-grade level when she enters the school and finishes the year on a sixth-grade level, then the receiving school should receive credit for raising the child's score by two grade levels but not be penalized because it received a child who was, and remains, behind after 1 year at the school. Significant growth without achieving grade-level proficiency status in the first year could serve as an alternative AMO for the purpose of making AYP.

For the purpose of making all special education programs accountable, assessment scores should be disaggregated on the basis of type of disability such as deaf or hard of hearing, learning disabled, etc. The educational needs of students vary greatly, depending on their disability category. A school that serves learning disabled children well may not serve children with hearing loss well, and vice versa. The public will not know how successful a school is in teaching each disability type without such disaggregation.

Finally, efforts to improve the consistency between NCLB and IDEA should continue and be fully implemented. When it comes to implementation, NCLB and IDEA provisions that affect testing of students with disabilities should be enforced, provisions such as the providing of accommodations, universal design, and availability of alternate assessments. With respect to improved consistency, one failure to align provisions has to do with age and graduation. According to IDEA, students may stay in school until age 21, whereas NCLB favors graduation in the typical number of years (i.e., by age 18). Clearly, there is an inconsistency between the two laws, which may result in schools being identified as in need of improvement when they may very well be providing appropriate and effective extended special education.

At the time of this writing, the reauthorization of NCLB, which was expected to be completed around fall 2007, is not complete. In April 2008, USDE proposed regulatory changes[19] that reflect the Administration's key priority areas for the NCLB reauthorization. Among other things, these include:

- Assessing higher-order thinking skills through multiple measures;
- Disaggregation of data;
- State reporting of National Assessment of Educational Performance scores;
- A standard definition of graduation rate;
- Allowing states to permit some students, who may take longer than the usual time to graduate, such as students with disabilities, to do so without penalty to the state;
- Using growth models to evaluate academic progress;
- Providing further support for supplemental educational services and parent choice to transfer their child to a higher performing school.

CONCLUSION

For too long, some groups of children—including deaf children—have not performed as well as others. But perhaps they performed as well as our society expected them to. NCLB does away with low expectations and implements a system of school accountability with uniform expectations. It provides an incentive to schools to make sure that all students succeed. It is a goal no one can disagree with. Congress and the USDE should continue on this quest to change the culture of America's schools (USDE, 2006a). At the same time, the culture of American schooling must become competently inclusive for all students, including deaf students, or this quest will fail.

REFERENCES

Associated Press. (2005, May 2). *Utah snubs federal No Child Left Behind Act.* Retrieved October 20, 2005 from http://www.msnbc.msn.com/id/7713931/

Cawthon, S. (2004). Schools for the deaf and the No Child Left Behind Act. *American Annals of the Deaf, 149* (4), 314–323.

19. Title I—Improving the Academic Achievement of the Disadvantaged; Proposed Rule, 73 *Fed. Reg.* 22020-22044 (April 23, 2008)

Education for All Handicapped Children Act of 1975, Pub. L. No. 94-142, 20 U.S.C. §§ 1400–1485.

Elementary and Secondary Education Act of 1965, Pub. L. No. 89-10, 20 U.S.C. § 6301 *et seq.*

General Accounting Office. (2005). *No Child Left Behind: Most students with disabilities participated in statewide assessments, but inclusion options could be improved.* Washington, DC: Author.

Gollan, J. (2005, October 20). Lagunitas district faces sanctions for alternative approach. *Marin Independent Journal.*

Graham, K., & Kummer, F. (2005, August 11). More N.J. schools miss mark. *Philadelphia Inquirer.*

Gustin, G. (2005, September 19). Schools ponder 'No-Child' penalties. *St. Louis Post-Dispatch.*

Harrison, K. (2005, September 22). Board of Ed supports NCLB lawsuit. *West Hartford News.*

Haycock, K. (2005, September 29). *Testimony before the House Education and Workforce Committee U.S. House of Representatives, hearing on "Closing the Achievement Gap in America's Schools: The No Child Left Behind Act."* Retrieved December 20, 2005, from http://www2.edtrust.org/EdTrust/Press+Room/Haycock+Testimony+9.29.05.htm

Individuals With Disabilities Education Act Amendments of 1997, Pub. L. No. 105-17, 20 U.S.C. § 1400 *et seq.*

Individuals With Disabilities Education Improvement Act of 2004, Pub. L. No. 108-446, 20 U.S.C. § 1400 *et seq.*

Jewell-Sherman, D. (2005, September 29). Testimony before the House Education and Workforce Committee U.S. House of Representatives, hearing on "Closing the Achievement Gap in America's Schools: The No Child Left Behind Act." Retrieved December 20, 2005, from http://republicans.edlabor.house.gov/archive/hearings/109th/fc/spellingsnclb092905/jewell-sherman.htm

Karchmer, M. A., & Mitchell, R. E. (2003). Demographic and achievement characteristics of deaf and hard of hearing students. In M. Marschark & P. E. Spencer (Eds.), *Oxford handbook of deaf studies, language, and education* (pp. 21–37). New York: Oxford University Press.

Loew, T. (2005, September 7). 26 district schools miss AYP targets. *Statesman Journal* (Oregon).

MacFarland, S. (2005, October 20). Utah schools chief to lobby education secretary. *Salt Lake Tribune.*

McNeill, B. (2005, August 25). For one elementary school, a frustrating year. *The Connection Newspapers.*

Maryland State Department of Education. (2005). *Implementation procedures for making AYP determinations for No Child Left Behind.* Baltimore, MD: Author.

Mills v. Board of Education, 348 F. Supp. 866 (D.C. 1972).

Mitchell, R. E., & Karchmer, M. A. (2006). Demographics of deaf education: More students in more places. *American Annals of the Deaf, 151* (2), 95–104.

Muller, E. (2005). *Deaf and hard of hearing: State infrastructures and programs.* Alexandria, VA: National Association of State Directors of Special Education.

National Center on Education Outcomes. (2005). *2005 state special education outcomes: Steps forward in a decade of change.* Minneapolis, MN: Author.

National Council of Teachers of English. (2004). *Status on implementation of the No Child Left Behind Act.* Retrieved October 12, 2005, from http://www.ncte.org/about/issues/national/views/116435.htm

National Education Association. (2005, April 20). *NEA stands up for children and parents, files first-ever national lawsuit against administration for not paying for education regulations* [Press release]. Retrieved October 20, 2005, from http://www.nea.org/newsreleases/2005/nr050420.html

National School Boards Association. (2003). Budget cuts threaten non-core programs. Retrieved November 16, 2005, from http://www.nsba.org/site/doc_sbn.asp?TRACKID=&VID=58&CID=1358&DID=32562

Ng, G. (2005). Judge Rules In 21-Year Special Ed Battle, Greg Ng, WBALTV Baltimore, August 12, 2005 retrieved from http://www.thewbalchannel.com/education/4846280/detail.html

No Child Left Behind Act of 2001, Pub. L. No. 107-110, 20 U.S.C. § 6301 *et seq.* (2002).

Olson, L. (2005). NCLB choice option going untapped, but tutoring picking up. *Education Week* (online edition). Retrieved September 7, 2005, from http://www.edweek.org/ew/articles/2005/03/16/27nclb.h24.html?querystring=low%20per forming%20school%20transfer

Pennsylvania Association for Retarded Children v. Commonwealth of Pennsylvania, 334 F. Supp. 1247 (E. Dist. Pa. 1971).

Raising Deaf Kids. (n.d.). Parents talk about School choices. Retrieved September 8, 2005, from http://www.raisingdeafkids.org/meet/parents/school.

Siegel, L. (2000). *The educational and communication needs of deaf and hard of hearing children: A statement of principle regarding fundamental systemic educational changes.* Greenbrae, CA: National Deaf Education Project.

Siegel, R.(2004, January 8). *Lyndon Johnson's war on poverty.* National Public Radio, All Things Considered [Broadcast]. Retrieved July 15, 2005, from http://www.npr.org/templates/story/story.php?storyId=1589660

Spellings, M. (2005, October 21). *Letter to Chief State School Officers.* Retrieved December 19, 2005, from http://www.ed.gov/policy/elsec/guid/secletter/051021.html

Spellings, M. (2005b). *Raising achievement: A new path for No Child Left Behind.* (2005). Prepared remarks for Secretary Spellings at Mount Vernon, VA, April 7, 2005. Retrieved October 20, 2005, from http://www.ed.gov/news/speeches/2005/04/04072005.html.

U.S. Census Bureau. (2005). School enrollment–social and economic characteristics of students: October 2005.Table 1. Retrieved March 12, 2008, from http://www.census.gov/population/www/socdemo/school/cps2005.html.

U.S. Department of Education (USDE). (2003). *25th annual report to Congress on the implementation of the Individuals With Disabilities Education Act.* Washington, DC: Author.

U.S. Department of Education (USDE). (2005a, June 13). *No Child Left Behind, supplemental educational services non-regulatory guidance.* Washington, DC: Author.

U.S. Department of Education (USDE). (2005b). *Raising achievement, a new path for No Child Left Behind.* Retrieved October 20, 2005, from http://www.ed.gov/policy/elsec/guid/raising/new-path.html

U.S. Department of Education (USDE). (2006a). *Overview, No Child Left Behind: A new era in education presentation.* Retrieved December 21, 2005, from http://www.ed.gov/nclb/overview/intro/presentation/index.html

U.S. Department of Education (USDE). (2006b). The No Child Left Behind Act: Challenging students through high expectations. Retrieved http://www.whitehouse.gov/news/releases/2006/10/20061005-2.html

U.S. Department of Education (USDE). (2007). Building on results: A blueprint for strengthening the No Child Left Behind Act. Retrieved May 20, 2008 from http://www.ed.gov/policy/elsec/leg/nclb/buildingonresults.html.

U.S. Department of Education (USDE). *Twenty-five years of progress in educating children with disabilities through IDEA.* Retrieved March 12, 2008, from http://www.ed.gov/policy/speced/leg/idea/history.html

U.S. House of Representatives, Hearing on "Closing the Achievement Gap in America's Schools: the No Child Left Behind Act" before the Committee on Education and the Workforce U.S. House of Representatives, September 29, 2005, Testimony of Deborah Jewell-Sherman, Ed.D., Superintendent, Richmond Public Schools, retrieved from http://edworkforce.house.gov/

2

Academic Achievement of Deaf Students

Ross E. Mitchell

The National Research Council (2001) identifies the practice of educational assessment as that which "seeks to determine how well students are learning and is an integral part of the quest for improved education. It provides feedback to students, educators, parents, policymakers, and the public about the effectiveness of educational services" (p. 1). Especially relevant to assessing the academic achievement of deaf students, this perspective assumes that the scores attained on standardized tests of academic achievement are valid and reliable indicators of what these students have learned; that the assessment results allow students as well as their families, teachers, and other interested parties to recognize their strengths and weaknesses; and that by identifying these strengths and weaknesses, families and schools have information that assists in designing and implementing programs and services that may improve the academic performance of these deaf students.

The latest reauthorizations of the two major federal education laws, namely, the No Child Left Behind Act of 2001 (hereafter NCLB) and the Individuals With Disabilities Education Improvement Act of 2004 (hereafter IDEA 2004), substantially incorporate the National Research Council's views on assessment.[1] That is, in addition to mandating a regime for school-based accountability that depends on the results of student test performance, current federal law encourages high-quality assessment practices that would provide detailed information about student academic performance and would be valuable for planning instruction and educational programming.

ACADEMIC ACHIEVEMENT RECORD

Two recent national studies provide important updates on the performance of deaf students on standardized assessments of academic achievement. The Gallaudet Research Institute established national norms for deaf and hard of hearing student performance on the Stanford Achievement Test Series, 10th edition (the National Deaf and Hard of Hearing Student Norms Project is described in Gallaudet Research Institute, 2004; Mitchell, Qi, & Traxler, 2008, in press), the fifth such study undertaken by the Gallaudet Research Institute over the last four decades (see also, e.g., Allen, 1986; Holt, Traxler, & Allen, 1992, 1997; Office of

1. For example, NCLB §1001.1; NCLB §§1111.b.3.C.ii, iii, xii, xv; and IDEA 2004 §614.b.3.A.

Demographic Studies, 1969; Traxler, 2000). At about the same time, SRI International conducted a similar study of deaf students' academic achievement as part of a comprehensive evaluation of the Individuals With Disabilities Education Act Amendments of 1997 (hereafter IDEA 1997) overseen by the Office of Special Education Programs (OSEP) within the U.S. Department of Education (e.g., see Blackorby et al., 2005; Wagner et al., 2003; Wagner, Newman, Cameto, & Levine, 2006; focusing solely on students with hearing impairment, see Blackorby & Knokey, 2006). These two studies are not identical in design, nor do they report achievement results from the same assessment instrument, but they are complementary. Together, the results of these studies highlight serious concerns about the academic achievement levels of deaf students.

Before presenting mathematics and reading achievement profiles for deaf students from the Gallaudet Research Institute and OSEP studies, two critical design differences need to be highlighted. First, the OSEP study did not specifically sample schools that enrolled students with hearing impairments (the applicable IDEA classification) whereas the Gallaudet Research Institute study used for its sampling frame a limited registry of schools and programs known to be serving deaf students. The consequence of this difference is that the Gallaudet Research Institute study is likely to overrepresent (a) deaf students with more severe hearing loss and (b) deaf students who attend schools for the deaf and other special programs that have relatively large numbers of deaf students (for a description of biases in the Gallaudet Research Institute study sampling frame, see Mitchell, 2004). Another way to look at this difference is that the OSEP study is likely to have a greater proportion of students who are hard of hearing compared with the Gallaudet Research Institute study. These prevalence differences between the two studies in severity of hearing loss and instructional program setting placement mean that achievement levels are expected to be higher for the OSEP study participants than for those in the Gallaudet Research Institute study (for a discussion of the relationship between achievement and deaf students' characteristics, see Karchmer & Mitchell, 2003).

Second, the OSEP study is longitudinal in its design whereas the Gallaudet Research Institute study is cross-sectional. As a result, except for replacements recruited because of attrition, the OSEP study is focused on a specific cohort of students identified for special education in 2000 regardless of their current eligibility for special education whereas the Gallaudet Research Institute study pertains to students tested in 2003, including students who were not identified until after 2000, had not entered the country until after 2000, or possibly had not become deaf until after 2000, but not including students who had exited special education before 2003. Moreover, the data from the OSEP study analyzed here are those collected during the second wave of data collection, which was closest in time to the Gallaudet Research Institute data collection activity. Because of study attrition and the difficulty of recruiting replacements, the achievement levels measured in the OSEP study are likely to be higher because, on average, more high-performing students remain in longitudinal studies. The cross-sectional Gallaudet Research Institute study is more likely to capture low-performing and mobile students. Despite these two important study design differences, certainly, there is significant overlap between the two study populations and, possibly, even identical participants. Nonetheless, there is no reason to expect the results of these studies to be identical.

Another important difference to highlight before presenting data summaries from the OSEP and Gallaudet Research Institute studies is that of the assessment instruments. The OSEP study used the Woodcock-Johnson III, which provides age-based norms. That is, the performance distribution is referenced to the age of the child taking the test batteries, not the child's grade in school. However, the Gallaudet Research Institute study used the Stanford Achievement Test Series, which provides grade-based norms. One has to assume an age-grade correlation to work with grade-based norms. In other words, Grade 2 norms are used for 8-year-olds, Grade 3 for 9-year-olds, Grade 4 for 10-year-olds, etc. With this very strong correlation, age-grade-based norms can then be used to compare the two groups of students on the two tests. The metric being used is the percentile rank collapsed into quartiles (i.e., 1st quartile is 1st–25th percentile, 2nd quartile is 26th–50th percentile, 2nd quartile is 51st–75th percentile, and 4th quartile is 76th–99th percentile).

OSEP Study

Two named studies within OSEP's IDEA 1997 evaluation measured academic achievement among deaf students identified for special education: the Special Education Elementary Longitudinal Study (SEELS) and the National Longitudinal Transition Study-2 (NLTS-2). Independent analyses of data from SEELS are summarized here. Data from the NLTS-2, which captures the high school age population and follows it beyond graduation, are not analyzed here, but published reports are summarized below. Analysis of data from the second wave of SEELS, which were collected in 2002, is reported here because the data were collected up to within a year preceding the Gallaudet Research Institute study and because the students were at the right ages for comparison purposes (i.e., at least age 8 years, specifically, ages 8 to 15 years).[2] The distributions of mathematics and reading achievement among these students with hearing impairment who were participating in SEELS in 2002 are summarized in Figure 2.1.

Each vertical bar in Figure 2.1 has four stacked segments, which represent the proportion of students whose scores correspond to each of the four quartiles of the general (hearing) population norms. If the score distribution of the deaf student population (more precisely, population of students with hearing impairment) were identical to the score distribution of the general population, then each of the four stacked segments would be exactly the same size, breaking at 25%, 50%, and 75% of students tested. However, the distributions differ dramatically. For

2. The data analyses reported here were run using *SPSS Complex Samples 15.0 for Windows* (SPSS, 2007) with the February 2007 release of the SEELS Waves 1, 2, and 3 public-use data file (U.S. Department of Education, 2007), Wave 2 data only. Analyses of the same data by SRI International were reported by Blackorby and Knokey (2006).

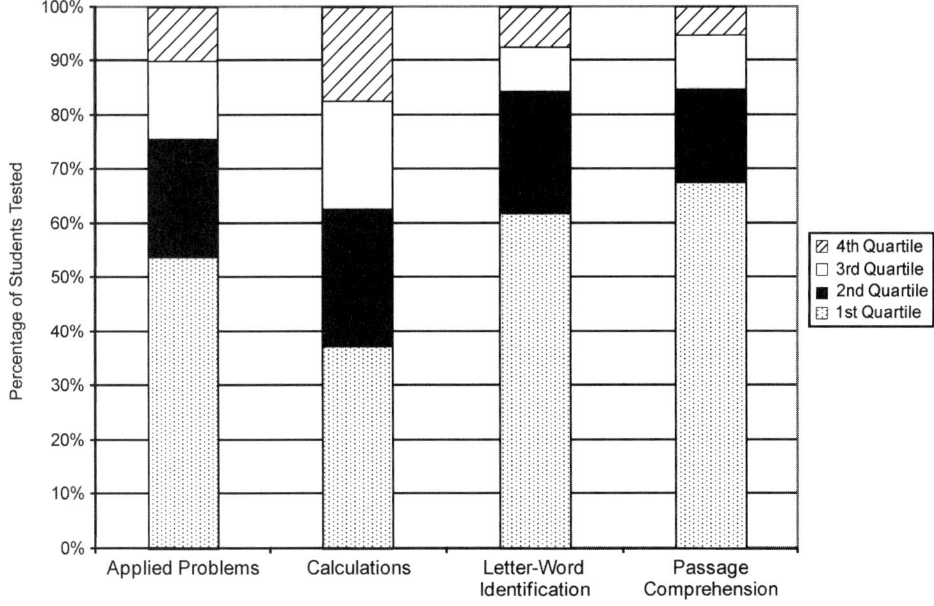

Figure 2.1. Distribution of mathematics and reading achievement among students with hearing impairment, ages 8–15 years, age-based general population norms, 2002. *Note:* From Special Education Elementary Longitudinal Study (U.S. Department of Education, 2007).

example, consider the first bar on the left, which is for the Applied Problems mathematics test. Nearly 54% of deaf students attained scores that corresponded to the lowest quartile of the general population (the lightly stippled white segment that is bounded at 0% and roughly 54%), which is more than twice what would have been expected if the two groups had similar achievement distributions. More than 75% of deaf students scored below the median of the general population (i.e., almost 22% scored in the 2nd quartile of the general population, represented by the solid black segment). Almost exactly 90% of deaf students scored in the first three quartiles of the general population distribution (i.e., almost 15% scored in the 3rd quartile of the general population, represented by the solid white segment). Only 10% of deaf students scored in the 4th quartile of the general population distribution (the densely stippled black segment bounded at roughly 90% and 100%). The median is typically considered the mark for being exactly at grade level (the boundary between the solid black and solid white segments), which means that just less than 25% of deaf students achieved at or above grade level on the Applied Problems mathematics test.

On the other test of mathematics, Calculations, deaf students come closer to, but are not in alignment with, the general population distribution of scores. About 37% of deaf students score at or above grade level (i.e., above the general population median). A similar proportion attain scores corresponding to just the 1st quartile of the general population. On the reading tests, the performance profiles are furthest out of alignment with the general population. For both Letter-Word Identification and Passage Comprehension, less than 16% of deaf students scored above the general population median. Slightly less than two-thirds achieved in the 1st quartile of the general population on Letter-Word Identification, and slightly more than two-thirds are in the 1st quartile on Passage Comprehension. These measures demonstrate a dramatic "achievement gap" between deaf students and their nondisabled peers.

For high school age students in the NLTS-2, Wagner and colleagues (2003) report that, on average, deaf students were 3.6 grades below grade level on tests of reading and 3.0 grades below grade level on tests of mathematics at the time of their most recent assessment. Just less than 20% of these students scored within one grade of grade level or better in reading while nearly 33% scored at least five grades below grade level. Almost 22% of the NLTS-2 sample of deaf students scored within one grade of grade level or better in mathematics while nearly 23% scored at least five grades below grade level.

Gallaudet Research Institute Study

From the Gallaudet Research Institute study, the most current deaf and hard of hearing student national norms for tests of reading and mathematics on the Stanford Achievement Test Series (hereafter referred to as the Stanford) are summarized in Figure 2.2.[3] Again, consider the first bar on the left, which is for the test of mathematics problem solving. Slightly more than 82% of deaf students attained scores that corresponded to the lowest quartile of the general population, which is more than three times what would have been expected if the two groups had similar achievement distributions. About 90% of deaf students scored below the median (50th percentile) of the general population (i.e., 8% scored in the 2nd quartile). Nearly 97% of deaf students scored in the first three quartiles of the general population distribution (i.e., 6% scored in the 3rd quartile). Only 3% of deaf students scored in the 4th quartile of the general population distribution. The median is typically considered the mark for being exactly at grade level, which means that just less than 10% of deaf students achieved at grade level on the test of mathematics problem solving. As expected, compared with the OSEP study, the results of the Gallaudet Research Institute study paint a more dismal picture of deaf students' academic achievement.

On the other test of mathematics, Procedures, deaf students come closer to, but are still quite far from alignment with, the general population distribution of scores. Less than 15% of deaf students are achieving at or above grade level (i.e., above the general population median). Almost 72% are in the 1st quartile of the general population score distribution. The performance profiles for the tests of reading vocabulary and reading comprehension are more profoundly skewed than that observed for mathematics problem solving. Well less than 10% of deaf stu-

3. The data analyses reported here were run using *SPSS Complex Samples 15.0 for Windows* (SPSS, 2007) with the unpublished data from the Stanford Achievement Test, 10th Edition, National Deaf and Hard of Hearing Student Norms Project (Gallaudet Research Institute, 2003).

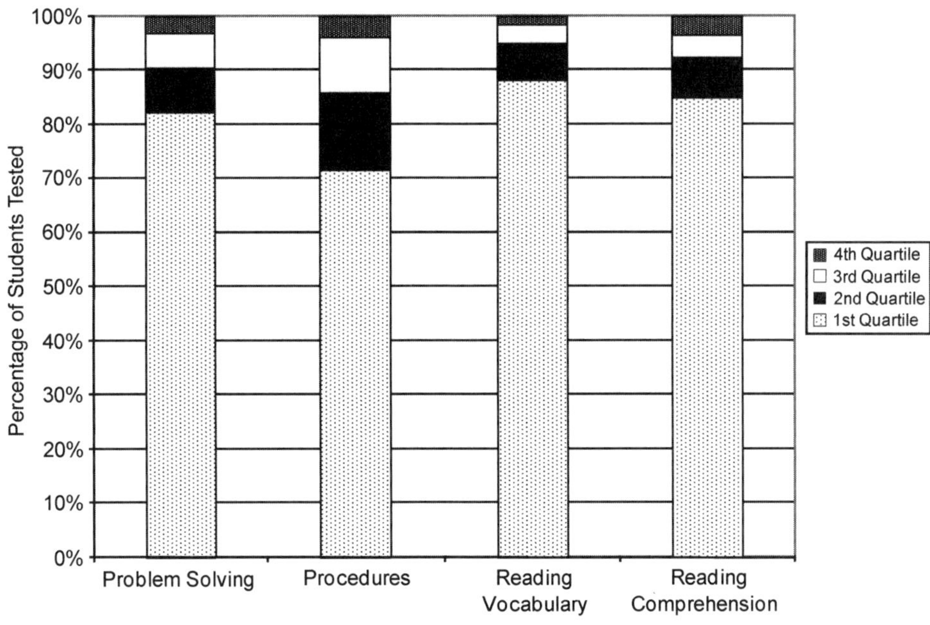

Figure 2.2. Distribution of mathematics and reading achievement among deaf students, ages 8–15 years, age-grade-based general population norms, 2003. *Note:* From National Deaf and Hard of Hearing Student Norms Project (Gallaudet Research Institute, 2003).

dents are at or above grade level on reading vocabulary and reading comprehension (less than 6% and 8%, respectively). Roughly seven of every eight students scores in the 1st quartile of the general population distribution (i.e., 88% on reading vocabulary and 85% on reading comprehension). The disparity between deaf students and their nondisabled peers is magnified by the selection biases of the Gallaudet Research Institute study. That is, by having a sample that amplifies the severity of disability and need for special programs, the Gallaudet Research Institute study emphasizes the dramatic achievement gap between this special population and the general population.

For high school age students taking the Stanford, on average, deaf students were 7.4 grades below grade level on tests of reading and 5.4 grades below grade level on tests of mathematics. Less than 10% of these students scored within 1.0 grade of grade level or better in reading while nearly 77% scored at least 5.0 grades below grade level. Almost 10% of the Gallaudet Research Institute study sample of deaf students scored within 1.0 grade of grade level or better in mathematics while nearly 53% scored at least 5.0 grades below grade level. Again, the sampling biases of the Gallaudet Research Institute sample draw attention to an even larger achievement gap between the general student population and deaf students with the greatest degrees of hearing loss or who are placed in programs designed to provide more specialized instructional services.

Historical Perspective

Putting these recent results into context, one can compare the current norms from the Gallaudet Research Institute study with those of deaf student performance on the Stanford over the last few decades. Karchmer and Mitchell (2003) note several studies that offer findings consistent with results from research using the Stanford; however, except for the Gallaudet Research Institute investigations using the Stanford, there are no other data that allow for historical comparison across multiple decades. Qi and Mitchell (2007) reviewed the distribution of scores relative to the general population and found that it has been nearly constant for both reading and mathematics. They found that performance in reading comprehension has held steady and has been quite low relative to the general population. The same is true for the type of content found on the current test of mathematics procedures. There are indications that there has been relative improvement in mathematics problem solving among older (high school age) deaf students since the 1990s, but part of the most recent (2003 norms for the 10th edition) improvement may be a consequence of eliminating an artificial ceiling in attainable scores that had been imposed on the design of earlier studies. In other words, the achievement gap between deaf students and the general population on the Stanford has remained large and effectively unchanged for more than three decades.

Another important historical perspective on the academic achievements of deaf students can be obtained by examining the two national longitudinal transition studies of special education students moving from their high school years to postsecondary education, employment, or other activities. These studies allow direct comparison among the groups of students identified by their disability categories. The relative performance of students with various disabilities can be assessed as well as any changes that have occurred over the intervening years. Explicit academic performance comparisons are made in a report by Wagner, Newman, and Cameto (2004) between the NLTS (data collected between 1985 and 1987) and NLTS-2 (data collected between 2001 and 2002) cohorts. These investigators found that "students with visual or hearing impairments tended to have the best grades overall, as well as among the largest increases over time in receiving mostly A's" (p. 4–8). Among students with disabilities, review of the NLTS and NLTS-2 studies leads to the conclusion that deaf students have been among the academically higher performing groups in both special education cohorts (though always exceeded by students with visual impairments) as measured by achievement testing (especially tests of mathematics), high school completion, and attendance at postsecondary educational institutions (National Research Council, 1997; Wagner et al., 2003; Wagner, Newman, Cameto, & Levine, 2005, 2006). That is, students with low-incidence disabilities have tended to outperform students identified by other, more prevalent primary disability categories. Moreover, students with low-incidence disabilities appear to have made tremendous gains among several indicators of academic achievement. However, this comparison is favorable only among students with disabilities. As discussed above, deaf students continue to lag far behind their nondisabled peers, especially on the recently elevated, if not decisive, indicator of academic achievement test scores.

CRITIQUE OF ASSESSMENT ASSUMPTIONS

Given the substantial achievement gap estimates from the OSEP and Gallaudet Research Institute studies, some discussion of assessment of deaf students is necessary. The accurate measurement of academic achievement depends on a number of considerations. In the case of deaf students, these considerations include important issues of language use and comprehension (see, e.g., Allen, White, & Karchmer, 1983; Baker, 1991; Chamberlain & Mayberry, 2000; Marschark, 2001; Paul & Quigley, 1990; Qi & Mitchell, 2007). Whether for the purpose of instructional feedback and program evaluation or punitive consequences of test-based accountability, accurately knowing what deaf students know presents a greater challenge than the demands placed on a system of assessment for their nondisabled, English-fluent peers.

As cited at the outset, the National Research Council (2001) emphasizes that educational assessment "seeks to determine how well students are learning." Elsewhere, however, the National Research Council (2004) highlights the challenges associated with testing students with disabilities and English language learners: "Many of these students have attributes—such as physical, emotional, or learning disabilities or limited fluency in English—that may prevent them from readily demonstrating what they know or can do on a test" (p. 1). In other words, when it comes to deaf students, test results may not accurately indicate how well they are learning. In a test-based accountability regime, this threat to validity undermines the entire enterprise. Unfortunately, "the existing base of research about the effects of accommodations on test performance and the comparability of scores obtained under standard and accommodated conditions is insufficient to provide empirical support for many of the decisions that must be made with respect to the testing of these students" (National Research Council, 2004, p. 2). There are some serious questions about just what causes the achievement gap identified in the recent Gallaudet Research Institute and OSEP studies and no unequivocal answers.

There are at least two clear directions for research that may lead to more accurate inferences from the assessment of academic achievement among deaf students. The first has nothing to do with test development, but has everything to do with valid inferences in a system of test-based school accountability. The first question raised by the National Research Council (2006, p. 145) for the purpose of examining systems for statewide assessment of science is whether any information is collected that establishes whether students have sufficient opportunity to learn. This question is an essential one, regardless of content area. Student attributes that may interfere with accurate assessment are not necessary to consider if the instructional program does not deliver the assessed content in a manner that can be learned.

Accommodating disabilities, including deafness, will not matter if the students do not or cannot know the material being tested. Given that federal special education law mandated access to the general curriculum only a decade ago, and many schools and programs serving students in special education did not take assessment participation seriously until after the passage of NCLB, a systematic approach to verifying adequate opportunity to learn would significantly improve the validity of inferences from statewide accountability assessments. If students do not have the opportunity to learn the content that an accountability exam attempts to assess (which assumes, correctly or not, that such exams can assess that learning) then results from such a test will provide little insight into what students actually have been learning in the classroom.

The second area for further research is language-based test accommodations (for an extended discussion of this topic, see Qi & Mitchell, 2007). For both students with disabilities and English language learners, "the assumption underlying the accommodation is that every student has a true level of competence in each tested subject area, and that a perfectly reliable and valid assessment will reveal that true performance. The accommodation is intended only to compensate for factors that prevent the student from demonstrating his or her true competence, and not to improve his or her performance beyond that level" (National Research Council, 2004, p. 35). In addition to being classified as one of several categories of students with disabilities, deaf students may be thought of, imperfectly, as English language learners because they may enter school either with prior proficiency in a signed language (see, e.g., Johnson, Liddell, & Erting, 1989; Meadow-Orlans, Mertens, & Sass-Lehrer, 2003; Mitchell & Karchmer, 2005; Mitchell, Young, Bachleda, & Karchmer, 2006; Padden & Humphries, 1988) or with delays in learning any language (see, e.g., Emmorey, Bellugi, Frederici, & Horn, 1995; Mayberry & Lock, 1998; Morford & Mayberry, 2000). Regardless of either the specific languages acquired or the timing of their acquisition, deaf students have limited access to spoken English language environments and receive instructional accommodations that do not depend on spoken English (e.g., teachers may interact with students directly through American Sign Language or through an interpreter using American Sign Language or some system of manual communication representing English). Typically, this limited access to spoken English negatively affects deaf students' abilities to respond effectively to written English tests.

Systematic investigation of tests that offer language simplification or translation into the discourse mode of the classroom would determine the efficacy of these accommodations and help eliminate any confoundedness between access to the assessment and other possible explanations of poor test performance (such as opportunity to learn). In other words, the assumption that students fully understand (a) the tasks they are asked to perform and (b) the nature of the responses requested is not necessarily a safe one. Appropriate language-based accommodations would improve the validity of inferences about learning by deaf students.

Without answers to questions of opportunity to learn and the efficacy of test accommodations, the National Research Council's (2001) remaining ambitions for educational assessment cannot be achieved with deaf students. In other words, validity and reliability remain to be determined; identifying students' strengths and weaknesses is more difficult; and feedback to program design and implementation, not to mention stakeholders (i.e., students, educators, parents, policymakers, and the public) will be more equivocal. Until high-quality assessment practices are brought to deaf education, it is going to be difficult to know what deaf students know. Or, at a minimum, schools serving deaf students will have great difficulty being responsive to a system of test-based accountability.

CONCLUSION

Current standardized assessment results indicate that there is a large achievement gap between deaf students and their nondisabled peers. This disparity has existed for decades and has changed little if at all. At the same time, performance indicators from other measures of academic achievement would suggest that deaf students are more successful in school and have translated that success into greater postsecondary education and employment opportunities. Either more deaf students are receiving inflated grades and easy passes to graduation and postsecondary opportunities or standardized assessments are failing to accurately measure the improved academic achievements of deaf students.

As discussed in this chapter's brief critique of assessment assumptions, there is good reason to believe that current standardized assessment practices may result in low-quality information about deaf students' learning, though the degree of disconnect between what deaf students know and their performance on tests of academic achievement is uncertain. Certainly, many students with low scores would continue to perform poorly even with appropriate accommodations because delayed language development or insufficient opportunity to learn have interfered with their ability to know the material being tested. Many other deaf students, however, may in fact know more than their test performances reveal. Valid inferences based on the test scores of students who have developed their academic proficiency through signed language rather than English language discourse are limited by the use of written English tests.

In the current era of test-based accountability, especially with the NCLB mandate that *all* students achieve proficient status on statewide accountability assessments by 2014, there is great reason to be concerned. Without some dramatic intervention that transforms the achievement profile of deaf students, eventually, these and others students in special education are likely to prevent schools from achieving 100% proficiency. Even with special allowances for students with severe cognitive disabilities (which is a category that applies to some but not all deaf students) and narrowing of the domain for which students will be held accountable for a larger share of students in special education, tremendous change is needed before all remaining deaf students achieve at the proficient level. Given the findings from the national longitudinal transition studies showing that significant progress has been made with deaf students over the last two decades, the central and elevated importance of performance on standardized tests of academic achievement is quite troubling. And though there is room for advancing the opportunity to learn, without fair and balanced consideration of multiple indicators of academic achievement, it is unclear whether test quality, assessment practices, and student performance will improve in time to prevent serious and potentially harmful disruption to the education of deaf students.

REFERENCES

Allen, T. E. (1986). Patterns of academic achievement among hearing impaired students: 1974 and 1983. In A. N. Schildroth & M. A. Karchmer (Eds.), *Deaf children in America* (pp.161–206). San Diego, CA: College-Hill Press.

Allen, T. E., White, C. S., & Karchmer, M. A. (1983). Issues in the development of a special edition for hearing-impaired students of the seventh edition of the Stanford Achievement Test. *American Annals of the Deaf, 128* (1), 34–39.

Baker, R. M. (1991). Evaluation of hearing-impaired children. In K. E. Green (Ed.), *Educational testing: Issues and applications* (pp. 77–107). New York: Garland.

Blackorby, J., & Knokey, A.-M. (2006). *A national profile of students with hearing impairments in elementary and middle school: A special topic report from the Special Education Elementary Longitudinal Study.* Menlo Park, CA: SRI International.

Blackorby, J., Wagner, M., Cameto, R., Davies, E., Levine, P., Newman, L., et al. (2005). *Engagement, academics, social adjustment, and independence: The achievements of elementary and middle school students with disabilities.* Menlo Park, CA: SRI International.

Chamberlain, C., & Mayberry, R. I. (2000). Theorizing about the relation between American Sign Language and reading. In C. Chamberlain, J. P. Morford, & R. I. Mayberry (Eds.), *Language acquisition by eye.* (pp. 221–259). Mahwah, NJ: Lawrence Erlbaum.

Emmorey, K., Bellugi, U., Frederici, A., & Horn, P. (1995). Effects of age of acquisition on grammatical sensitivity: Evidence from on-line and off-line tasks. *Applied Psycholinguistics, 16,* 1–23.

Gallaudet Research Institute. (2003). Stanford Achievement Test, 10th Edition, National Deaf and Hard of Hearing Student Norms Project, non-public data file. Washington, DC: Gallaudet Research Institute, Gallaudet University.

Gallaudet Research Institute. (2004). *Norms booklet for deaf and hard-of-hearing students: Stanford Achievement Test, 10th Edition, Form A.* Washington, DC: Gallaudet University.

Holt, J. A., Traxler, C. B., & Allen, T. E. (1992). *Interpreting the scores: A user's guide to the 8th Edition Stanford Achievement Test for educators of deaf and hard of hearing students.* (Gallaudet Research Institute Technical Report No. 92-1). Washington, DC: Gallaudet University.

Holt, J. A., Traxler, C. B., & Allen, T. E. (1997). *Interpreting the scores: A user's guide to the 9th Edition Stanford Achievement Test for educators of deaf and hard-of-hearing students.* (Technical Report No. 97-1). Washington, DC: Gallaudet University, Gallaudet Research Institute.

Individuals With Disabilities Education Act Amendments of 1997, Pub. L. No. 105-17, 20 U.S.C. § 1400 *et seq.*

Individuals With Disabilities Education Improvement Act of 2004, Pub. L. No. 108-446, 20 U.S.C. § 1400 *et seq.*

Johnson, R. E., Liddell, S. K., & Erting, C. J. (1989). *Unlocking the curriculum: Principles for achieving access in deaf education.* (Working Paper No. 89-3). Washington, DC: Gallaudet Research Institute, Gallaudet University.

Karchmer, M. A. & Mitchell, R. E. (2003). Demographic and achievement characteristics of deaf and hard of hearing students. In M. Marschark & P. E. Spencer (Eds.), *Oxford handbook of deaf studies, language, and education,* (pp. 21–37). New York: Oxford University Press.

Marschark, M. (2001). *Language development in children who are deaf: A research synthesis.* Alexandria, VA: National Association of State Directors of Special Education. (ERIC Document Reproduction Service No. ED455620)

Mayberry, R. I., & Lock, E. (1998, May). *Critical period effects on grammatical processing: Privileged status of the first language.* Paper presented at the American Psychological Society Convention, Washington, DC.

Meadow-Orlans, K. P., Mertens, D. M., & Sass-Lehrer, M. A. (2003). *Parents and their deaf children: The early years.* Washington, DC: Gallaudet University Press.

Mitchell, R. E. (2004). National profile of deaf and hard of hearing students in special education from weighted survey results. *American Annals of the Deaf, 149* (4), 336–349.

Mitchell, R. E., & Karchmer, M. A. (2005). Parental hearing status and signing among deaf and hard-of-hearing students. *Sign Language Studies, 5* (2), 83–96.

Mitchell, R. E., Qi, S., & Traxler, C. B. (2008, in press). *Stanford Achievement Test, 10th Edition, national performance norms for deaf and hard of hearing students: A technical report.* Washington, DC: Gallaudet Research Institute, Gallaudet University.

Mitchell, R. E., Young, T. A., Bachleda, B., & Karchmer, M. A. (2006). How many people use ASL in the United States? Why estimates need updating. *Sign Language Studies, 6* (3), 306–335.

Morford, J. P., & Mayberry, R. I. (2000). A reexamination of "early exposure" and its implications for language acquisition by eye. In C. Chamberlain, J. P. Morford, & R. I. Mayberry (Eds.), *Language acquisition by eye,* (pp. 111–127). Mahwah, NJ: Lawrence Erlbaum.

National Research Council. (1997). *Educating one and all: Students with disabilities and standards-based reform.* L. M. McDonnell, M. J. McLaughlin, & P. Morison (Eds.), Committee on Goals 2000 and the Inclusion of Students with Disabilities, Board on Testing and Assessment, Commission on Behavioral and Social Sciences and Education. Washington, DC: National Academies Press.

National Research Council. (2001). *Knowing what students know: The science and design of educational assessment.* Committee on the Foundations of Assessment, J. Pelligrino, N. Chudowsky, & R. Glaser (Eds.), Board on Testing and Assessment, Center for Education. Division of Behavioral and Social Sciences and Education. Washington, DC: National Academies Press.

National Research Council. (2004). *Keeping score for all: The effects of inclusion and accommodation policies on large-scale educational assessments.* Committee on Participation of English Language Learners and Students with Disabilities in NAEP and Other Large-Scale Assessments, J. A. Koenig & L. F. Bachman (Eds.), Board on Testing and Assessment, Center for Education, Division of Behavioral and Social Sciences and Education. Washington, DC: The National Academies Press.

National Research Council. (2006). *Systems for state science assessment.* Committee on Test Design for K–12 Science Achievement, M. R. Wilson and M. W. Bertenthal (Eds.), Board on Testing and Assessment, Center for Education, Division of Behavioral and Social Sciences and Education. Washington, DC: The National Academies Press.

No Child Left Behind Act of 2001, Pub. L. No. 107-110, 115 Stat. 1425 (2002).

Office of Demographic Studies. (1969). *Academic achievement test performance of hearing impaired students.* Washington, DC: Gallaudet College.

Padden, C. A., & Humphries, T. (1988). *Deaf in America: Voices from a culture.* Cambridge, MA: Harvard University Press.

Paul, P. V., & Quigley, S. P. (1990). *Education and deafness.* New York: Longman.

Qi, S., & Mitchell, R. E. (2007, April 10). *Large-scale academic achievement testing of deaf and hard-of-hearing students: Past, present, and future.* Paper presented at the annual meeting of the American Educational Research Association, Chicago, Illinois.

Traxler, C. B. (2000). The Stanford Achievement Test, 9th Edition: National norming and performance standards for deaf and hard-of-hearing students. *Journal of Deaf Studies & Deaf Education, 5* (4), 337–348.

U.S. Department of Education. (2007, February). Special Education Elementary Longitudinal Study, Waves 1, 2, and 3 public-use data file. Washington, DC: Office of Special Education Programs, U.S. Department of Education.

Wagner, M., Marder, C., Blackorby, J., Cameto, R., Newman, L., Levine, P., et al. (2003). *The achievements of youth with disabilities during secondary school. A report from the National Longitudinal Transition Study-2 (NLTS2).* Menlo Park, CA: SRI International.

Wagner, M., Newman, L., & Cameto, R. (2004). *Changes over time in the secondary school programs of students with disabilities. A report of findings from the National Longitudinal Transition Study and the National Longitudinal Transition Study-2 (NLTS2).* Menlo Park, CA: SRI International.

Wagner, M., Newman, L., Cameto, R., & Levine, P. (2005). *Changes over time in the early postschool outcomes of youth with disabilities. A report of findings from the National Longitudinal Transition Study (NLTS) and the National Longitudinal Transition Study-2 (NLTS2).* Menlo Park, CA: SRI International.

Wagner, M., Newman, L., Cameto, R., & Levine, P. (2006). *The academic achievement and functional performance of youth with disabilities. A report from the National Longitudinal Transition Study-2 (NLTS2).* (NCSER 2006-3000). Menlo Park, CA: SRI International.

3

Accommodations to Improve Instruction and Assessment of Deaf Students

Betsy J. Case

Raising academic standards for all students and measuring student achievement to hold schools accountable for educational progress are central strategies for promoting educational excellence and equity in American schools. The No Child Left Behind Act (NCLB) of 2001 was designed to support state efforts to establish challenging standards, to develop assessments that are aligned with those standards, and to build accountability systems for districts and schools that are based on educational results. Students with disabilities are required by federal law (Section 504 of the Rehabilitation Act of 1973, Title II of the Americans With Disabilities Act of 1990, Title I of the Elementary and Secondary Education Act, and the Individuals With Disabilities Education Improvement Act of 2004 [IDEA 2004]) to take the same assessments as the general population of students. Both NCLB and IDEA 2004 "require that students with disabilities be provided accommodations, when appropriate and documented on the student's Individualized Education Program (IEP) or Section 504 plan. Because assessment is often associated with direct individual benefits (e.g., promotion, graduation) and is an integral part of accountability systems, it is imperative for researchers to look closely at the accommodations allowed in instruction and assessment" (Case, 2003, p. 2).

Accommodations in assessment and instruction are especially important to students who are deaf because they generally do not have ready access to standard English as they enter school. As a result, their educational progress is often delayed. To understand the appropriate selection of accommodations for this population, professionals, parents, and policymakers need to understand the implications of being deaf as they affect education.

IMPLICATIONS OF BEING DEAF

Linguists and developmental psychologists generally believe that children must acquire basic competence in using a language between the ages of 1 and 3 if they are to build a good foundation for later intellectual development. Hearing loss

---

This chapter is based on B. Case. (2005). *Accommodations to improve instruction and assessment of students who are deaf or hard of hearing.* Harcourt policy paper. San Antonio, TX: Pearson Education.

typically has a significant effect on the acquisition of a spoken language such as English, but the extent of the effect varies according to when the child becomes deaf, how severe the deafness is, and how resourceful the child's parents or caretakers are in providing rich and accessible language interaction. The remainder of this section deals primarily with assessment problems experienced by students whose hearing loss has resulted in significant difficulty learning English in its written and oral forms.

Mounty (2001) summarized the primary reason this student population faces distinct challenges with assessments:

> At the heart of this difficulty is the reality that often English functions as a nonnative language within this population. Because English is auditorily based, deaf and hard of hearing individuals do not have full access to it across situations.

Rudner (1978, cited in Gordon & Stump, 1996) states that standardized testing presumes a certain level of English proficiency that is not necessarily present among students who are deaf. The presumption of a certain level of verbal language ability presents several problems with respect to these students: (a) difficulties with English, (b) proficiency in diverse modalities of communications, (c) deficient reading skills, (d) culturally related experiential differences, and (e) consequent uncertainty with respect to the validity and reliability of these students' test results.

Difficulties with English. Students who are deaf or severely hard of hearing generally have great difficulty understanding spoken English without some type of accompanying or alternative accommodation that is visually comprehensible. If these students were born deaf or lost their hearing at a very early age, then they often have missed out on crucial developmental milestones and experiences. The result is that they come to school developmentally delayed in learning English and often lagging behind in any form of language development. Interestingly, a substantial amount of research suggests that deaf children with deaf parents are less likely than deaf children with hearing parents to experience irreparable delays in English acquisition, partly because their deaf parents are often quite proficient at establishing early and effective communication with their deaf children (typically by promoting sign language development through sign language use) and partly because they themselves have come to learn English in spite of hearing loss. Consequently, these parents know how to make what they have learned understandable to a deaf child. Nevertheless, for most deaf students, the fact is that standardized tests presume more familiarity with common English usage than these students generally attain in comparison with hearing peers of the same age. Thus, on average, they are at a distinct disadvantage when taking these tests. Those learning English primarily as a topic of discussion shared through American Sign Language (ASL) are, in essence, learning English as a second language. Taking into consideration the expressive and receptive modalities most familiar to these students, which differ significantly from those of English-based hearing students, the need for accommodations becomes more apparent.

Diverse modalities of communication. Students who are profoundly deaf or severely hard of hearing are taught in a wide variety of modalities, depending on their individual abilities and needs and the communication policies of their schools. When interacting with the children at home, the parents of these students often (but not always) try to reinforce the communication practices used with their children at school. These modalities include auditory-oral approaches in which students learn to speak and speechread and to relate written English to spoken English in ways resembling as much as possible the way hearing children learn to read and write. For example, Cued Speech, or Cued English, is a unique form of oral instruction in which hand signals are used to differentiate vowels and consonants that look alike when speechread. The Sign-Supported English approach includes various forms of signed English—such as Signed English or Signing Exact English—in which signs are produced in English word order as words are simultaneously spoken. Signing while speaking is often described as Simultaneous Communication, or "Sim-Com," which in one form or another has been the primary communication method used in so-called "total communication" programs. Bilingual education for deaf students uses ASL for through-the-air classroom discussion, and English is taught as a second, written—rather than spoken—language. Signs in ASL are presented in the order inherent to that language and do not necessarily match English word order.

Each approach has benefits and limitations as well as a cadre of advocates and supporters. The diversity of these modalities makes development of assessments for deaf students significantly challenging. The need for accommodations is paramount for both expressive and receptive communication.

Although a variety of methods are used to communicate with deaf students face to face, English is used for reading and writing because there is not a widely accepted written form of ASL. Furthermore, the grammar and structure of ASL differs significantly from that of the English taught in schools for the general population, so students who use ASL as their primary means of communication essentially learn English as a foreign language in school.

Deficient reading skills. With the hindered access to English that many of these students face, students who are deaf often lag behind general education students in reading and mathematics—but especially in reading. It has been typical for deaf students to be many years behind their general education peers. For example, the average performance on tests of reading comprehension for deaf students at the age of 15 is roughly six grade equivalents lower than their hearing peers of the same age (Karchmer & Mitchell, 2003). Because reading is auditorily based—printed letters associated with phonemes that most hearing readers have heard—learning to read has been especially problematic for deaf students.

Culturally related experiential differences. Hearing loss and deafness are more than functional issues; they are also cultural. The use of sign language as well as other cultural elements sets deaf students apart from hearing peers in general education (Moores, 2002). This difference occurs because, "in general, students with significant hearing loss encounter greater difficulty in comprehending and using the English language than do their peers" (Luetke-Stahlman, 1998, p. 316). Because deaf children do not have a well-developed vocabulary and awareness of English grounded in years of hearing and using the spoken language, "literacy development typically does not proceed at a pace considered average for hearing students" (Schirmer, 2001, p. 74).

ACCOMMODATIONS TO IMPROVE INSTRUCTION, LEARNING, AND ASSESSMENT

The 2004 reauthorization of IDEA contains the mandate that all children with disabilities should participate in statewide and districtwide assessments. It states that "children with disabilities are included in general state and district-wide assessment programs with appropriate accommodations, where necessary" (IDEA, 2004, p. 118). The legislation does not clarify what "appropriate" means. Furthermore, the legislation and common practice tend to confuse the terms "accommodations" and "modifications."

The term *accommodation* has been used interchangeably with the term *modification,* and there is a lack of consensus as to their formal meanings (Thurlow, Hurley, Spicuzza, & El Sawaf, 1996). Consequently, what is deemed an accommodation in one state may be considered a modification in another. In an attempt to clarify the two concepts psychometrically, Hollenbeck, Tindal, Harniss, and Almond (1999) built on the theories of Phillips (1993, 1994) to define the two as separate and distinct concepts.

Accommodations are changes made in the test presentation or response method so students can demonstrate what they know about the content without requiring any changes to the construct of the content being measured, the grade level, or performance requirements. Phillips (1994) also posited that there must be a differential boost or differential access. Fuchs (1999) noted that an accommodation is justified when students with disabilities perform higher because of the test alteration than students without disabilities receiving the same alteration.

Modifications are defined as changes in the test (how it is given, completed, or what construct is being measured) that work equally well for all students. The resulting modified score would not be interpreted in the same way as a score would be when the test is given under standardized conditions. A frequently used example is one in which a student is asked to read a passage by him- or herself and then answer questions about the story. A modification would be that the story is read to the child, which changes the construct from silent reading comprehension to a listening comprehension measure.

Frequently, confusion arises in the distinction between which changes made to an assessment qualify as accommodations and which changes qualify as modifications. A major source of this confusion is the policy differences among states. For example, some states allow students who are deaf to answer questions in sign language whereas other states do not. Sometimes, these signed answers are videotaped, to be transcribed by an interpreter at a later time; more frequently, a test administrator who understands sign language simply writes in English what the student has signed as the student takes the test. Some states may allow a student to take a test using a computer. Typically, the decision as to whether a change is considered an accommodation or a modification depends on the policy of the state. Some states decide that the student has to read the test whereas other states agree that the youngster may have the passage signed to him or her, if necessary. Every state sets its own policy on these issues. Another source of this confusion is IDEA 2004, which uses the terms interchangeably. Regardless, the definitions given above are what are used psychometrically.

SELECTING ACCOMMODATIONS AND MODIFICATIONS

Currently, members of the Individualized Education Program (IEP) team are charged with determining the accommodation (or accommodations) or modification (or modifications) that a student with a disability requires and may use during classroom instruction and assessments. Often, the decisions are made by IEP team members who have not received adequate training. Further, there is a lack of consistency in the selection of accommodations and modifications from school to school and from district to district. To rectify this situation, the U.S. Department of Education has charged each state with developing a decision-making model that would provide guidance for choosing appropriate accommodations and modifications and that would train administrators and teachers to use the approach. A major challenge is for each state to create a decision-making model or process that helps IEP team members decide which is appropriate—an accommodation (testing alterations that are based on the needs of the child but that do not alter the construct being measured) or modifications (testing alterations that change the content or performance level of what is being assessed). Another challenge is for IEP teams to know whether or not a particular accommodation works for a specific student.

Yet another challenge is that the effect of the accommodation must be empirically measured to meet the technical standards of NCLB, for example, measured in a way that demonstrates how the accommodation retains the original construct of the question. The burden of providing such evidence falls on each state. Hence, it is important to use the psychometric definitions of accommodations and modifications.

Defining Accommodations for Deaf Students

Tindal and Fuchs (1999) have defined accommodations as "changes in standardized assessment conditions to 'level the playing field' for students by removing the construct-irrelevant variance created by their disabilities. Valid accommodations produce scores for students with disabilities that measure the same attributes as standard assessments measured in non-disabled students" (p. 7).

Harcourt Assessment, Inc., (Harcourt) uses the accommodations taxonomy listed in Table 3.1, which was developed by the National Center on Educational

Table 3.1. Harcourt Accommodations Taxonomy

Administration[a]	Changes to how the assessment is given, that is, the way in which students are told how to take the test
Setting	Changes to where the assessment is given
Timing/Scheduling[b]	Changes to when the assessment is given
Presentation Format	Changes to how the assessment is given, that is, how the test items are presented to the student
Response Format	Changes to how a student responds to the assessment
Other	Use of dictionaries, word lists, glossaries

Notes: a. National Center on Educational Outcomes combines Setting and Administration whereas Harcourt separates them.

b. National Center on Educational Outcomes separates Timing and Scheduling whereas Harcourt combines them.

Outcomes at the University of Minnesota. We have modified the taxonomy of administration, setting, timing or scheduling as indicated by the table notes.

AN EMPIRICAL BASIS FOR DEFINING ACCOMMODATIONS

In addition to using the taxonomy of accommodations, Harcourt has used Tindal's (Tindal & Fuchs, 1999) classification of research approaches to examine the validity of test accommodations. The approaches are classified as descriptive, comparative, or experimental.

Descriptive approach. With a descriptive approach, accommodations are analyzed logically to consider the disability along with the characteristic of the assessment. According to Tindal and Fuchs (1999), large print is considered to be valid for a student with visual disabilities because it allows access to printed information and lets the student demonstrate what he or she knows by preserving the meaningfulness of the measured content.

Comparative approach. With a comparative approach, extant databases are analyzed to gain insight into how accommodations may affect students with disabilities. Koretz (1997) and Koretz and Hamilton (1999) used this approach. Both studies indicated that accommodations, at times, overestimated the academic competence of students with disabilities (Tindal & Fuchs, 1999). Harcourt has used this method of data review. Although the methodology permits interesting insights into the effects of accommodations, the approach often leaves unanswered important questions about validity of specific accommodations.

Experimental approach. In an experimental approach, the effects of accommodations are examined with controlled research designs, which examine effects for students with and without disabilities, with and without accommodations (Tindal & Fuchs, 1999). Harcourt reviewed the studies reported in Tindal and Fuchs

(1999), Elliott (2001), Koretz and Hamilton (1999), and Thurlow, Elliott, and Ysseldyke (1998). In addition, Harcourt is in the process of developing and conducting similar studies.

HOW VARIOUS ACCOMMODATIONS FOR DEAF STUDENTS MAY BE REGARDED

For the most part, when students who are deaf use accommodations that are marked as getting "universal" acceptance in Table 3.2, the administration of the assessment to them is regarded as having the same validity as standard administrations to students who do not require accommodations. In this situation, the scores that they receive from the assessment are almost always considered to be valid and can be aggregated with those of students in the general population. Accommodations should be used in classroom instruction before testing to ensure that the construct measured represents the content area rather than the student's ability to use the accommodation. Available evidence indicates that most of the accommodations listed in Table 3.2 are considered to be "incidental to the construct intended to be measured by the test" (AERA, APA, & NCME, 1999, p. 101). Note that in Table 3.2, when states differ on whether the change is accepted as an accommodation or modification (depending on the construct measured), a footnote indicates whether the inconsistency is a result of psychometric arguments or other kinds of policy decisions.

NOTES ON PRESENTATION FORMAT OF ACCOMMODATIONS FOR DEAF STUDENTS

Over the years, the Gallaudet Research Institute has developed tips for administering assessments to students who are deaf.[1] The following material is adapted from the Administration Procedures for the *Stanford Achievement Test Series,* 9th edition (Traxler, 2000).

Many deaf students do poorly on achievement tests, not because they lack skills necessary to make correct test item responses, but because they do not understand the tasks that they are required to perform. Communicating the intent of the tasks required for the tests is of paramount importance.

The method of communication to be used in the administration of the test is the method normally used in the instructional context with the students being tested (e.g., speech only, a combination of speech and signs, sign only, etc.). Throughout the directions for administering at each test level, directions such as "say," dictate," "listen carefully," "read," etc. are meant to be interpreted within the context of this "usual method" of communication used with the students being tested.

---

1. Accommodations for administration are a major heading in Harcourt's taxonomy, presented in Table 3.1.

Table 3.2. Consistency Among States With Respect to Acceptance of Accommodations Used With Deaf Students

Accommodation	Acceptance	
	Universal	Inconsistent
Administration		
▪ Teachers may sign, use Cued Speech, or communicate through a sign language interpreter any directions or other information normally read aloud to students.	X	
▪ Audio amplification devices (hearing aids, FM systems, cochlear implants) may be used to help students who benefit from such devices for hearing directions.	X	
▪ Directions may be repeated.		X[a]
▪ Directions may be simplified.		X[a]
Setting		
▪ Test in a regular classroom.	X	
▪ Test in a small group of students with similar needs.	X	
▪ Test individually in a study carrel where environmental conditions (special lighting, adaptive furniture, noise buffers, etc.) can be created to ensure the student will not be distracted.	X	
▪ Test in a separate location such as a home or hospital setting where environmental conditions appropriate to the student's needs can be created.	X	
Timing/Scheduling		
▪ Provide extended time for student(s) to finish the test.	X	
▪ Schedule breaks between subtests.	X	
▪ Allow frequent breaks within a subtest.	X	
▪ Schedule test for time of day most beneficial to student(s).	X	
▪ Break up testing over more than one day.	X	
Presentation Options		
▪ Special test forms in which items biased against students who are deaf have been replaced with similarly difficult, standards-based items that are without such bias	X	
▪ Signed presentation of test items (*except* for reading comprehension passages and questions), supported by scripts to help ensure accuracy and uniformity among teachers or interpreters	X	

Table 3.2. Continued

Accommodation	Acceptance	
	Universal	Inconsistent
■ Signed presentation of test items (*including* for reading comprehension passages and questions), supported by scripts to help ensure accuracy and uniformity among teachers or interpreters		X[b]
■ Video, streaming video, or DVD of signed translation of test items (*except* for reading comprehension passages or items)	X	
■ Video, streaming video, or DVD of signed translation of test items (*including* for reading comprehension passages or items)		X[b]
■ Amplified audio recordings of test items (*except* for reading comprehension passages and questions)	X	
■ Amplified audio recordings of test items (*including* for reading comprehension passages and questions)		X[b]
Response Options		
■ Students generally respond to test questions by writing or marking in their test booklet, even when they are responding to signed questions.	X	
■ A special pencil, pen, or pencil grip may be used.	X	
■ Computer-administered testing allows student to use keyboard instead of paper and pencil.		X[b]
■ Students unable to demonstrate knowledge in writing may respond to questions by signing, using whatever form of signing is typically used by the student, whereupon a scribe may translate the signed response into written English.		X[b]
■ Visual aids (graph paper, templates, rulers) may be used to solve problems.	X	
■ A calculator with programming capability disabled may be used (allowed for mathematics problem solving at some grade levels).	X	
Cross-Category (may include stimulus and response)		
■ Augmentative, assistive, or adaptive technology		X[b]

Notes: a. Policies are different across the states.
b. Problematic because of psychometric argument or evidence.

Although flexibility is allowed in communicating the test instructions to students, the individual test items should not be altered in any way. Thus, no one should give individual assistance to students after the testing has begun. For dictated subtests, those dictating should try to stay as close as possible to the format of the item as it is presented in the teacher directions.

The following comments will alert those administering tests to some of the important issues related to administering dictated subtests (some of these comments pertain only to situations in which signs are used as the mode of communication):

- In dictated spelling tests, the target word should not be fingerspelled.
- Certain words and phrases, used mainly in the mathematics items, may cause special problems for students who are deaf and hard of hearing. When previewing the test, those administering the tests should consider carefully how these concepts will be best communicated to these students. These words and phrases may include:
  - "left" or "left over" (e.g., How many are left?)
  - "many more" (e.g., How many more?)
  - "odd number," "family of facts," etc.
- It is recommended that for the mathematics tests—and for other subtests with a special vocabulary—the teacher of that subject administer the test.
- Verb tense is a potential source of confusion in dictated items. Understanding a time sequence may be important to solving a problem. For example, in the item
  Jane's cat had 5 kittens. Jane gave 3 kittens away. How many kittens does Jane have now?
  the understanding of tense is crucial to the understanding of the problem. Here again, those administering the test should consider carefully how to communicate these test items.
- Some dictated test items contain words in the item stems that, if signed, reveal the correct answer to the student. This situation is especially true in mathematics problem-solving tests. Words such as *circle, triangle,* and *square* should be communicated in such a way that they do not reveal the correct answer.
- Technical terms, such as words that refer to the metric system (e.g., *millimeter, grams, liter*) should also be communicated in such a way that they do not reveal the correct answer.
- Idioms, figures of speech, and metaphorical expressions appear occasionally throughout dictated items. These expressions are commonly understood by hearing children at very young ages, but they may not be familiar to deaf students. Those administering the test should present these items in a way

that ensures that the students understand the idiomatic content of the expressions.

- In a dictated mathematics test, there are long sentences with subordinate clauses and phrases. Those administering the tests should consider carefully how these relationships might be best communicated to the students using the mode that they normally use (i.e., ASL, Signed English).

SUMMARY

Assessing students who are deaf presents significant challenges in addition to the ones associated with testing in general. Confounding factors for testing deaf students include inconsistent understanding of what is an accommodation and what is a modification, proficiency in English, the test administrator's knowledge of the approach the student uses to communicate, and the skill level of the test taker in communication.

Accommodations are a way of leveling the playing field on accountability assessments. If chosen wisely, accommodations enable students to show what they know without affecting the validity of the test results.

REFERENCES

American Educational Research Association (AERA), American Psychological Association (APA), & National Council on Measurement in Education (NCME). (1999). *Standards for educational and psychological testing.* Washington, DC: Author.

Americans With Disabilities Act of 1990 Pub. L. No. 101–336 § 2, 104 Stat. 328 (1991).

Case, B. J. (2003). *Accommodations on Stanford 10 for students with disabilities.* San Antonio, TX: Harcourt Assessment.

Elementary and Secondary Education Act of 1965, Pub. L. No. 89–10, 20 U.S.C. 6301 *et seq.*

Elliott, S. N. (2001). Including students with disabilities in assessments. *ECE Today, 8* (3).

Fuchs, L. S. (1999). *Curriculum-based measurement: Updates on its applications in standards-based assessment systems.* Charlotte, NC: Council for Exceptional Children.

Gordon, R. P., & Stump, K. (1996). Assessment of individuals with hearing impairments: Equity in testing procedures and accommodations. *Measurement and Evaluation in Counseling and Development, 29* (2), 111–118.

Hollenbeck, K., Tindal, G., Harniss, M., & Almond, P. (1999). *The effect of using computers as an accommodation in a statewide writing test.* Eugene, OR: University of Oregon, Behavioral Research and Testing.

Individuals With Disabilities Education Improvement Act of 2004. Pub. L. No. 108–446, §612, 2686 Stat. 118 (2004).

Karchmer, M. A., & Mitchell, R. E. (2003). Demographic and achievement characteristics of deaf and hard of hearing students. In M. Marschark & P. E. Spencer (Eds.), *Oxford handbook of deaf studies, language, and education,* (pp. 21–37). New York: Oxford University Press.

Koretz, D. (1997). *The assessment of students with disabilities in Kentucky* (CSE Technical Report No. 431). Los Angeles, CA: University of California, Center for the Study of

Evaluation, National Center for Research on Evaluation, Standards, and Student Testing.

Koretz, D., & Hamilton, R. (1999). *Assessing students with disabilities in Kentucky: The effects of accommodations, format and subject.* (CSE Technical Report No. 498). Los Angeles, CA: University of California, Center for the Study of Evaluation, National Center for Research on Evaluation, Standards, and Student Testing.

Luetke-Stahlman, B. (1998). *Language issues in deaf education.* Hillsboro, OR: Butte Publications.

Moores, D. F. (2002). The law of unexpected consequences. *American Annals of the Deaf, 147* (2), 84–87.

Mounty, J. L. (2001). *Standardized testing: Considerations for testing deaf and hard-of-hearing candidates.* Washington, DC: Gallaudet University. Retrieved March 17, 2008, from http://gri.gallaudet.edu/TestEquity/stantest.html

No Child Left Behind Act of 2001, Pub. L. No. 107–110, 115 Stat. 1425 (2002).

Phillips, S. E. (1993). Testing accommodations for disabled students. *Education Law Reporter, 80,* 9–32.

Phillips, S. E. (1994). High-stakes testing accommodations: Validity versus disabled rights. *Applied Measurement in Education, 7* (2), 93–120.

Rehabilitation Act of 1973, Pub. L. No. 93–112, 87 Stat. 394 (Sept. 26, 1973), codified at 29 U.S.C. § 701 *et seq.*

Rudner, L. M. (1978). Using standard tests with the hearing impaired: The problem of item bias. *Volta Review, 80,* 31–40.

Schirmer, B. (2001). *Psychological, social, and educational dimensions of deafness.* Needham Heights, MA: Allyn & Bacon.

Thurlow, M. L., Elliott, J. L., & Ysseldyke, J. E. (1998). *Testing students with disabilities.* Thousand Oaks, CA: Corwin Press.

Thurlow, M., Hurley, C., Spicuzza, R., & El Sawaf, H. (1996). *A review of the literature on testing accommodations for students with disabilities* (Minnesota Report No. 9). Minneapolis, MN: University of Minnesota, National Center on Educational Outcomes. Retrieved March 17, 2008, from http://education.umn.edu/NCEO/OnlinePubs/MnReport9.html

Tindal, G., & Fuchs, L. (1999). *A summary of research on test changes: An empirical basis for defining accommodations.* Lexington, KY: Mid-South Regional Resource Center.

Traxler, C. B. (2000). *The Stanford Achievement Test,* 9th Edition: National norming and performance standards for deaf and hard-of-hearing students. *Journal of Deaf Studies and Deaf Education, 5* (43), 337–348.

4 Using Universal Design Research and Perspectives to Increase the Validity of Scores on Large-Scale Assessments

Martha L. Thurlow, Christopher Johnstone, Sandra J. Thompson, and Betsy J. Case

Contemporary American educational culture is dominated by accountability requirements for all students, including students who are deaf. The No Child Left Behind (NCLB) Act of 2001 requires states to ensure that all students meet certain expected levels of academic proficiency and that all schools meet goals for Adequate Yearly Progress (AYP). These requirements are reinforced and supported by the 2004 reauthorization of the Individuals With Disabilities Education Act (IDEA)—the Individuals With Disabilities Education Improvement Act of 2004 (IDEA 2004). The Individuals With Disabilities Education Act Amendments of 1997 (IDEA 1997) was the first federal law requiring that students with disabilities, including those who are deaf or hard of hearing, participate in state- and district-wide assessments; that alternate assessments be developed for students with cognitive disabilities so severe that they are unable to participate in regular assessments; and that performance be reported publicly with the same frequency and in the same detail as for students without disabilities.

Students in Grades 3–8 and in one grade in high school (state's choice) currently are tested in either English language arts or reading and mathematics to meet NCLB accountability requirements. Beginning in 2007, students also are tested in science at three levels (Grades 4–6, 7–8, and high school). Most states continue to administer these assessments in a paper-and-pencil format, although several states are working toward various forms of online administration (Thompson, Johnstone, Thurlow, & Altman, 2005).

Arguments both for and against the merits of large-scale assessment as a measure of accountability have permeated educational literature, yet NCLB itself enjoyed fairly consistent bipartisan support during its first 5 years. Accepting that testing is at worst a stubborn reality in schools and at best an incentive to improve instruction for all students, advocates and teachers are challenged to assist stu-

---

The preparation of this manuscript was supported, in part, by a cooperative agreement (H326G000001) between the U.S. Department of Education, Office of Special Education Programs, and the University of Minnesota (National Center on Educational Outcomes). Opinions expressed herein are those of the authors, however, and do not necessarily reflect those of the U.S. Department of Education or offices within it.

dents who are deaf in accessing standardized tests that are usually designed for and field tested with hearing students.

For some deaf students, standardized testing does not pose a problem (Luckner & Muir, 2001). On average, however, this population has perennially performed below grade level on standardized achievement tests (Karchmer & Mitchell, 2003). In those states that document performance by category of disability, poor performance of students who are deaf has been consistently noted (Luckner, 2004). Reasons for the lack of success on tests by so many deaf students rest, in part, on students' reading abilities, which typically fall well below grade-level expectations (Traxler, 2000). Educators of deaf children, in other words, face enormous challenges in their efforts to help these students meet grade-level proficiencies.

Issues related to low achievement on standardized tests, however, may also be a result of the tests themselves. Johnstone, Miller, and Thompson (2005) conducted research involving 21 deaf students in Grades 4 and 8 in which the students used sign language to explain their understanding of mathematics test items. Among the items presented to students, 13% of errors were caused by distraction because of item wording and 6% of errors were caused by distraction because of item graphics. Such data indicate the need for improving not only the educational experiences for deaf students but also the tests we use to assess educational achievement.

A recent innovation is that of specifically designing assessments to be accessible for a wider variety of students. These assessments are referred to as universally designed assessments. Research is being conducted on increasing access for students with all types of characteristics, including students who are deaf. Through this research, ways to improve access to tests have been found for all students, producing more valuable and reliable results. The application of universal design concepts to assessments is a process of designing tests from the beginning to be accessible to all types of students, possibly reducing (but not eliminating) the need for accommodations or other special forms of access.

The importance of the concept and intent of universally designed assessments is reflected in both NCLB and IDEA 2004. The following requirement appears in NCLB regulations:

> [Assessments must be] designed to be accessible and valid with respect to the widest possible range of students, including students with disabilities and students with limited English proficiency. (Section 200.2(b)(2))

An explicit reference to and requirement for universal design appears in IDEA 2004:

> The state educational agency or (in the case of a district-wide assessment) the local educational agencies shall, to the extent feasible, use universal design principles in developing and administering any assessments. (Section 612(a)(16))

These kinds of emphases within federal law show that because all students are obliged to participate in assessments and schools are held accountable for their performance, there is a commitment to ensuring that the assessments will be fair and reliable measures of what students know and are able to do, regardless of their disability.

UNIVERSALLY DESIGNED ASSESSMENTS

Universally designed assessments are those that are designed to be inclusive and valid, contain minimal bias, are amenable to accommodations, have clear and intuitive procedures, and are comprehensible and legible (Thompson, Johnstone, & Thurlow, 2002). Tests that are universally designed may require less need for accommodation because they are designed with accessibility in mind from the very start. Although research on universal design of assessments is still in its nascence, there are clear indications from universal design literature that this specific approach may be useful in addressing many of the challenges that still exist in assessments for students who are deaf (despite widespread use of accommodations). The purpose of this chapter is to describe elements of universally designed assessments and related research, particularly as they relate to increased assessment access for deaf students.

It is important to note that each of these elements must be grounded in the recognition that tests are based on certain constructs that they are intended to measure. The construct takes on a primary role in defining what is malleable and what is not in working on an assessment to make it more universally designed. What the test is intended to measure cannot be changed, nor can the grade level of the intended construct. Yet, there are many things that tests are not intending to measure that actually contribute to what is measured. Knowing what is and is not part of the intended construct is essential to working on universal design, and sticking to the ground rule that the construct cannot be changed in the name of universal design is essential. In this effort, those creating universally designed assessments must consider five key parameters: making assessments inclusive and valid, introducing minimal bias, making assessments amenable to accommodations, creating clear and intuitive procedures, and making assessments comprehensible and legible.

Making Assessments Inclusive and Valid

IDEA 1997, NCLB, and now IDEA 2004 require all students enrolled in public schools to participate either in general assessments, with or without accommodations, or in alternate assessments designed for students with the most significant cognitive disabilities. Students who are deaf may be tested in any one of these ways, depending on their cognitive skills and need for accommodations.

Most states field-test potential items for use in large-scale assessments to study item characteristics before they are actually used in testing. Through a survey of state directors of special education, the National Center on Educational Outcomes (NCEO) found that only 20 states include accommodated formats in their field tests to help ensure accessible items (Thompson, Johnstone, Thurlow, et al., 2005). However, field test items are not usually given to all students, so students representing a group as small as the deaf student population may not be included in field tests. When included in field tests, deaf students are sometimes combined with other small groups of students such as those with visual impairments, even though issues with test items are very different for these two groups.

Furthermore, the statistics that are typically used to determine whether items are functioning differentially for particular populations are problematic for low-incidence groups such as students who are deaf. In a recent review of items that functioned differently between deaf and hearing students, Johnstone, Thompson, Moen, Bolt, and Kato (2005) found that items that were problematic for deaf students were typically not problematic for hearing students. Likewise, items that were problematic for hearing students (including students from other disability categories) were typically not problematic for students who are deaf.

These results suggest that there is a danger in examining populations of students that are highly heterogeneous as a single group (Sireci, Li, & Scarpati, 2003). When students with several types of characteristics or disabilities are collapsed into a single group, statistics become more reliable, but may have reducted practical value. The educational needs of students who are deaf may or may not (depending on whether secondary disabilities are present) be similar to those of a student with an orthopedic impairment, a traumatic brain injury, or autism, for example. This problem is complicated by the fact that, even if deaf populations were singled out for analysis, students who are deaf themselves represent a very heterogeneous group with varying access needs.

Introducing Minimal Bias

One of the most significant challenges of assessments facing deaf students is possible bias in items. Alverman and Phelps (2002) identified four types of bias that typically arise in instruction and assessment found in English language arts. These biases, which may also be present for students who are deaf, include (a) content bias (when the content is reflective of the mainstream society), (b) linguistic bias (when the vocabulary used is unnecessarily difficult for people whose primary language is not English), (c) functional bias (when questions are asked in a way that seems to have no purpose or value for people from diverse cultures), and (d) consequential bias (when the stakes are unnecessarily high for students from particular populations).

One method of detecting bias is by reviewing items. Typically, states have "bias" or "sensitivity" review teams that review assessment items before field testing to minimize bias. These teams, however, may not always have a deaf person or a person with a deaf perspective present. Data from the 2005 survey of state special education directors indicated that a little more than half of states ($n = 27$) had multiple disability representatives on sensitivity review panels. Conversely, 11 states had no disability representation on sensitivity review panels, and 8 states had one person who represents all disability perspectives (Thompson, Johnstone, Thurlow, et al., 2005). Cultural sensitivity panels contain representatives from various ethnic groups, but do not typically consider issues of Deaf culture.

Those states that do consider deaf perspectives during the deliberations of sensitivity panels are more likely to find and revise or replace items that contain a form of bias. For example, a teacher from a school for the deaf recently attended a universal design review of her state's high school exit exam and found that several items and language arts passages required students to understand sound references to respond to test questions. Noting that this task was impossible for students who are deaf, items were flagged and indicated as problematic in a public report to the state (Wise et al., 2005).

In another state, a test was released that contained items requiring students to select words that "sounded alike" even though the words were spelled differently. Perhaps because information was not solicited from deaf stakeholders before the release of the test, the state might have to "retrofit" the examination by using a decision tree such as the one shown in Appendix 4A. The questions in Appendix 4A were developed by NCEO in collaboration with the Partnership for Accessible Reading Assessments, a project conducting research on how to increase the accessibility of reading assessments for students with various disabilities that affect reading. The questions specifically address those situations where disability precludes the performance of a skill required by a reading assessment.

Although universal design review addresses bias that exists against deaf students because of the requirements for certain items, universal design reviews may also reduce unfair *advantages* to students who are deaf, advantages that arise, for example, when tests are translated into American Sign Language (ASL). Data from a validation study of universal design considerations (Thompson, Johnstone, Anderson, & Miller, 2005) and a study that used "cognitive lab" (think aloud) methods (Johnstone, Miller, et al., 2005) indicated that some items, when translated into sign language, may give away the answer to students who are deaf. For example, during a cognitive lab study, several deaf students were asked to answer a question that related to a geometrical term. The ASL sign for the term demonstrated exactly the shape that students were supposed to know. Such an issue may have been ameliorated if a person fluent in ASL had reviewed the item before release and chosen to fingerspell rather than sign that concept.

Making Assessments Amenable to Accommodations

One method for increasing access to assessments for students who are deaf is through accommodations (see Case, this volume). Accommodations are typically defined as "changes in standardized assessment conditions introduced to level the playing field for students by removing the construct-irrelevant variance created by their unique characteristics" (Tindal & Fuchs, 1999, p. 8). Sireci et al. (2003) explained the validity of accommodations through an "interaction hypothesis," or the theoretical assumption that test accommodations will lead to improved test scores for students who need the accommodations but will not for students who do not need these accommodations.

Theoretically, accommodations should remove any of the nonconstruct-related portions of an assessment that may be difficult to access because of a student's deafness. The most common accommodations used by students who are deaf are (a) sign language accommodations (an interpreter provides test information in

ASL or an English-based sign system), (b) extended time (a student is allowed to take a test, with or without an interpreter, for a longer-than-usual period of time), (c) separate location (a student may take a test in a separate room to minimize distractions), and (d) computer administration (a student may take a paper-based test on a computer to increase access). At least one state is experimenting with Web-based delivery with video streams of ASL. Deaf students who are proficient readers of print may not need additional tools to access assessments. Table 4.1 shows the number of states that have policies that allow, in certain circumstances, or that prohibit some of the accommodations that deaf students might use.

Creating Clear and Intuitive Procedures

Students should be able to understand the instructions and procedures of the assessment, regardless of their disability. Keeping instructions consistent from one part of a test to another, using simple words and phrases, and allowing multiple standardized explanations of instructions are some examples of ways to create clear and intuitive assessment procedures.

Some states allow only test instructions to be signed. The rest of the test must be read visually by the student. Noteworthy is the fact that not all states allow the directions to be signed to students (Clapper, Morse, Lazarus, Thompson, & Thurlow, 2005; Lazarus, Thurlow, Lail, Eisenbraun, & Kato, 2006). Generally, it is the reading test for which signed instructions are not allowed. Clear instructions that are intuitive and easy to follow, however, are very important for all students on reading tests.[1]

Making Assessments Comprehensible and Legible

Universal design also applies to the legibility of test items for print readers and to comparability when using sign language interpreters. Legibility refers to clear print that is at least as large as 12 points, that presents text in commonly used fonts, and that uses other features (such as bolding text, using straight lines of text rather than curved text, for example) that make visual print reading as clear as possible. Comparability when using sign language interpreters refers to the importance of having guidelines for sign language interpreters to follow.

Because the use of sign language interpreters introduces human variability into the testing situation, the potential for challenges to the validity and comparability of resulting scores is greatly increased. Consequently, the availability of guidelines that direct the work of these individuals, and the specificity of language in these guidelines, is critically important to states, students, and the individuals who work as access assistants themselves (Clapper, Morse, Thurlow, & Thompson, 2005a). In 2005, 11 states had assessment administration guidelines for sign language interpreters. NCEO has a manual available to assist in the development or enhancement of guidelines for access assistants (Clapper, Morse, Thurlow, & Thompson,

1. See http://www.readingassessment.info for more information.

Table 4.1. Number of States That Allow or Prohibit Specific Accommodations

Number of States	Allowed	Allowed with implications for scoring, aggregation, or both	Allowed in certain circumstances	Allowed in certain circumstances & Allowed with implications for scoring, aggregation, or both	Prohibited
Directions interpreted by means of sign language	45	2	0	2	0
Questions interpreted by means of sign language	13	0	21	8	0
Amplification equipment	42	0	0	0	0
Audio/Video equipment	16	0	8	4	2
Computer or machine	37	3	2	3	1
Responses signed to sign language interpreter	20	1	7	1	0
Pointing	21	0	2	1	0
Extended time	29	3	9	4	2
Breaks	39	2	4	1	1
Multiple sessions	35	3	1	0	0
Individual administration	46	0	0	0	0
Small group	47	0	0	0	0
Carrel	40	0	0	0	0
Separate room	38	0	0	0	0
Seat location/proximity	38	0	0	0	0

Source: Clapper, Morse, Lazarus, et al. (2005).

2005b). Whether a state already has guidelines or is still in the process of establishing them, this manual will provide structure to the process and many examples of criteria already included by states.

Another area of challenge is the difference in the various types of sign language. For instance, Signed English has ending markers such as *-ly, -s, -ed* whereas ASL does not. ASL is a linguistically complete language showing no grammatical similarities to English. For instance, "Suddenly, it rained" in English might be signed "HIT RAIN" in ASL.

MOVING THE THEORY OF UNIVERSAL DESIGN INTO REALITY FOR DEAF STUDENTS

Additional work is being done to take the concept of universal design as it applies to large-scale assessments and move it from a theoretical concept to one that can be easily applied by practitioners. The elements of universal design identified by Thompson, Johnstone, et al. (2002) were examined by a team of experts through a Delphi methodology (Thompson, Johnstone, Anderson, et al., 2005). The experts included individuals in the areas of assessment and content areas as well as population experts. One of those population experts was a professor at Gallaudet University who knows deaf students and who for many years not only has worked with them but also has conducted research on their language acquisition, assessment performance and challenges, and their educational progress. Together, these experts validated a list of what were called "considerations" for universally designed assessments.

Among the most relevant considerations for deaf students that were identified through the Delphi methodology were (a) ensuring that reading or mathematics passages did not rely on sound references for students to answer questions correctly, (b) ensuring that constructs such as rhyming were minimized or eliminated from tests, and (c) ensuring that sign language interpretation of test items would neither change the construct of the test nor make items unnecessarily difficult or easy for deaf students. It was agreed that tests reflected universal design when all of the test items truly test the intended constructs, respect the diversity of the assessment population, have language that is comprehensible to a wide range of students, have print and images that are clear and remain consistent if they are presented in alternative formats (such as American Sign Language), and are deemed acceptable for all students (Thompson, Johnstone, Anderson, et al., 2005).

CHALLENGES OF ASSESSING DEAF STUDENTS

Although progress is being made toward improved assessment techniques for all students, the current state of assessment for students who are deaf appears to be inconsistent. Deaf perspectives are often overlooked in both test development and in the examination of field test results. Such inconsistencies reveal a need for universal design concepts to be embedded in all facets of test design and administration.

The use of accommodations can be controversial. Research over the past 8 years revealed that studies of accommodations have inconsistent results in terms of both effectiveness and validity (Johnstone, Thompson, Thurlow, & Altman, 2005; Thompson, Blount, & Thurlow, 2002; Tindal & Fuchs, 1999). Despite the controversies surrounding accommodations, there is still a need to accommodate tests for students who are deaf, especially when the design of the test reflects the culture, communication patterns, and sensory experiences of hearing populations. The need for accommodations, however, may decrease if tests begin to reflect the diversity of the entire assessment population, including deaf students.

As noted above, universal design is an approach that can be embedded throughout all testing processes, beginning with the early stages of item development. During the item development phase, test designers are more likely to derive valid information from students who are deaf if they are able to consider the perspectives and experiences of these students. When deaf representatives are included on panels that review item bias sensitivity, the assessments that are subsequently developed are more likely to reflect the abilities, experiences, and unique perspectives of students who are deaf. Provided that constructs are not changed by making changes to tests, test vendors can make significant contributions to the design of items by including advocates for deaf students.

Likewise, test vendors and states can have a better idea of the capabilities of students who are deaf by specifically including such students in field testing. Because deaf students make up such a small segment of the population, they are often overlooked in field testing samples. If such students are included in field testing, their scores can be calculated in comparison with their hearing peers to determine whether particular items are potentially problematic. Although the differential item functioning (DIF) statistics that are typically used to determine item functioning are not very useful for low-incidence groups such as students who are deaf, Johnstone, Thompson, Moen, et al. (2005) suggested using multiple approaches such as item ranking, item total correlation, DIF statistics (using contingency tables), and DIF statistics (using item response theory). Each of these four methods alone is questionable, but collectively, they may demonstrate patterns across analyses related to potential problems with an item.

Finally, as part of test administration, states should ensure that accommodation policies count ASL and other sign systems as valid accommodations and that students who are deaf (unless they have a comorbid cognitive disability) are included in the general education assessment. Scores from the assessments can be reviewed using the analysis techniques described in this chapter.

If states are seeing items that appear to function differently for deaf populations and hearing populations, they may also conduct cognitive labs at any point in the testing process. Cognitive labs are a method of tapping into students' mental processing while they complete items (Ericsson & Simon, 1994). Students who speak aloud or use ASL while they are completing items are typically able to communicate how the design of an item affects how they approach and solve the item. In such studies, bias, distracters, and unnecessarily complex vocabulary are easily detected.

According to requirements of contemporary educational policies, students who are deaf are required to demonstrate the same levels of proficiency as those who are not deaf. Thus, it is critical that test designers and states orient themselves to the challenges faced by deaf students. Improvements such as universal design approaches may help students to better demonstrate their academic abilities on large-scale assessments.

REFERENCES

Alverman, D., & Phelps, S. (2002). *Content reading and literacy: Succeeding in today's diverse classrooms.* Boston: Allyn and Bacon.

Clapper, A., Morse, A., Lazarus, S., Thompson, S., & Thurlow, M. (2005). *2003 state policies on assessment participation and accommodations for students with disabilities.* (Synthesis Report No. 56). Minneapolis, MN: University of Minnesota, National Center on Educational Outcomes.

Clapper, A., Morse, A., Thurlow, M., & Thompson, S. (2005a). *Access assistants for state assessments: A study of state guidelines for scribes, readers, and sign language interpreters.* Minneapolis, MN: National Center on Educational Outcomes.

Clapper, A., Morse, A., Thurlow, M., & Thompson, S. (2005b). *How to develop state guidelines for access assistants: Scribes, readers, and sign language interpreters.* Minneapolis, MN: National Center on Educational Outcomes.

Ericsson, K. A., & Simon, H. (1994). *Protocol analysis: Verbal reports as data* (2nd ed.). Cambridge, MA: MIT Press.

Individuals With Disabilities Education Act Amendments of 1997, Pub. L. No. 105-17, 20 U.S.C. § 1400 *et seq.*

Individuals With Disabilities Education Improvement Act of 2004, Pub. L. No. 108-446, 20 U.S.C. 1400 *et seq.*

Johnstone, C., Miller, N., & Thompson, S. (2005). *Using the think aloud method (cognitive labs) to evaluate test design.* Minneapolis, MN: National Center on Educational Outcomes.

Johnstone, C., Thompson, S., Moen, R., Bolt, S., & Kato, K. (2005). *Analyzing results of large-scale assessments to ensure universal design* (Technical Report No. 41). Minneapolis, MN: National Center on Educational Outcomes.

Johnstone, C., Thompson, S., Thurlow, M., & Altman, J. (2005). *A summary of research on the effects of accommodations: 2002–2004.* Minneapolis, MN: National Center on Educational Outcomes.

Karchmer, M. A., & Mitchell, R. E. (2003). Demographic and achievement characteristics of deaf and hard of hearing students. In M. Marschark & P. E. Spencer (Eds.), *Oxford handbook of deaf studies, language, and education,* (pp. 21–37). New York: Oxford University Press.

Lazarus, S. S., Thurlow, M. L., Lail, K. E., Eisenbraun, K.D., & Kato, K. (2006). *2005 state policies on participation and accommodation policies* (Synthesis Report 64). Minneapolis, MN: University of Minnesota, National Center on Educational Outcomes.

Luckner, J. L. (2004). *Issues–Education of students who are deaf or hard of hearing.* Greeley, CO: The National Center for Low Incidence Disabilities.

Luckner, J. L., & Muir, S. (2001). Successful students who are deaf in general education settings. *American Annals of the Deaf, 146* (5), 450–461.

No Child Left Behind Act of 2001, Pub. L. No. 107-110, 115 Stat. 1425 (2002).

Sireci, S. G., Li, S., & Scarpati, S. (2003). *The effects of test accommodations on test performance:*

A review of the literature (Research Report No. 485). Amherst, MA: Center for Educational Assessment.

Thompson, S., Blount, A., & Thurlow, M. (2002). *A summary of research on the effects of test accommodations: 1999 through 2001* (Technical Report No. 34). Minneapolis, MN: University of Minnesota, National Center on Educational Outcomes.

Thompson, S., Johnstone, C., Anderson, M., & Miller, N. (2005). *Considerations for the development and review of universally designed assessments* (Technical Report No. 42). Minneapolis, MN: National Center on Educational Outcomes.

Thompson, S., Johnstone, C., & Thurlow, M. (2002). *Universal design in large-scale assessments* (Synthesis Report No. 44). Minneapolis, MN: National Center on Educational Outcomes.

Thompson, S., Johnstone, C., Thurlow, M., & Altman, J. (2005). *2005 state special education outcomes: Steps forward in a decade of change.* Minneapolis, MN: National Center on Educational Outcomes.

Thurlow, M .L., Liu, K. K, Lazarus, S. S., & Moen, R. E. (in press). *Questions to ask to determine how to move closer to universally designed assessments from the very beginning, by addressing the standards first and moving on from there.* Minneapolis, MN: Partnership for Accessible Reading Assessments.

Tindal, G., & Fuchs, L. (1999). *A summary of research on test changes: An empirical basis for defining accommodations.* Lexington, KY: University of Kentucky, Mid-South Regional Resource Center.

Traxler, C. B. (2000). The *Stanford Achievement Test,* 9th edition: National norming and performance standards for deaf and hard-of-hearing students. *Journal of Deaf Studies and Deaf Education, 5* (4), 337–348.

Wise, L. L., Becker, D. E.(Sunny), Harris, C. D., Taylor, L. R., Johnstone, C. J., Miller, N. A., et al. (2005). *Independent evaluation of California High School Exit Examination (CAHSEE): 2005 evaluation report* (Vol. 1). Prepared for California Department of Education. Retrieved March 20, 2008, from http://www.cde.ca.gov/ta/tg/hs/documents/year6vol1.pdf

APPENDIX 4A

Set of Questions to Ask to Determine How to Move Closer to Universally Designed Assessments From the Very Beginning, by Addressing the Standards First and Moving on From There

Question: How should a state or district handle a situation in which a student's disability precludes the performance of a skill required by a reading assessment? Examples might include the following:

- Students who are deaf are required by the state or district assessment to match the sounds of words.
- Students who are blind are required by the state or district assessment to select objects of the same color.
- Students who are dyslexic are required by the state or district assessment to decode a passage about which the questions are ones of understanding.

Answer: There are several issues for the state or district to address. Each of these issues should be considered in turn to determine how to deal with this situation.

1. **Does the skill in question reflect a standard that is to be assessed?** It is possible that a skill has slipped into an assessment that is not reflective of a state or district standard, so this possibility should be checked first. If it does not reflect a standard, then remove measurement of the skill from the assessment. If it does reflect a standard, then go to Consideration 2.
2. **Is there a clear match between the breadth and depth in the standard and how the standard is reflected on the test?** It may be that the assessment is not adequately aligned to the standard and that the standard development committee would agree that the skill should not be included in the way it is currently assessed. If this possibility is the case, then remove measurement of the skill from the assessment. If it is not, then go to Consideration 3.
3. **Is there an accommodation that can be used by a student, even though it might not be used for other aspects of the assessment?** For example, could a student read a Braille version of a question, have the question presented in sign language, or use a text reader instead of proceeding in the manner that had originally been intended? If such an accommodation is possible and the same skill is still measured, then assess the standard using an appropriate accommodation for the skill in question. If it is not possible, then go to Consideration 4.
4. **Is there an alternative skill that could be used for students whose disability precludes performance of the skill?** For example, instead of identifying words that sound the same, could students who are deaf identify words that have similar meanings? If there is an alternative skill and it is considered feasible, then allow the alternative skill to be on the assessment for certain students. If alternative skills are not considered appropriate and feasible, then go to Consideration 5.
5. **Is there a way to score the assessment so the student and the school are not punished because the student's disability precludes performance on the skill?** For example, do not simply assign an automatic zero or lowest possible score to the student, but consider other scoring possibilities instead. One scoring possibility to consider is imputing a score for the missed skill.

Measuring English proficiency in areas such as speaking and listening when assessing students with disabilities who are also English language learners will have similar challenges. Decisions about how to include English language learners with disabilities whose English proficiency and disabilities preclude the skill being measured in exactly the same way as other students (e.g., an English language learner who is deaf taking the listening test) require careful consideration of the questions identified above. Just as it is for other students with disabilities, the critical decision point will be whether decision makers are willing to recognize that a skill may have to be accommodated (e.g., taking information in from sign language can be considered listening for those who cannot hear). The difficulty becomes how far along a continuum a skill can be considered the same when a disability is considered. For example, can responding by means of a sign language be considered "spoken language" for those students who have been deaf since birth? These kinds of policy decisions require much discussion among personnel responsible for assessment, curriculum, special education, and English as a second language or bilingual education.

Source: Adapted from Thurlow, Liu, Lazarus, & Moen (in press).

5

Alternate Assessments: Leaving No Child Behind Amid Standards-Based Reform

Elizabeth Towles-Reeves

Imagine that you begin your day with an 8:00 a.m. Individualized Education Program (IEP) team meeting. You may be a school administrator, school psychologist, general education teacher, special education teacher, or speech/language therapist who, on a daily basis, works with deaf or hard of hearing students. You may be a parent of a student who is deaf or hard of hearing. With your full cup of coffee and necessary paperwork, you walk into the child's yearly IEP meeting ready to discuss current intellectual, achievement, adaptive functioning, IEP objectives, instructional strategies, and large-scale educational assessment participation options for this student. As you sit down and look around the table at all the stakeholders in this student's life, you wonder how the team will make good decisions about instruction, accommodations, and assessment for this student who has unique and specialized needs for support. You find yourself wondering, where do we even begin to talk about these issues?

Many teams find themselves wondering this same question, and it seems like a daunting task. For this particular team, the most difficult question is deciding the best method for enabling this student to participate in large-scale educational assessments. The administrator, who is also the student's principal, wants to make sure the student takes the most appropriate assessment so the scores are accurate and can be reported for accountability purposes. The general and special education teachers—realizing that the goals of the IEP emphasize learning academic, grade-level content standards in language arts, mathematics, and science—are considering how the standards on the assessment can best be embedded in instruction. Related service providers are intent on their goal to ensure that the student uses the appropriate accommodations, if necessary, during both instruction and assessment. Parents' goals, of course, encompass all these concerns. They want to make sure their child is treated fairly, given access to the general curriculum, and assessed appropriately. They want their child to be able to demonstrate profi-

The author of this chapter would like to acknowledge the reviews of earlier versions of this chapter, and the very helpful suggestions and comments of the following individuals, whose thinking contributed greatly to improving the final product: Dr. Harold Kleinert, Dr. Jacqui Kearns, and Ms. Tara Stevens.

ciency in academic content areas, but they also want their child to learn important functional skills that will be of benefit in daily functioning.

To better understand the large-scale assessment participation options for students with disabilities, especially those who are deaf or hard of hearing, we will explore the following topics: (a) current status of alternate assessments, (b) key points of special education reform related to the evolution of alternate assessments, (c) current alternate assessment options for students with disabilities, and (d) consideration of each alternate assessment option through student vignettes for students who are deaf or hard of hearing.

THE CURRENT STATUS OF ALTERNATE ASSESSMENT

Before defining alternate assessments, it is important to understand the differences between the following three terms: (a) *academic content standards,* (b) *academic achievement standards,* and (c) *alternate academic achievement standards.* These three terms are critical to discerning the intricacies between alternate assessment options for students with disabilities while at the same time conceptualizing the requirements of key legislative educational reform efforts.

Academic content standards define what all students should know and be able to do. These standards should contain coherent and rigorous content that promotes teaching of higher-order skills. Academic content standards are often grade or grade-band specific for grades 3–8 (U.S. Department of Education, 2004), as shown in the following examples:

- A reading academic content standard—Students will describe characters, plot, and setting within a passage.
- A mathematics academic content standard—Students will solve equations.

Academic achievement standards are summary descriptions of how well a student demonstrates proficiency in a content domain. Academic achievement standards are often described in at least three levels (e.g., Basic, Proficient, or Advanced) (U.S. Department of Education, 2004), as shown in the following examples:

- A proficient reading academic achievement standard—Student applies information appropriately to solve the problem, analyze the situation, and/or draw conclusions.
- A basic mathematics achievement standard—Student rarely demonstrates appropriate use of mathematical reasoning.

An *alternate academic achievement standard* is defined as "an expectation of performance that differs in complexity from a grade-level achievement standard" (U.S. Department of Education, 2005a, p. 20). Alternate academic achievement standards allow for achievement standards that are *linked* to grade-level content to promote access to the general curriculum. Alternate achievement standards also include descriptors of what student work reflecting the achievement looks like at basic, proficient, or advanced levels. Alternate achievement standards should be *linked* to academic content standards and defined in a way that supports individual growth across grade levels (U.S. Department of Education, 2004). It is important to remember that "while required to link to grade-level content standards, the alternate assessment judged against alternate achievement standards will not be required to meet the same depth, breadth, and complexity as grade-level achievement standards" (National Alternate Assessment Center, 2005, p. 12). In addition, states may choose to develop multiple alternate achievement standards if the data describing the population of students taking the assessment suggests a need for multiple sets of achievement standards.

Defining Alternate Assessments

Alternate assessment is the primary means through which students with the most significant cognitive disabilities participate in measures of educational assessment and accountability. Most states currently offer one type of alternate assessment, while a small number of states offer two or three alternate assessment options (Thompson & Thurlow, 2003). Lehr and Thurlow (2003) report that states vary considerably in the approaches they use for alternate assessments. Nevertheless, these approaches generally have in common that they are very different from those used for states' general assessments (i.e., paper-and-pencil formats).

There are three alternate assessment approaches currently used by states. The first is a portfolio or body of evidence approach, which is a purposeful and systematic collection of student work evaluated and judged against predetermined scoring criteria. A second approach is a checklist or rating scale that requires teachers to identify whether students are able to perform certain skills or activities. These assessments base scores on the number of skills the student is able to perform successfully. Third, the performance assessment approach is a direct measure of a skill in a one-to-one assessment format (e.g., in reading, responding to questions about characters and plot from fictional text). Performance assessments (often referred to as performance event assessments) range in structure from prescribed directions for administration and scoring to a more flexible approach tailored to students' needs (Roeber, 2002).

States are given the freedom to develop their alternate assessment system to fit appropriately within their own large-scale assessment system. Therefore, variations in the types of approaches across states (e.g., portfolio versus performance event versus checklist) and variations within approaches (e.g., within portfolio assessments from one state to the next) is typical. For example, the portfolio assessment in Kentucky is very different from the performance assessment used in Colorado. At the same time, the portfolio assessment in Kentucky looks very different from the portfolio assessment in Massachusetts.

The Population of Learners for Which Alternate Assessments Are Designed

Currently, states may choose to develop two types of alternate assessments: alternate assessments based on grade-level achievement standards and alternate assessments based on alternate achievement standards. Both are designed for a very small percentage, yet unique, population of students.

Students taking alternate assessments based on grade-level achievement standards. Alternate assessments based on grade-level achievement standards are designed for a very small percentage of the total student population. However, there is little research to date on these types of assessments, and the population of students taking such assessments is still unknown. These assessments are particularly important to students who, because of their significant disability, which is *not* cognitive in nature, still cannot participate in the regular state assessment even with appropriate accommodations. Because of the complexity, severity, or exceptional nature of their disabilities, these students require an alternate assessment based on grade-level achievement standards. These alternate assessments must measure the same grade-level achievement as students taking the regular state assessment, but through a different assessment format and context. At this time, few states have developed alternate assessments based on grade-level achievement standards, but according to the Individuals With Disabilities Education Improvement Act of 2004 (IDEA 2004), all have the right and obligation to develop such assessments to meet the needs of qualifying individual students.

Students taking alternate assessments based on alternate achievement standards. Alternate assessments based on alternate achievement standards are purposefully designed for a very small percentage of the student population for whom traditional paper-and-pencil assessments, even with appropriate accommodations, would result in an inappropriate measure of student progress within the general education curriculum. Generally, less than 1% of the total student population (i.e., those students who have the most significant cognitive disabilities) participates in the alternate assessment based on alternate achievement standards. Students participating in these alternate assessments have a variety of special education labels such as autism, mental retardation, and multiple disabilities (U.S. Department of Education, 2005b). The majority of students who take an alternate assessment may have one of these three special education labels. However, it is important to remember that not all students receiving special education services in each of these categories require an alternate assessment. Conversely, students identified in *other* IDEA categories, should they have a significant cognitive disability, could also qualify for an alternate assessment based on alternate achievement standards.

IEP Team Decisions

For each student with a disability, the student's IEP team decides how the student will participate in the state assessment system. Still, the process of choosing the appropriate assessment for an individual student varies considerably from state to state. The IEP team, by law, is directed by state participation guidelines for the alternate assessment. The team must ensure that each student "participates in a way that accurately portrays the student's achievement of knowledge and skills so as to hold accountable the educational system responsible for the student's learning" (National Center on Educational Outcomes, 2003, p. 4). Students who take alternate assessments based on grade-level achievement standards present a dilemma to states required by law to assess all students using valid and reliable methods. As mentioned earlier, few states have developed alternate assessments based on *grade-level* achievement standards. This situation places students eligible for this type of assessment in a difficult and vulnerable position because their IEP teams are forced to choose from assessment options with little data to support their use.

IEP teams should *always* first consider students for the general assessment system with appropriate accommodations before the alternate assessment. These IEP team decisions are ones that should be taken very seriously; for example, in some states, the option of receiving a regular high school diploma is tied to participation in the general assessment. Consideration of the appropriate assessment for each student also is of utmost importance for accountability purposes.

Characteristics of Students Currently Participating in Alternate Assessments

As mentioned previously, students currently participating in alternate assessments that are based on alternate achievement standards typically have special education labels of autism, mental retardation, or multiple disabilities (U.S. Department of Education, 2005b). However, labels naturally do not accurately describe the true characteristics of the student (e.g., how he or she prefers to communicate or receive information, motor abilities, health conditions). There is currently little research that identifies the characteristics of students taking alternate assessments. However, one study has provided preliminary data on the characteristics of students taking alternate assessments that are based on alternate achievement standards. The Colorado Alternate Assessment Collaborative conducted a pilot study investigating the development of two new types of alternate assessments (Almond & Bechard, 2005). Findings revealed that (a) of the 165 students in the study, 142 had mental retardation, but more than one-third of the students also had two or more significant disabling conditions; (b) most students' instructional objectives fell into the categories of functional living and communication skills or English language arts and mathematics; (c) exactly 49 students used 1–4 assistive technologies during day-to-day instruction, 41 used 5–7 technologies, and 46 students used 8–11 assistive technologies represented most often by printed or picture schedules and word cards, a word book, or word wall; (d) although 10% of students did not use words to communicate, almost 40% used 200 words or more in functional communication; and (e) there was a range of physical movement and level of support required by students in this study (Almond & Bechard, 2005).

Although this information provides only a snapshot of the characteristics in this one sample, it is currently the only research to date with respect to characteristics of students participating in alternate assessments based on alternate achievement standards. The National Alternate Assessment Center is currently investigating the characteristics of students taking alternate assessments based on alternate achievement standards, but it is in the early stages of organizing this study (Towles-Reeves, Kearns, Kleinert, & Kleinert, in press; Kearns, Towles-Reeves, Kleinert, & Kleinert, 2008) . Further research is necessary to better understand the characteristics of this heterogeneous population of students.

Future Research in Alternate Assessment

The field of alternate assessment requires future research in many areas because there are still numerous issues we need to resolve to improve the outcomes of students taking alternate assessments that are based on both grade-level and alternate achievement standards. Browder et al. (2003) note six recommendations for the direction of future research:

- Validate performance indicators with content area experts and stakeholders.
- Use a format for alternate assessment that produces data for instructional decisions.
- Link alternate assessments to the IEP so students and parents can participate in setting the level of expectation.
- Train teachers in how to incorporate alternate assessment in daily practice.
- Use best measurement practice for scoring and reporting alternate assessments and collecting and reporting data on technical quality.
- Use alternate assessment outcomes for program evaluation and ongoing quality enhancement. (See the Browder et al. (2003) article for more in-depth discussion of future research necessary in understanding and improving alternate assessments.)

KEY SPECIAL EDUCATION REFORM EFFORTS

Educational accountability systems have been in place for years within state departments of education (Linn, 2000). However, every state must now operate an accountability system (as a result of the No Child Left Behind Act of 2001) that imposes high stakes on schools, districts, and states. Accountability systems are defined as "systems used to achieve specific educational goals by attaching to performance indicators certain consequences meant to effect change in specific areas of functioning" (Council for Chief State School Officers, 2004, p. 4). Today, critical issues for accountability systems center on states' abilities to include students with disabilities in the appropriate assessment systems and to report outcomes for all students in reading, mathematics, and science.

According to the U.S. Department of Education (a), there are three reasons why students with disabilities should be included in state assessment and accountability systems. First, it is the law. Second, students with disabilities benefit from receiving the instruction necessary to successfully participate in state assessment systems. Third, the appropriate measurement of students' achievement and inclusion within the accountability system ensures appropriate allocation of resources dedicated to help students with the most significant cognitive disabilities succeed in school. Other advocates note additional benefits to including students with disabilities in accountability systems: improved instruction for these students and higher expectations for student learning (Browder et al., 2003; Thurlow & Johnson, 2000; Wehmeyer, Lattin, & Agran, 2001).

It is important to review key points of educational reform legislation to understand accountability systems and how current alternate assessments have evolved into their current status. The Individuals With Disabilities Education Act Amendments of 1997 (IDEA 1997), the No Child Left Behind Act of 2001 (NCLB), and the Individuals With Disabilities Education Improvement Act of 2004 (IDEA 2004) are all significant pieces of legislation that demand holding all students with disabilities to high expectations while holding teachers, schools, and states accountable for the learning of those students. The following information is meant to provide readers with key points of each of the aforementioned federal laws. For a more in-depth look at IDEA 1997, IDEA 2004, and NCLB, please refer to Chapter 1 of this book.

The reauthorization of IDEA in 1997 ushered in a new era in the education field highlighting educational results and improved outcomes for students with disabilities. This legislation mandated that all students with disabilities be included in state and districtwide educational assessments.[1] An alternate assessment was required for those students who could not participate in the general assessment, even with appropriate accommodations.[2] Before IDEA, few states had considered including students with the most significant cognitive disabilities in large-scale educational assessment. In fact, most of these students were excluded from testing systems altogether (Elliott, 1997). The purpose of the call for alternate assessments within the large-scale educational assessment system was to ensure that schools were held accountable for the learning of all students, including those with the most significant cognitive disabilities (Browder & Spooner, 2002; Kleinert & Thurlow, 2001; Thompson & Quenemoen, 2001).

Requirements of more recent legislation such as NCLB demand that the content of alternate assessments be based on grade-level academic content standards derived from the state content standards appropriate for all students. The passage of NCLB built on earlier requirements of IDEA by mandating that states measure the progress of all students in the content areas of language arts, math, and science on academic content standards. NCLB also emphasizes that scores of alternate assessments be valid for individual and aggregated reporting of student scores by student groups according to poverty, race and ethnicity, disability category, and limited English proficiency. Although NCLB specifies that academic content standards are to be the foundation of the content for any large-scale educational assessment, the way students show progress on those content standards may need to be simplified in breadth, scope, and complexity for students taking alternate assessments. Therefore, NCLB allows for the development of alternate

1. 612(a)(17)(A).
2. 612(a)(17)(A)(i-ii).

assessments based on grade-level achievement standards and alternate achievement standards.

The reauthorization of IDEA in 2004 continues to strengthen the requirements set forth in previous legislation as states work furiously to ensure that students with disabilities are appropriately included in state assessment and accountability systems while also ensuring that the scores are reliable and valid for high-stakes decision making for students, schools, and states. This reauthorization emphasizes raising expectations for students with disabilities through challenging academic standards.[3] Legislation also mandates that if states choose to develop alternate assessments based on alternate achievement standards, then they must align (or be linked) to academic content standards at grade-level.[4] Now that we recognize why alternate assessments exist, it is important to understand the differences between the current two options for students with disabilities.

ALTERNATE ASSESSMENT PARTICIPATION OPTIONS FOR STUDENTS WITH DISABILITIES

There are currently multiple participation options in large-scale educational assessment systems for all students with disabilities. Students may participate in (a) the regular state assessment without accommodations, (b) the regular state assessment with accommodations, (c) the alternate assessment based on grade-level achievement standards, or (d) the alternate assessment based on alternate achievement standards. [There is currently a fifth option, alternate assessments based on modified achievement standards, but the final regulations were not published at the time this chapter was written.] For the purpose of this chapter, we will focus solely on options c and d. Table 5.1 outlines the two alternate assessment options available to students with disabilities. This table also describes the foundation for content, evaluation of performance, and participation eligibility for each assessment option. All students are to be working toward grade-level content standards. For that reason, alternate assessments are to be based on the state's *grade-level* academic content standards as described in Column 2 of Table 5.1. However, not all assessment options are to be judged against the same *achievement* standards as outlined in Column 3. Alternate assessments may be judged against grade-level achievement standards or alternate achievement standards. Alternate assessments based on alternate achievement standards should still be *linked* to grade-level content standards. Column 4 of Table 5.1 outlines the differences in participation options based on the individual needs of the student. The child's IEP team decides the type of assessment most appropriate for the student. Only students with disabilities needing an alternate assessment format may participate in the alternate assessment based on grade-level achievement standards. The alternate assessment

3. 612(a)(16)(C)(ii)(I).
4. 612(a)(16)(C)(ii)(II).

Table 5.1. Alternate Assessment Participation Options for Students with Disabilities

Alternate Assessment Option	Foundation for Content	How Performance Is Evaluated	Who Can Participate
Alternate Assessment Judged Against Grade-Level Achievement Standards	State's Academic Content Standards	Grade-Level Achievement Standards	Any student with a disability
Alternate Assessment Judged Against Alternate Achievement Standards	State's Academic Content Standards	Alternate Achievement Standards	Students with significant cognitive disabilities

Source: Adapted from Browder (2005).

based on alternate achievement standards is reserved for students with the most significant cognitive disabilities.

Table 5.2 was extracted from the U.S. Department of Education nonregulatory guidance on alternate assessments based on alternate achievement standards (U.S. Department of Education, 2005a). This table outlines the maximum participation rates (or "caps") and proficiency calculations for the purpose of evidencing Adequate Yearly Progress (AYP). This table is supplemental to Table 5.1 in that it explicates both IDEA and NCLB regulations for (a) including students as participants in state alternate assessments and (b) including students in the accountability system for purposes of meeting AYP. The first column in Table 5.2 outlines the type of alternate assessment option that is available, the foundation for content, and where the use of accommodations is appropriate. The second column outlines how students with disabilities, but *not* those with the most significant cognitive disabilities, may participate in each type of assessment and how scores would count for AYP purposes.

The final column summarizes how students with the most significant cognitive disabilities may participate in each alternate assessment and how scores would count for AYP purposes. For alternate assessments based on alternate achievement standards, a maximum of 1% of all students' scores in that state can be counted as proficient for the purposes of AYP, though there is no limit on the number of students who can *participate* in the alternate assessment based on alternate achievement standards. However, if more than 1% of the total student population takes the alternate assessment on alternate achievement standards in all grades assessed at the local and state levels *and* scores proficient, then the state must develop a process to ensure that only 1% of all students' scores for this assessment are counted as proficient when calculating AYP. The rest of the scores

Table 5.2. Requirements for Use of Alternate Assessment Results in AYP Calculations

Type of Assessment	Students With Disabilities, But *Not* the Most Significant Cognitive Disabilities	Students With the Most Significant Cognitive Disabilities
Alternate Assessment Based on Grade-Level Achievement Standards		
• Aligned with grade-level achievement standards • With approved accommodations and a valid score	• Must be considered a participant through IEP process • May be proficient in AYP calculations	• Applicable in a state that does not establish alternate achievement standards • Student would be considered a participant and achievement would be measured against grade-level achievement standards
Alternate Assessment Based on Alternate Achievement Standards		
• Based on alternate achievement standards • With approved accommodations and a valid score	• If a state permits these students to be assessed based on alternate achievement standards, then it would *not* be consistent with regulation	• Student is a participant (as designated by the IEP team) and proficient score may be included as proficient in AYP calculations, subject to 1.0% cap.

Source: Adapted from U.S. Department of Education (2005a).

for students taking alternate assessments based on alternate achievement standards, above the 1%, are calculated as not meeting proficiency for the purposes of AYP. Placing a cap on the number of students who can be counted as proficient in AYP calculations ensures that only those students appropriate for an alternate assessment based on alternate achievement standards are participating in that assessment.

ALTERNATE ASSESSMENT PARTICIPATION OPTIONS FOR STUDENTS WHO ARE DEAF OR HARD OF HEARING

For students with disabilities, there are two alternate assessment participation options as currently outlined in Tables 5.1 and 5.2. However, this chapter has yet to consider the complexities of these assessment options in relation to deaf or hard of hearing students. The following section is set up with a short overview of the type of assessment, two student vignettes to illustrate the diversity of students who are deaf or hard of hearing that may participate in each type of assessment, and guiding considerations or questions to be used when deciding which alternate assessment option is most appropriate for students with unique and specialized needs for support.

Alternate Assessments Judged Against Grade-Level Achievement Standards

Students who are deaf or hard of hearing may participate in an alternate assessment based on grade-level achievement standards. In this participation option, students with disabilities need an alternate format in which to document their progress rather than a multiple choice, paper-and-pencil test that is most often used by states as the regular state assessment. Students requiring this type of assessment do not have significant cognitive disabilities that preclude a modification in the scope and complexity of academic content but do have disabilities that are significant enough in nature to require an alternate assessment to evaluate their acquisition of that content. This assessment option should be considered only after the regular state assessment with and without accommodations is found not to be appropriate for this student.

Student Vignette: Amy

Amy is a fourth-grade student who became hearing impaired at the age of almost 3 due to viral meningitis. After the viral meningitis was treated, she was left with a moderate to severe hearing loss in both ears. Amy uses hearing aids to increase clarity but also uses an audio amplification device (an FM system) within the classroom. Both of Amy's parents communicate orally with her. Amy communicates with other family members, peers, and teachers through speechreading and oral language. The FM system helps her to better understand her teachers and other students within the classroom. Amy was also diagnosed with Asperger's syndrome at the age of 6; this condition manifests itself in her significant inability to attend and maintain concentration over long periods of time necessary to participate and successfully complete a regular state assessment with or without accommodations. Amy also has repetitive motor mannerisms (i.e., hand flapping), which makes it difficult for her to participate in the regular state assessment. Amy experiences many difficulties in reading and writing English, which add to her difficulties in academic areas not only in language arts but also in mathematics and science. In the classroom, she requires extra time on instructional activities; reduced amounts of work; and a screen reader, which converts text to synthesized speech that is directly channeled into her FM system. Because of Amy's inability to maintain concentration coupled with her hearing impairment and difficulties in the classroom, she participates in the alternate assessment based on grade-level achievement standards.

Student Vignette: Danny

Danny is a seventh-grade student. He was born with cerebral palsy (CP) and a comorbid hearing impairment in both ears, due to lack of oxygen before and during birth. Danny wears hearing aids to increase acuity. Danny is also nearsighted and wears corrective lenses. Because of the CP, Danny also uses a wheelchair for mobility. Danny's parents, teachers, and peers communicate with him using an augmentative communication device, Pathfinder, that he controls with a laser headpointer. The device converts his messages to speech as controlled through the headpointer and has successfully improved his communication with everyone. Danny has been using the device for 2 years and has made significant strides in the classroom. Now that Danny has a consistent communication system, his frustration level with completing work within the classroom has decreased significantly, and his teachers and parents have noted tremendous gains in academic learning. Danny uses his assistive communication device to develop classroom projects and participate in general education classes. Given Danny's intense physical and sensory needs, Danny participates in the alternate assessment based on grade-level achievement standards.

Considerations or Guiding Questions

First, does the student receive special education services under one of the IDEA disability categories?

- If no, then the student cannot be considered for the alternate assessment based on grade-level achievement standards.
- If yes, then the student should first be considered for the regular state assessment with or without accommodations before being considered for the alternate assessment based on grade-level achievement standards.

Second, can the student show progress on grade-level content measured by grade-level achievement standards, *but has difficulty in taking the regular state assessment because of the format of the test and the student's disability* (e.g., paper-and-pencil multiple choice test requiring extended periods of time to complete each test section)?

- If no, then the student should be considered for the regular state assessment, though the student may still require accommodations to address other assessment needs.
- If yes, then the student should first be considered for the regular state assessment with accommodations. However, if the student requires an alternate format because of his or her disability but can still show proficiency through grade-level achievement standards, then the alternate assessment based on grade-level achievement standards is most likely appropriate for this student.

Alternate Assessments Judged Against Alternate Achievement Standards

An alternate assessment based on alternate achievement standards is another option for assessment participation available to students who are deaf or hard of hearing. This assessment is reserved for students with the most significant cognitive disabilities. As a result, a student who is deaf or hard of hearing may participate in this assessment option only if the student also has a significant cognitive impairment.

Student Vignette: Annie

Annie is an eighth-grade student. She lives with her parents who adopted her when she was age 16 months. She was born with multiple disabilities. Annie has median facial cleft syndrome, which resulted in total blindness at birth and a progressive hearing loss. She has also been diagnosed with Charcot-Marie tooth disease, a degenerative disease requiring her to wear leg braces and adaptive footwear. Because of Annie's developmental needs, she has undergone 35–40 surgeries since birth to correct facial structures. It is hoped that Annie will soon have a surgery to close her palate. At this point, she is able to ingest only baby food. Annie is able to communicate verbally with her teachers and family, although her speech is sometimes unintelligible to persons who are not familiar with her. In addition, Annie uses some gestures to communicate. In her day-to-day activities and within the classroom, Annie does not use any assistive technology devices to help her communicate. Annie does have access to the general education curriculum and is fully included in her classes. However, she has difficulty in many of the following areas: remembering new information, generalizing learned skills to appropriate contexts, self-regulating her behavior, and synthesizing skills. Annie also has limited motor response repertoires and special health-care needs that may limit participation in school activities from time to time. Annie's cognitive functioning, measured through intellectual, achievement, and adaptive functioning tests by a school psychologist, falls in the moderate to severe intellectual disability range. Because of these difficulties in cognition, Annie's special health-care needs, and her progressive hearing loss and blindness, the most appropriate assessment option is the alternate assessment based on alternate achievement standards.

Student Vignette: Frank

Frank is a tenth-grade high school student. Frank was born with a profound hearing loss. At the age of 11, he was diagnosed with Usher's syndrome. Frank's educational, achievement, and adaptive tests have consistently indicated that his cognitive functioning is in the moderate intellectual disability range. Frank can do many things independently (e.g., eat, bathe, play video games), but he continues to need some supervision in his daily routine (e.g., choosing appropriate clothing, choosing healthy meals). Before his sixth-grade year, Frank was educated at a regular school, mostly in a self-contained, special education classroom. For the past 5 years, Frank has attended his state school for the deaf. At the school for the deaf, Frank has built on his communication system but still uses limited, unconventional gestural cues to communicate with family, peers, and teachers. In the classroom, Frank struggles with generalization, remembering new information, and synthesizing skills. He requires direct, systematic language instruction to expand his mode of communication. Because of Frank's level of cognitive functioning and his performance in the classroom, he participates in the alternate assessment based on alternate achievement standards.

Considerations or Guiding Questions

First, does the student have a significant cognitive disability?

- If no, then this student should be considered for other assessment options. The assessment option of an alternate assessment based on alternate achievement standards is *not* appropriate for individuals who do not have significant cognitive disabilities.
- If yes, all other assessment options should still be considered for this student before considering the alternate assessment based on alternate achievement standards. If the student has a significant cognitive disability, then the alternate assessment based on alternate achievement standards may be the most appropriate assessment option. The essential element in this decision is whether the student's achievement would be more fairly measured against alternate achievement standards as opposed to grade-level achievement standards, while maintaining that the student is held to high expectations.

As noted earlier, individual states have participation guidelines for each large-scale educational assessment participation option within the state. These guidelines, along with the questions outlined above, should be considered when choosing the most appropriate option for all students with disabilities, including those who are deaf or hard of hearing.

CONCLUSION

Although the area of alternate assessments for students with hearing loss, deafness, and multiple disabilities is a complex one indeed, it is important to remember the intent of these new laws: that all students have the right to an education where they are given access to the general curriculum and are held to high expectations for their achievement. This chapter is not meant to discuss every situation related to choosing appropriate alternate assessment options for deaf or hard of hearing students. However, it is hoped this chapter will help readers to better understand why alternate assessments exist and how important it is to carefully consider large-scale assessment participation for all students, especially for those who are deaf or hard of hearing.

REFERENCES

Almond, P., & Bechard, S. (2005). *In-depth look at students who take alternate assessments: What do we know now?* Retrieved June 5, 2008, from http://www.measuredprogress.org/resources/inclusive/articlespapers/StudentsTakingAltAssess.pdf.

Browder, D. (2005, July). *Instruction and learning for students with alternate and modified achievement standards.* Presentation at the Office of Special Education Programs Project Directors' Conference, Washington, DC.

Browder, D., & Spooner, F. (2003). Understanding the purpose and process of alternate assessment. In D. Ryndak, & S. Alper (Eds.), *Curriculum and instruction for students with significant disabilities in inclusive settings* (pp. 51–72). Boston, MA: Allyn & Bacon.

Browder, D. M., Spooner, R., Algozzine, R., Ahlgrim-Delzell, L., Flowers, C., & Karvonen, M. (2003). What we know and need to know about alternate assessment. *Exceptional Children, 70,* 45–61.

Council for Chief State School Officers. (2004). A framework for examining the validity in state accountability systems. Washington, DC: Author.

Elliott, J. (1997). Invited commentary. *Journal of the Association for Persons With Severe Handicaps, 22,* 104–106.

Individuals With Disabilities Education Act of 1990, Pub. L. No. 101-476, 20 U.S.C. §§ 1400–1485.

Individuals With Disabilities Education Act Amendments of 1997, Pub. L. No. 105-17, 20 U.S.C. § 1400 *et seq.*

Individuals With Disabilities Education Improvement Act of 2004, Pub. L. No. 108-446, Part B. (2004).

Kearns, J., Towles-Reeves, E., Kleinert, H., Kleinert, J. (2008). *Alternate achievement standards assessments: Understanding the student population.* Ms.

Kleinert, H., & Thurlow, M. (2001). An introduction to alternate assessments: Historical foundations and essential parameters. In H. Kleinert & J. Kearns (Eds.), *Alternate assessment: Measuring outcomes and supports for students with disabilities,* (pp. 1–15). Baltimore: Paul H. Brookes.

Lehr, C., & Thurlow, M. (2003). *Putting it all together: Including students with disabilities in assessment and accountability systems* (NCEO Policy Directions No. 16). Minneapolis, MN: University of Minnesota, National Center on Educational Outcomes. Retrieved October 16, 2005, from http://education.umn.edu/NCEO/OnlinePubs/Policy16.htm.

Linn, R. L. (2000). Assessment and accountability. *Educational Researcher, 29*(2), 4–16.

National Alternate Assessment Center. (2005, June). *Access and alignment to grade level content for students with significant cognitive disabilities.* Pre-session conducted at the meeting of the Chief Council for State School Officers, San Antonio, TX.

National Center on Educational Outcomes. (2003). Accountability for assessment results in the No Child Left Behind Act: What it means for children with disabilities. Minneapolis, MN: University of Minnesota, National Center on Educational Outcomes. Retrieved October 16, 2005, from http://cehd.umn.edu/nceo/OnlinePubs/NCLB disabilities.pdf.

No Child Left Behind Act of 2001, Pub. L. No.107-110, 115 Stat.1425 (2002).

Roeber, E. (2002). *Setting standards on alternate assessments* (NCEO Synthesis Report No. 42). Minneapolis, MN: University of Minnesota, National Center on Educational Outcomes. Retrieved October 16, 2005, from http://education.umn.edu/NCEO/On linePubs/Synthesis42.html.

Thompson, S., & Quenemoen, R. (2001). Eight steps to effective implementation of alternate assessments. *Assessment for Effective Intervention, 26*(2), 67–74.

Thompson, S., & Thurlow, M. (2003). *2003 state special education outcomes: Marching on.* Minneapolis, MN: University of Minnesota, National Center on Educational Outcomes. Retrieved October 16, 2005, from http://education.umn.edu/NCEO/On linePubs/2003StateReport.htm.

Thurlow, M. L., & Johnson, D. R. (2000). High stakes testing of students with disabilities. *Journal of Teacher Education, 51,* 305–314.

Towles-Reeves, E., Kearns, J., Kleinert, H., & Kleinert, J. (in press). An analysis of the learning characteristics of students taking alternate assessments based on alternate achievement standards. *Journal of Special Education.*

U.S. Department of Education. (2004). *Standards and assessments peer review guidance: Information and examples for meeting requirements of the No Child Left Behind Act of 2001.* Washington DC: U.S. Department of Education, Office of Elementary and Secondary Education.

U.S. Department of Education. (2005a). *Alternate achievement standards for students with the most significant cognitive disabilities: Non regulatory guidance.* Washington DC: U.S. Department of Education, Office of Elementary and Secondary Education.

U.S. Department of Education. (2005b). *Education week analysis of data from the Office of Special Education Programs, Data Analysis System.* Washington, DC: Author.

Wehmeyer, M. L., Lattin, D., & Agran, M. (2001). Achieving access to the general curriculum for students with mental retardation: A curriculum decision-making model. *Education and Training in Mental Retardation and Developmental Disabilities, 36,* 327–342.

6

NCLB and Schools for the Deaf: Integration Into the Accountability Framework

Stephanie W. Cawthon

The philosophy behind the No Child Left Behind Act (NCLB) of 2001 is that education will be improved if there are (a) clear expectations of educational goals, (b) measurement of student progress, and (c) consequences for schools and districts that do not meet educational goals. Forte-Fast and Hebbler (2004) refer to this philosophy as a "Grand Theory of Action," or the reasons why an accountability system will, ultimately, achieve its goal of increased student achievement. They identify four main steps in the accountability system:

1) **Performance indicators**—How do we measure what students have learned?
2) **Decision rules**—What action is taken based on results from the performance indicators?
3) **Consequences**—What is the outcome of this evaluation and how will it help improve student achievement?
4) **Goals**—What is the overall intent of this accountability system?

The goal of NCLB is for all students to become proficient in core content areas by 2014. In a sense, the four steps above "work backwards" from the desired outcome of student proficiency. This chapter will focus specifically on the first two steps in the process: performance indicators, or measures of student achievement, and decision rules on what actions to take based on those assessment data. For further discussion of the last two steps in the Grand Theory of Action, see Forte-Fast and Hebbler (2004).

NCLB outlines an accountability framework for states to follow to reach the goal of student proficiency. Many of these requirements are quite specific. For example, states are to develop a comprehensive plan that includes accountability reporting at the school, district, and state level. Second, and relevant to this discussion, a minimum of 95% of students from every subgroup, including students with disabilities, must participate in assessments (which means, essentially, that all students except for those with excused absences must take the tests). Although proficiency targets can begin low and gradually rise, schools must strive to meet a goal whereby 100% of students achieve proficiency in math and reading by 2014, including the students in subgroups such as students with disabilities, English language learners, and major ethnic groups.

The specific approach to this framework, including decisions about what test to use and how to define proficiency, is left to the states to define. There is, therefore, a great deal of variability between states in what NCLB looks like and how much progress students have made toward meeting educational goals. Palmer and Coleman (2004) discuss several factors that contribute to the differences in how NCLB is implemented. First, this legislation is meant to layer on top of accountability frameworks already in place at the state level. Most states already had some of the elements of NCLB before the law existed, including content standards, goals for student achievement, standardized assessments, alternate assessments, school indicators, and report cards. NCLB was not meant to replace the state systems, but to integrate them into a high-stakes accountability framework. State approaches to each of the key NCLB components therefore reflect, in part, the previous system already in place in each respective state. Much of the overall discussion of the effect of NCLB includes state-level analysis of policies in each of these realms (e.g., Palmer & Coleman, 2004; Porter, Linn, & Trimble, 2005; Thurlow & Wiley, 2004; Wiley, Thurlow, & Klein, 2005).

This chapter focuses on the state-level assessment and data reporting policies as they relate to students who are enrolled at schools for the deaf. Research questions guiding this analysis are as follows:

1. What do current (spring 2007) state policies say about how schools for the deaf are included in state accountability frameworks? How have these policies changed since spring 2004?
2. In states that include schools for the deaf in their accountability frameworks, how are they evaluated using state decision rules about student performance?
3. How are students at schools for the deaf performing on state assessments in math and reading, and how are these scores integrated into the accountability framework?

This chapter will use findings to discuss what factors related to assessment policies and data reporting may affect how schools for the deaf are integrated into state NCLB accountability frameworks.

ACCOUNTABILITY PLANS

As with the Cawthon (2004) analysis on NCLB and schools for the deaf, the information about state policies for this chapter was gleaned from the individual Consolidated State Application Accountability Workbooks (i.e., accountability plans) found on the Department of Education Web site.[1] The purpose of these accountability plans is for state officials to describe their plans for implementing NCLB policies and guidelines. Some examples of areas covered include policies (who is tested), measurement (what tests will be used), and benchmarks (definitions of proficiency and Adequate Yearly Progress, or AYP). Nearly all of the accountability plans have been revised since the time of the last analysis to reflect changes in state processes and legislation. States now appear to have reached a stable place

1. These documents are located at http://www.ed.gov/admins/lead/account/saa.html#plans.

in terms of their accountability frameworks; this stage is therefore an apt time to conduct a reanalysis of these policies and to discuss their implications for schools for the deaf.

The review of accountability plans focused on Principle 1.1: A single statewide Accountability System applied to all public schools and Local Education Agencies. This section goes on to ask states to enumerate how all students, including those in special schools such as schools for the deaf, are included in the state assessment and accountability framework. State policies were designated as responding to this principle in one of four ways:

- Data for students at schools for the deaf will be reported at the host school. (Host Schools)
- Data for students at schools for the deaf will be reported at the referring or sending district. (Referring District)
- Data for students at schools for the deaf will be aggregated to the district or state level. (Aggregated)
- Data for students at schools for the deaf are not reported because of state statute. (Exempt)

Table 6.1 summarizes state data reporting policies for schools for the deaf as found in their accountability plans (current as of spring 2007). The lines in bold font indicate those states with changes in accountability policies from 2004 to 2007.

There are 44 states with state-funded schools for the deaf. Table 6.1 demonstrates that the majority of states have maintained the same policies that they had in the previous analysis. As of the most recent revisions to the state accountability plans, many (29 of 44, or 66%) have policies that have student data reported at the host school for the deaf. A smaller proportion, (7 of 44, or 16%) report student data at the sending or referring school or district. Four states have policies that allow for either host-school or referring-school data reporting schemes. Two states (Oklahoma and Alabama) have statutes that exempt schools for the deaf from state testing. The remaining state, Tennessee, aggregates data for students at schools for the deaf to the state level for accountability purposes.

There are several shifts that have occurred in the past 3 years. Only one state, Oregon, went from policies that report student data at the host schools for the deaf to those that report them back to the sending or referral districts. In contrast, four states (Idaho, Illinois, Rhode Island, Wisconsin) have shifted from a "referring" school policy in 2004 to a "host" school reporting policy by 2007. Four additional states (Delaware, Massachusetts, New Jersey, and Pennsylvania) have added flexibility to their plans by expanding them to include multiple options depending on the context of the decision to attend the school for the deaf. For example, the Pennsylvania state policy indicates that it is not *where* the student is taught that is the deciding factor, but *how* the placement decision was made. As laid out in the Pennsylvania Accountability Plan,

Table 6.1. State NCLB Data Reporting Policies, 2004 and 2007

State	2004 Reporting Policy	2007 Reporting Policy
Alabama	Exempt[d]	Exempt
Alaska	Host[a]	Host
Arizona	Host	Host
Arkansas	Host	Host
California	Host	Host
Colorado	Host	Host
Connecticut	n/a	n/a
District of Columbia	n/a	n/a
Delaware	**Referring[b]**	**Referring or Host**
Florida	Host	Host
Georgia	Host	Host
Hawaii	Host	Host
Idaho	**Referring**	**Host**
Illinois	**Referring**	**Host**
Indiana	Host	Host
Iowa	Exempt	Exempt
Kansas	Host	Host
Kentucky	Referring	Referring
Louisiana	Host	Host
Maine	Host	Host
Maryland	Host	Host
Massachusetts	**Referring**	**Referring, Host or Aggregated**
Michigan	Host	Host
Minnesota	Host	Host
Mississippi	Host	Host
Missouri	Referring	Referring
Montana	Host	Host
Nebraska	n/a	n/a
Nevada	n/a	n/a
New Hampshire	n/a	n/a
New Jersey	**Host**	**Referring or Host**
New Mexico	Host	Host
New York	Referring	Referring
North Carolina	Host	Host
North Dakota	Host	Host
Ohio	Referring	Referring
Oklahoma	Exempt	Exempt
Oregon	**Host**	**Referring**
Pennsylvania	**Referring**	**Referring or Host**
Rhode Island	**Referring**	**Host**

(*continued*)

Table 6.1. Continued

State	2004 Reporting Policy	2007 Reporting Policy
South Carolina	Host	Host
South Dakota	Referring	Referring
Tennessee	Aggregated[c]	Aggregated
Texas	Host	Host
Utah	Host	Host
Vermont	n/a	n/a
Virginia	Host	Host
Washington	Host	Host
West Virginia	Referring	Referring
Wisconsin	**Referring**	**Host**
Wyoming	n/a	n/a

Note: n/a = Not applicable. These states do not have a state-administrated school for the deaf. Bold font indicates those states with changes in accountability policies from 2004 to 2007.

a. School for the deaf is designated as exempt from state testing.

b. State policy indicates that it will compute AYP analysis for the school for the deaf.

c. State policy indicates that it will compute school for the deaf student data in sending, or referral school or district.

d. State policy indicates that it will aggregate school for the deaf student data at the district or state level.

Students who are assigned by a school or district to receive their educational services outside their attendance area will have their scores attributed to the attendance area school for purposes of reporting and accountability; the scores of those who change schools voluntarily will be attributed to the school they are attending. (Pennsylvania Accountability Workbook, 2004, p. 7)

Delaware leaves it up to the district to decide whether to have the scores of students attending special schools be sent to the referring school or be reported at the host school:

In schools that serve students from other schools, where the students are "tuition-based" special needs students, the district has the option of tracking the students back to the school of residence or to make the school that is providing the instruction the accountable school. Whatever option the district decides for accountability purposes in 2006, the district will do the same in 2007. The NCLB Stakeholder group will re-examine the issue in 2007. (Delaware Accountability Workbook, 2007, p. 10)

The trend in state accountability plans is therefore toward individual accountability for the host schools, with some additional flexibility in how local agencies implement state policies. The distinction between "host school" and "referring school" policies is very important in the overall discussion of the philosophy of accountability for students who are deaf or hard of hearing. Who is responsible for the educational outcomes of students with disabilities—those who place them in the educational setting or the staff in the placement location? The answer to this question could feasibly be argued in either direction. For example, if a special services school is considered to have the same accountability for its students as regular education schools and districts, then a "host" policy reflects that assumption. Alternatively, if the special services school is considered to be providing services in lieu of the regular district, one that may not have the requisite resources available, then the "referring" policy is more aligned to that function. In many cases, both assumptions are true, which is perhaps why the U.S. Department of Education has allowed states to decide how to establish accountability for schools that provide specialized services for students. It will be interesting to see whether state choices toward more flexibility are continued in states such as Pennsylvania or are considered by others as NCLB evolves.

There were some important changes in the language used in response to the Principle 1.1 component of the state accountability plans. In the 2004 analysis, the text in the accountability plans was often unclear as to how schools for the deaf would specifically be included in the accountability framework (Cawthon, 2004). Many state policies required extensive follow-up communication with both the superintendents of schools for the deaf and state-level administrators in special education and assessment. In contrast, the language in the revised accountability plans was far more detailed and explicit. Although there were still a few states that needed to make further clarification, on the whole, states specifically identified data reporting procedures for students who attend state schools for the deaf. As an example, here is the current text for Principle 1.1 in the Arkansas Accountability Plan:

Arkansas has three State-supported schools that receive no local funds. These schools include:

1. Arkansas School for the Blind (K-12)
2. Arkansas School for the Deaf (K-12)
3. Arkansas School for Mathematics and Sciences (11–12)

The Arkansas School for the Blind and Arkansas School for the Deaf are residential special purpose schools serving students from across the state who have these disabilities. Some students attending have multiple disabilities. All, 100%, of these students participate in the state assessment system. A small percentage takes the Benchmark tests with no accommodations, most take the regular assessments with accommodations, and all others complete the alternate portfolio assessments. Scores for these schools are reported publicly as are scores at other schools. Both of these schools have in the past and will continue to participate fully in the State Accountability system, the scores will be included in the report card and AYP for these schools will be determined in the same manner as at any other school. However, since these schools serve a special population, are residential schools serving students from throughout the state, and are established by state statute, some sanctions may not apply. (Arkansas Accountability Plan, 2006, p. 1)

The Arkansas plan is a good example because it clearly articulates (a) that the state runs a school for the deaf, (b) that students participate in the state assessment system, (c) how the type of assessment participation may vary to meet the needs of students with disabilities, and (d) that each school will report data publicly within the AYP framework established for all schools in the state. This kind of specificity, though not ubiquitous, is growing in the state responses to Principle 1.1 in the Accountability Plans. Details such as these allow the deaf education community to have a clear idea of the goals and procedures states will follow when accounting for students who are enrolled at schools for the deaf.

State NCLB policies for how student data are reported are the primary way in which variability between states is established. The majority of states report data for students at schools for the deaf at their host institutions but a significant proportion report data at the referring school or district. States with referring policies subsume students who are served by schools for the deaf into the broader "students with disabilities" category at the school and district level. Although a few states have shifted this policy over the past year, there have not been significant changes between 2004 and 2007. It is with the states that have host reporting policies that we continue our analysis of the effect of NCLB on schools for the deaf.

ADEQUATE YEARLY PROGRESS

The NCLB legislation outlines a goal for all students to be proficient in core content areas within the decade. Although the goal for student proficiency is not new, NCLB is unique in its high-stakes accountability framework built around student achievement on key performance indicators. Because NCLB is meant to be implemented over a long time frame (now 7 years), it is important to monitor for progress along the way. AYP is the term used to describe whether a school (or district or state) is showing enough movement toward the end goal of 100% proficiency for its student body. In a sense, AYP is a measure of growth, of increased levels of student achievement on standardized tests over the previous year (or years).

As part of the NCLB accountability framework, schools are designated as either "meeting" or "not meeting" AYP goals. Each state accountability plan defines what these goals are and how schools can meet them. Relating back to the accountability system concepts described earlier, these accountability plans lay out the decision rules that the state will follow when reviewing the results on the performance indicators (assessments). In general, a school must meet all test participation, student proficiency, attendance and graduation (where relevant) criteria to meet AYP. Schools that do not meet AYP for several years in a row are subject to school improvement measures such as providing tutoring to students, allowing parents to choose another school, or reconstituting the school. These accountability measures are meant to provide guidelines for school improvement based on continued participation and progress on state assessments (Linn, 2003). (For a technical discussion of important elements in developing an accountability framework, see Winter & La Marca, 2001.)

Cawthon (2004) found that most schools for the deaf met both the criteria for test participation (at least 95% of eligible students) and for rates of attendance and graduation. However, very few schools for the deaf received an AYP designation with respect to the school's report card. A total of 11 schools for the deaf were included in the AYP framework 3 years ago, with 3 schools meeting AYP and 8 schools not meeting AYP. An additional 16 schools in 13 states had an NCLB report card but did not receive an AYP designation.

Table 6.2 lists the current (as of spring 2007) AYP status for schools in 34 states that report student assessment data at host schools for the deaf (including those with flexible reporting policies). Most states use the standard language of "met" or "did not meet" AYP; some, however, include other designations such as "academic warning" or "not in need of improvement." Those states with "not reported" either did not provide a report card for the school for the deaf on the public Web site for test results or did not include an AYP designation on the available report card. Unless otherwise noted, the AYP designation is for the state school for the deaf and corresponds to all grades (elementary, middle, and high school). In addition, all designations are those that apply to schools during the 2006–07 school year (usually based on 2005–06 assessment scores).

The overall picture of AYP designations has shifted toward greater representation in state AYP frameworks. A total of 18 states (out of a possible 34 states with policies to report student data at the host school) do provide some level of information about the specific AYP status of their schools for the deaf. Within these states, 22 schools have a designation within the state AYP frameworks, two times more than the number of schools with AYP designations a year earlier (n = 11). Seven schools for the deaf met AYP goals for their respective states of Arkansas, Colorado, Kansas, Louisiana, Montana, Rhode Island, and Washington. The language used to describe a school that made AYP varied from a positive identification (e.g., "this school made AYP") to a descriptive phrase such as "not identified as in need of improvement." The remaining 15 schools with an AYP status were designated as not meeting AYP requirements according to state criteria, up from 8 schools in 2004 (Cawthon, 2004). Although the *number* of schools with an AYP status has doubled, the *proportion* of schools meeting AYP goals has remained stable (about one third) over the past 3 years.

Even with the increase in information discussed above, these data represent only half of the potential AYP designations for schools for the deaf. A total of 16 states that have a "host" school reporting policy (or flexible policy) for student assessment data did not include the school for the deaf in the AYP reporting framework. The reasons for this action vary from state to state. Some, such as those with flexible policies, opt to send scores to the referring district instead of electing to report scores at the school for the deaf. Other states such as Texas plan to report in accordance with NCLB in the future, but do not currently provide a report card with an AYP designation. Perhaps the number of states with report cards for schools for the deaf will increase in the future as NCLB implementation

Table 6.2. AYP Status for States With Host School or Flexible Reporting Policies

State	Adequate Yearly Progress Status
Alaska	Not reported
Arizona	Arizona School for the Deaf: Not Reported
	Phoenix Day School: Not Reported
Arkansas	Not identified as in need of improvement
California	Fremont: Did not meet AYP
	Riverside: Did not meet AYP
Colorado	Met AYP
Delaware	Academic Review
Florida	Did not meet AYP
Georgia	Atlanta Area School: Did not meet AYP
	Georgia School for the Deaf: Did not meet AYP
Hawaii	Did not meet AYP
Idaho	Did not meet AYP
Illinois	Not Reported
Indiana	Did not meet AYP
Kansas	Met AYP
Louisiana	Met AYP
Maine	Not reported
Maryland	Columbia: Did not meet AYP
	Frederick: Did not meet AYP
Massachusetts	Not reported
Michigan	Not reported
Minnesota	Not reported
Mississippi	Not reported
Montana	Not identified as in need of improvement
New Jersey	Not reported
New Mexico	Did not meet AYP
North Carolina	Eastern North Carolina: Did not meet AYP
	North Carolina: Did not meet AYP
North Dakota	Not reported
Ohio	Not reported
Pennsylvania	Not reported
Rhode Island	Moderately performing
South Carolina	Did not meet AYP
Texas	Not reported
Utah	Not reported
Virginia	Not reported
Washington	Met AYP
Wisconsin	Not reported

continues and data reporting mechanisms become more systematized to manage special service schools.

Alternative Frameworks

There are two alternative frameworks proposed by states that warrant further attention: The Small Schools Process in Montana and the inclusion of Individualized Education Program (IEP) objectives in South Carolina (see Foster, this volume). Both of these frameworks offer relevant, but distinctly different, mechanisms for evaluating student progress in core content areas.

Small Schools Process, Montana

In this year's review of school report cards, the first unique AYP framework identified is Montana's Small Schools Process. This alternative framework is unique in that it proposes to address small schools using data sources different from the standardized assessments used for larger schools. When student enrollment is smaller than the minimum number needed to protect the identities of students, states opt not to calculate test scores for that group. As NCLB moves toward annual testing, the number of students per grade, particularly at schools with smaller enrollment, will likely fall below that minimum group size. The small schools process is therefore likely to yield more information than will be available using only the standardized assessment reports.

In its state accountability plan, Montana outlines this different framework meant for schools with small enrollments:

> Montana will make AYP determinations for all public schools and districts based primarily on state assessment data. Montana proposes to make AYP determinations for small schools where the total number of test scores is below the minimum number of 30 in all student groups based on a tiered process, using the state assessment/AYP data for each school and district along with a broader, qualitative review of school and subgroup performance data and other information related to student achievement where necessary to ensure the most valid and reliable AYP determinations (Small Schools Process). (Montana Accountability Plan, 2006, p. 53)

It is the "broader, qualitative review" of student achievement and school progress that is most striking about the proposed Small Schools Process. Although the designations (met AYP, did not meet AYP, school improvement measures) remain the same, the process by which those designations are determined is different. The Small Schools Process is being dovetailed into the Montana All Schools Accountability Process (Montana Department of Public Instruction, 2005). In addition to quantitative measures such as student performance on both criterion-referenced and norm-referenced tests, attendance, and graduation, Montana proposes to include a qualitative review of school effectiveness in its AYP decisions (Montana Department of Public Instruction, 2005). This review includes an evaluation of how schools are working with their own action plans, providing professional development for teachers, and strengthening areas within their school curriculum.

Mastery of IEP Objectives = 96% for 2005–2006

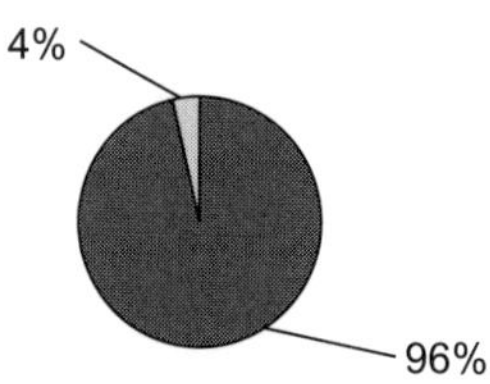

% Mastered by Gender		% Mastered by Ethnicity		% Mastered by Free Meals Status	
Male	96%	White	97%	Free/Reduced	96%
Female	97%	African-American	96%	Paid	96%
		Hispanic	94%		
		Other	97%		

Figure 6.1. South Carolina master of IEP objectives report. From South Carolina Department of Education, Education Oversight Committee (2006).

In a sense, the qualitative review of effectiveness parallels the process of assessing student progress on IEP objectives. The entire process then assigns scores to each component, quantitative and qualitative, with consideration for improvement over previous achievement levels. It is these composite scores and final reports that are used to determine AYP status for each school or district.

Inclusion of IEP Objectives, South Carolina

The second alternative framework was used by the school for the deaf in South Carolina. In addition to the standard school report card developed for all public schools in the state, the report card for the school for the deaf integrates information that is specific to students who attend special schools: mastery of IEP objectives and academic gains on alternate assessments. The school did not previously receive an AYP designation because it had an insufficient sample for NCLB subgroups and statewide testing data, but it has received the AYP rating for the past two academic years (South Carolina Department of Education, 2006, p. 2). The South Carolina School for the Deaf and Blind did not meet AYP goals for student performance on standardized assessments. However, the report card is unique in that it provides other relevant information about how their students show proficiency in reading and mathematics.

The IEP objectives analysis uses language similar to that found in typical report cards, with a focus on "percentage of IEP objectives mastered" by students. Data are provided for students overall and for subgroups according to NCLB guidelines. The IEP objectives mastery data are shown in Figure 6.1.

These data show that students are showing progress on the objectives established by their IEPs. This use of data represents an approach to evaluating student progress that uses principles of instruction and assessment more in line with the Individuals With Disabilities Education Act (IDEA) than with the standardized

ACADEMIC GAINS COMPOSITE 92% FOR 2005–2006		
N= 309	English/Language Arts	Mathematics
Academic Gains	*% Students w/Gains*	*% Students w/Gains*
Gender		
Male	92%	93%
Female	90%	93%
Ethnic Group		
African-American	93%	94%
Hispanic	100%	97%
White	87%	92%
Other	92%	94%
Meal Status		
Free/Reduced	91%	93%
Paid	92%	96%

Figure 6.2. Brigance assessment results for South Carolina School for the Deaf from South Carolina Department of Education, Education Oversight Committee (2006).

approach of NCLB. Using IEP objectives on a school report card thus has important implications in the overall perspective of how to include students with disabilities in an accountability framework. Although this practice is not an explicit part of the accountability plan, it is a good example of how states might incorporate IDEA practices into NCLB accountability.

The second data source used on the South Carolina School for the Deaf and Blind report card is results from the Brigance Alternate Assessments. These data are described not in terms of absolute measures of proficiency, but in terms of progress in core content areas. Academic gains for 2005–06 are shown in Figure 6.2.

For the 2005–06 academic year, students showed similar levels of overall improvement for both English/Language Arts and Mathematics on Brigance assessments (92% composite improvement score). As with the data for mastery of IEP objectives, the data for academic gains show subgroups required for NCLB reporting, including gender and ethnicity. Although the terminology and criteria for evaluating schools on student achievement are not the same as those laid out in NCLB guidelines, this reporting format does reflect similar accountability goals.

The Controversy of Alternate Assessments

Alternate assessments are a controversial aspect of NCLB implementation for students with disabilities. Why? NCLB places a limit on what percentage of a school's enrollment can use alternate assessments and still have those scores counted toward the proficiency rate in that subject area. Originally, this limit was 1% of the student population; this rate has now been increased to 3% under certain circumstances (*Federal Register*, April 9, 2007). The intent of these limits is to encourage schools to use alternate assessments only with students with the most severe disabilities. The remaining students are to participate in standardized assessments, with accommodations if necessary. There are some underlying issues that affect how alternate assessments are integrated into accountability policies (Quenemoen & Thurlow, 2002). For example, does proficiency on an alternate assessment parallel similar scores on a standardized assessment? Does allowing a student to participate in an alternate assessment increase the likelihood that his or her scores will be counted as part of school accountability?

These questions motivate both sides of the debate on how alternate assessments might allow students with disabilities to meaningfully participate in a state accountability framework. Quenemoen and Thurlow (2002) emphasize the importance of technically sound assessments and a clear process by which scores on alternate assessments are included in accountability decisions. Technical quality issues such as validity in constructs measured and reliability in scoring are just as important for alternate assessments as they are for standardized tests (Shepard, 1993). The current policy discourages participation in alternate assessments for students who are deaf or hard of hearing because they are usually above and beyond the maximum percentage of students that can participate and have their scores counted. The effect of using alternate assessments in AYP decisions will depend, therefore, on how states define proficiency on these tests and their integration into the overall framework.

STUDENT PROFICIENCY

The first portion of this chapter focused on the state reporting policies and AYP designations under NCLB for students at schools for the deaf. As noted by Moores (2004), these policies have a significant effect on what we know about students who are deaf and how they are doing on state assessments. Schools for the deaf educate a significant proportion of the deaf population (Gallaudet Research Institute, 2005; Mitchell, 2004). Furthermore, schools for the deaf focus specifically on the linguistic and educational needs of this population. It is therefore vitally important to know how students at schools for the deaf are doing in core content areas measured by NCLB.

Cawthon (2004) provided a summary of the number of publicly funded schools for the deaf that had a report card on their respective state Web sites. Of these, eight states had a report card that included student performance data on state assessments in math and reading. This figure had nearly tripled by 2007, just 3 years! As of spring 2007, a total of 21 states have report cards for schools for the deaf that include some student performance data on state assessments in reading and mathematics. With few exceptions, all of the states that reported data as of spring 2004 also had report cards in spring 2007. Although this increase still does not include all of the states ($n = 34$) that have a policy for reporting data at the host school level, it is a significant jump from the previous analysis.

Student proficiency data in the NCLB required areas, reading and math, is shown in Table 6.3. Assessment results for individual grades are shown when school-wide composite scores were not available. An asterisk indicates that the sample size was too small to meet the minimum required number of scores to report test results. Student proficiency on state assessments in reading and math cover a broad range. There are several examples of schools for the deaf with proficiency levels at 10% or fewer. There are also examples where at least half of

Table 6.3. Student Proficiency Rates at Schools for the Deaf

School for the Deaf	Grades	Proficiency in Reading (%)	Proficiency in Math (%)
Alaska	3	*	*
	4	*	*
	5	40.0 or less	40.0 or less
	6	40.0 or less	40.0 or less
	7	*	*
	8	*	*
	9	40.0 or less	40.0 or less
	10	66.7	*
Arizona			
Arizona School for the Deaf	3	4.0	0.0
	4	0.0	12.0
	5	15.0	16.0
	6	3.0	0.0
	7	0 8	12.0
	8	0.0	8.0
	High School	0.0	14.0
Phoenix Day School			
	3	6.0	0.0
	4	0.0	0.0
	5	0.0	0.0
	6	0.0	0.0
	7	13.0	13.0
	8	33.0	41.0
	High School	4.0	4.0
Arkansas	3	*	*
	4	*	*
	5	*	*
	6	0.0	0.0
	7	0.0	0.0
	8	0.0	0.0
	11	*	*
California			
Fremont	All grades	18.1	22.8
Riverside	All grades	9.0	16.2
Colorado	Grades 3–8	*	*
	9	13.0	13.0
	10	0.0	0.0
Delaware	All grades	*	*
Florida	Elementary	6.0	8.0
	Middle	6.0	0.0
	High	0.0	10.0

(*continued*)

Table 6.3. Continued

School for the Deaf	Grades	Proficiency in Reading (%)	Proficiency in Math (%)
Georgia			
Georgia School for the Deaf	All grades	0.0	0.0
Hawaii	All grades	*	*
Idaho	All grades	25.7	17.14
Indiana	All grades	36.4	53.5
Kansas	Elementary	60.0	60.0
	6	68.3	89.2
	7	40.0	20.0
	8	46.0	9.0
	10	not tested	53.0
Louisiana (made AYP with confidence interval)	All grades	15.6	31.3
Maryland			
Columbia	All grades	38.8	34.3
Frederick	All grades	47.2	67.9
Montana	Elementary	10.5	10.5
New Mexico	All grades	18.5	9.1
North Carolina			
Morganton Campus	Grades 3–8	27.5	29.4
Eastern North Carolina	Grades 3–8	21.3	10.6
Rhode Island	All grades	27.0	32.0
South Carolina	All grades	57.1	54.5
Texas	3	*	40.0
	4	*	67.0
	5	*	100.0
	6	*	*
	7	*	*
	8	*	*
	9	40.0	43.0
	10	56.0	18.0
	11	60.0	25.0

(continued)

Table 6.3. Continued

School for the Deaf	Grades	Proficiency in Reading (%)	Proficiency in Math (%)
Washington	3	*	*
	4	*	33.0
	5	17.0	17.0
	6	29.0	17.0
	7	*	*
	8	*	*
	10	11.0	0.0

Note: An * indicates that the number of scores was too small to meet the state threshold for reporting disaggregated data. States in bold made AYP for the 2006–07 school year. Assessments and grades vary from state to state; comparisons across assessments are not appropriate for these data. Proficiency rates include the percentage of students passing standards and meeting benchmarks of Proficient and above, or those designated as "passing" state standard. Data for individual grades or grade levels are reported when an aggregate "all students" summary is not available. Data obtained from state departments of education Web sites. A summary of links to these websites can be found at *http://www.education.umn.edu/NCEO/TopicAreas/Reporting/StatesReporting.htm.*

a school's students demonstrated proficiency on the state assessment. These results show there is a wide range of student achievement on standardized assessments, but that some schools are on their way to reaching the NCLB goals of 100% proficiency in core content areas.

Under NCLB, states set annual benchmarks for the proportion of students within each school that have reached proficiency on the state assessment. These benchmarks typically start low but will be increased in future years until all students need to demonstrate proficiency (a benchmark of 100%). These benchmarks are thus important because they are used, in part, to define whether a school's students are meeting achievement goals. Those schools that made AYP in their states are indicated in bold in Table 6.3. However, just as the data reporting policies vary by state, so do both the definitions of proficiency and the benchmarks for annual progress (Linn, 2003; Porter et al., 2005). This variation is evident in the range of proficiency scores that result in a school meeting AYP benchmarks (e.g., Kansas versus Louisiana).

Student proficiency data is not always included in the same reporting format as a school's AYP status. States sometimes report the student assessment information in one mechanism and the AYP designation in another. Only 12 state report cards connect student assessment results and school AYP status in a single document. Of these, Louisiana is the only state with a complete NCLB report card where the school for the deaf made AYP. The other six states that made AYP (or are not noted as in need of improvement) may have both NCLB report cards and assessment data, but they are reported separately. There are several elements that contribute to an AYP designation, including but not exclusively, student assessment scores. It is not always clear, therefore, whether math and reading assessment results are directly connected to a school's having met state AYP goals.

There are a number of important issues that arise from a summary of proficiency data across schools for the deaf. The first is a note from the previous Cawthon (2004) paper: These proficiency data reflect only those assessments used for NCLB accountability frameworks and reported on school report cards at state Web sites. This table should not be interpreted to mean that students at schools for the deaf other than those shown here do not participate in state assessments. Students participate in a wide range of school and state assessments that are used in other reporting formats unconnected to NCLB. The remaining discussion of student proficiency scores will address two main issues: sample size and confidence intervals.

Sample Size

One of the first patterns to notice when reviewing Table 6.3 is that there are many schools for which student proficiency and state benchmark information is not reported because of "Insufficient sample" (indicated with an asterisk in the table). There are three main reasons that explain why data may not be available for schools for the deaf: small student enrollment in the assessed grade, no students tested in that grade, and the use of another assessment framework. The most common reason for missing data is the small sample size. Each state sets its own guidelines for how many students must be within each group to meet the "minimum *n*" for data reporting. This minimum can vary a great deal from state to state, ranging from 5 in Maryland to 100 in California (Erpenbach, Forte-Fast, & Potts, 2003). Most states have a minimum *n* of either 30 or 40 (ASR-CAS Joint Study Group on Adequate Yearly Progress, 2002; Porter et al., 2005). Some states such as California and Colorado have higher minimum group sizes for meeting AYP criteria for different subgroups, including students with disabilities. Although many schools for the deaf enroll more than the minimum for data reporting, it is often the case that there are not enough students in the assessed grade (e.g., Grade 8 or Grade 10) to meet these requirements. States therefore opt to protect the privacy of students by not reporting proficiency data for these grades. These measures are required by the Family Educational Rights and Privacy Act (FERPA) of 1974.

The problem of small sample sizes is exacerbated by a shift from schoolwide data reporting to individual grade reports or assessment results. NCLB now requires states to test all students in Grades 3–8, with one additional grade in high school. With the increase in testing, there is a corresponding increase in the amount of information to be made available to the public. Summarizing student proficiency results across all grades and on all tests is a formidable task. Yet when the minimum sample sizes used by states is larger than the average class size at a school for the deaf, then the test results go unreported in the NCLB school report cards or state summaries of student proficiency in core content areas.

Report cards that do not report proficiency rates because of small sample sizes can use other indicators to demonstrate progress under NCLB. Some states aggregate results across all grade levels to give an overall composite score for the school. Other states are developing multiyear aggregates of data to meet minimum subgroup size. Yet, on school report cards, the most common tool to indicate student progress for small groups is the use of state benchmarks in the core content areas. States can use this overall summary of performance without revealing more specific information about student proficiency scores. This approach allows for the education community to know more about where the school's relative strengths and weaknesses are without violating privacy guidelines for students in schools with small enrollments.

Confidence Intervals

Some states have begun to include confidence intervals in AYP calculations to allow for error inherent in calculating the percentage of students who are achieving scores above the threshold to be considered proficient (Forte-Fast, Blank, Potts, & Williams, 2002; Porter et al., 2005). Confidence intervals are used to help account for measurement error when comparing a small group of students with the larger population (the state as a whole) by placing an upper and lower bound on the "true" or error-free percentage of those who are proficient. In general, a smaller group has more variance in its scores than a larger group, making the AYP determination less accurate for the smaller group. Some states provide a single confidence interval, typically 95%, for all schools and districts (Porter et al., 2005). In these cases, if all the students were to take the same (or similar) test repeatedly, then the percentage achieving proficiency would be expected to be within the confidence interval 95% of the time.

By using a confidence interval to set proficiency benchmarks in their accountability plan, states define how they will calculate the range of the percentage of those who are proficient that is required for schools to meet the benchmarks, not just a single percentage. To see what this range looks like in practice, consider a hypothetical data display for subgroup scores with confidence intervals such as those that are shown in Figure 6.3. The average (mean) scores for each group of students are displayed along with the 95% confidence interval for those scores (the range surrounding the scores). The width of the confidence interval in its simplest form depends on the size of each group and the percentage achieving proficiency. In this example, the first group actually has the fewest members, resulting in a wider confidence interval than in the other two groups. This group therefore has a greater range of scores that would meet the state criteria for statistically passing AYP. Although rare, this example of the range falling at or below 0% proficient is possible when confidence intervals are used with small sample sizes.

There are strengths and drawbacks to the use of confidence intervals. Strengths include the ability to incorporate sample size into the AYP criteria calculations, an important factor when considering the statistical properties of student proficiency measurement. A second strength is that benchmarks move from cutoff points to a target range of scores. This shift allows for greater flexibility in the accountability framework and for schools or subgroups that are within statistically similar scores to receive a positive AYP designation. However, there are also some drawbacks to the use of confidence intervals, particularly when used in conjunction with very

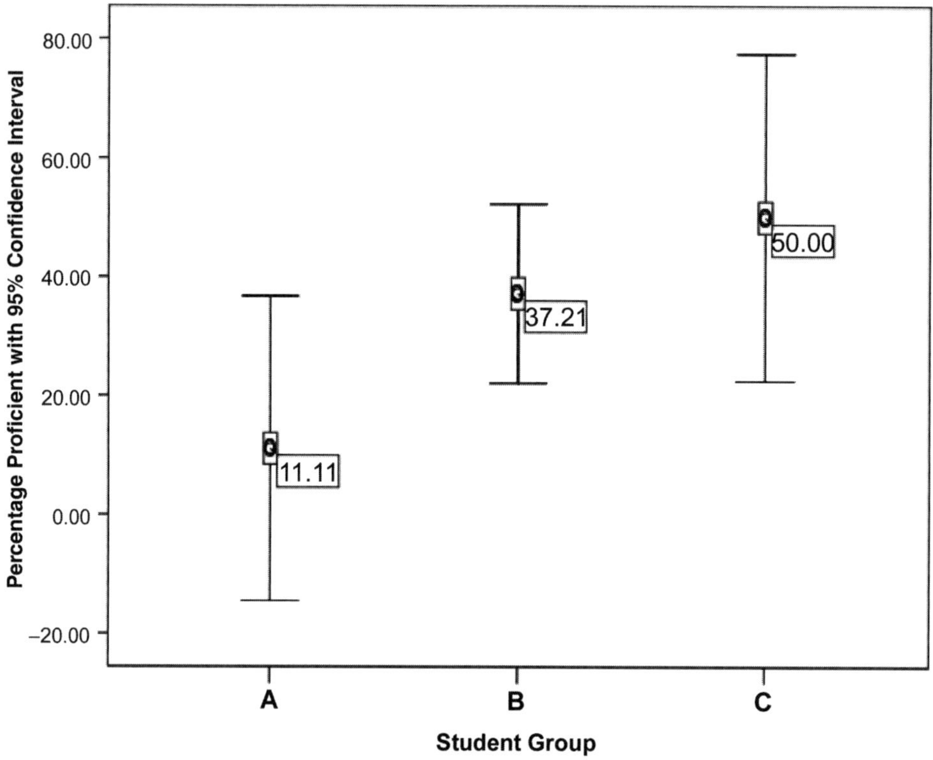

Figure 6.3. Example of confidence interval display for subgroup proficiency scores. Average (mean) scores for each group are displayed in boxes.

small group sizes. When the number of members in a group is very small, the confidence interval can span such a wide range that it renders the score and its interpretation meaningless.

As an example, the state of Maryland uses confidence intervals and has a small minimum group size: five students. For the 2004 school year, Maryland had a target proficiency rate of 46.1% in reading. The overall proficiency rate for school for the deaf (Frederick campus) (n = 93 students) was 37% with a confidence interval of 21.9%–47.3%. The school did not meet the target proficiency rate but did fall within the confidence interval, therefore meeting AYP requirements. This case reflects a reasonable use of confidence intervals that can be applied to large groups.

However, the subgroup analysis led to much wider confidence intervals. Two of the subgroups had fewer than 15 members, leading to very wide confidence intervals in AYP calculations. In one case, the percentage of proficient for the group was 0%, but the confidence interval ranged from −11.7% to 80.9%. Although the group's proficiency rate fell within this range, it is difficult to say that they met the goal of 46.1% proficiency in reading for the year. This example is an extreme one, but it is given to illustrate an important point: When group sizes become so small that the confidence intervals spread across the entire range of possible outcomes, it is misleading to say that the subgroup has met AYP criteria.

Improper use of the confidence interval can lead to an overestimation of student proficiency on state assessments. It is important, therefore, to consider group size, proficiency rates, and the use of confidence intervals when interpreting benchmark information on state report cards.

CONCLUSION

This chapter has reviewed three main components of state NCLB frameworks as they relate to schools for the deaf: State data reporting policies, AYP designations, and student proficiency data. The conclusion to this chapter will once again consider the original research questions put forth in the introduction.

1. What do current (spring 2007) state policies say about how schools for the deaf are included in state accountability frameworks? How have these policies changed since spring 2004? There have not been significant changes in the overall patterns of state policies for data reporting as they relate to schools for the deaf. In total, 64%, or 29 states, have a "host" school reporting policy for schools for the deaf, and an additional four states have a flexible host or referring school policy. The remaining states report student data for these schools elsewhere, either at the referring school or aggregated to the state level. The implication of these findings is that the majority of information about student proficiency and the effect of NCLB will focus on the states that have a "host" reporting policy for the schools for the deaf. There may also be some interesting developments in policies that allow for local decisions about where student scores are included in the accountability framework.

2. In states that include schools for the deaf in their accountability frameworks, how are they evaluated using state decision rules about student performance? This second research question looks at the decision rules that states have outlined about how they designate AYP status for schools in their accountability framework. The number of schools for the deaf that received an AYP designation has doubled in the past year to 22 schools nationwide. Although a similar proportion, roughly 65%, of the schools did not meet AYP, this increase in data reporting demonstrates that more schools for the deaf are being integrated into state NCLB accountability frameworks. However, only half of the states with a "host" reporting policy provide report cards and AYP designations for their schools for the deaf; there may be a significant increase in information available about this element of the NCLB framework in upcoming years.

Two alternative frameworks for evaluating school progress were noted in this chapter. The first was the use of a mixed-methods design that used both quantitative and qualitative methods for determining AYP. This "Small Schools Process" allows schools with less than the minimum sample size to participate in the AYP process without violating FERPA requirements. Montana is currently in the process of implementing this comprehensive model in all of its schools. The second alternative framework was integration of alternate assessments into a schools' report card and evaluation. Alternate assessments are not commonly a significant piece of a school's NCLB evaluation. In fact, NCLB regulations discourage the use of alternate assessments for all students but those with the most significant disabilities. South Carolina School for the Deaf and Blind includes both IEP objectives and alternate assessments in its report of student progress. Schools for the deaf may certainly benefit if alternate assessments become a formalized component of AYP decisions.

3. How are students at schools for the deaf performing on state assessments in math and reading, and how are these scores integrated into the accountability framework? The final piece of this analysis focused on student performance on state assessments used in their respective NCLB frameworks. On the whole, students at schools for the deaf do not meet the state benchmarks for achievement in math and reading. However, there are some significant factors that affect what the field can say about student achievement and meeting state benchmarks. First, there are often not enough students in each subgroup, or each grade level, to make a statistically sound estimate of student performance. FERPA guidelines also prevent states from reporting student test data when groups are below their established guidelines for minimum group size data reporting. Second, many states use confidence intervals when comparing school (or subgroup) performance against state benchmarks. Although there are many advantages to using confidence intervals, when they are coupled with small group sizes, it becomes difficult to interpret these findings meaningfully. It will be important for states to carefully review the effect of their data analysis policies on both the over- and under-identification of schools that are in need of improvement.

Palmer and Coleman (2004) outline a number of steps that states will go through in the implementation of the accountability system. These steps include the implementation of the strategies, evaluation of its effectiveness, and updates to the system as needed. Now that NCLB has been in place for a few years and states have more fully developed their AYP designation process, it is an appropriate time to critically evaluate accountability system effectiveness. Evaluation can include a close look at the reliability and validity of the measures used to determine student achievement and school progress. For example, are the sample sizes for data reporting and AYP calculations large enough to provide reliable conclusions? Do school report cards clearly indicate the reporting elements of NCLB and how AYP designations are made? Through this kind of review, states and federal agencies can work together to demonstrate where NCLB legislation is having a positive effect, and where accountability plans may need to be revised to result in a more effective implementation of the law.

As with states and schools overall, schools for the deaf can also contribute to the review and evaluation of the existing NCLB accountability framework. One of the goals of NCLB was to ensure that all students, including students with disabilities, are included in this education reform. As one of the few agencies serving students with disabilities that can be included in the NCLB framework as a single entity, schools for the deaf can be a model for how other schools can integrate student scores and demonstrate progress in their proficiency goals. This analysis shows that it is essential to look beyond the AYP designations and identify the decision-making process behind those results. Factors such as data reporting requirements, state benchmarks, and use of statistical measures such as confidence intervals all contribute to the broader picture of how students at schools for the deaf are faring under NCLB.

REFERENCES

Arkansas State Department of Education (2006). Arkansas Consolidated State Application Accountability Workbook. Available at *http://www.ed.gov/admins/lead/account/stateplans03/index.html.*

ASR-CAS Joint Study Group on Adequate Yearly Progress. (2002). *Executive summary: Making valid and reliable decisions in determining adequate yearly progress.* Washington, DC: Council of Chief State School Officers.

Cawthon, S. (2004). Schools for the deaf and the No Child Left Behind Act. *American Annals of the Deaf, 149* (4), 314–323.

Delaware State Department of Education (2007). Delaware Consolidated State Application Accountability Workbook. Available at *http://www.ed.gov/admins/lead/account/stateplans03/index.html.*

Erpenbach, W., Forte-Fast, E., & Potts, A. (2003). *Statewide educational accountability under NCLB.* Washington, DC: Council of Chief State School Officers.

Family Educational Rights and Privacy Act (FERPA) of 1974, 20 U.S.C. Sec 1232g; 34 CFR Part 99.

Office of the Federal Register, National Archives and Records Administration (April 9th, 2007). Federal Register, Vol. 72, No. 67.

Forte-Fast, E., Blank, R., Potts, A., & Williams, A. (2002). *A guide to effective accountability reporting.* Washington, DC: Council of Chief State School Officers.

Forte-Fast, E., & Hebbler, S. (2004). *A framework for examining validity in statewide accountability systems.* Washington, DC: Council of Chief State School Officers.

Gallaudet Research Institute (January, 2005). *Regional and national summary report of data from the 2003–2004 Annual Survey of Deaf and Hard of Hearing Children and Youth.* Washington, DC: GRI, Gallaudet University.

Individuals With Disabilities Education Act of 1990, Pub. L. No. 101-476, 20 U.S.C. §§ 1400–1485.

Individuals With Disabilities Education Act Amendments of 1997, Pub. L. No. 105-17, 20 U.S.C. § 1400 *et seq.*

Individuals With Disabilities Education Improvement Act of 2004, Pub. L. No. 108-446, Part B. (2004).

Linn, R. L. (2003). Accountability: Responsibility and reasonable expectations. *Educational Researcher, 32* (7), 3–13.

Mitchell, R. (2004). National profile of deaf and hard of hearing students in special education from weighted survey results. *American Annals of the Deaf, 149* (4), 336–349.

Montana Department of Public Instruction. (2005). *Montana all schools accountability process.* URL: http://www.opi.mt.gov/PDF/5YearPlan/06–07scoringGuide.pdf.

Moores, D. (2004). The future of education of deaf children: The implications of population projects. *American Annals of the Deaf, 149* (1), 3–4.

No Child Left Behind Act of 2001, Pub. L. No. 107-110, 115 Stat. 1425 (2002).

Palmer, S., & Coleman, A. (2004). *Blueprint for building a single statewide accountability system.* Washington, DC: Council of Chief State School Officers.

Pennsylvania State Department of Education (2004). Pennsylvania Consolidated State Application Accountability Workbook. Available at *http://www.ed.gov/admins/lead/account/stateplans03/index.html.*

Porter, A., Linn, R., & Trimble, S. (2005, April). *The effects of state decisions about NCLB Adequate Yearly Progress targets.* Paper presented as part of the symposium "Challenges, Contributions, and Consequences of State Accountability Systems," at the Annual Meeting of the National Council on Measurement in Education, Montreal, Canada.

Quenemoen, R., & Thurlow, M. (2002). *Including alternate assessment results in accountability decisions* (Policy Directions No. 13). Minneapolis, MN: University of Minnesota, National Center on Educational Outcomes. Retrieved September 28, 2005, from http://education.umn.edu/NCEO/OnlinePubs/Policy13.htm.

Shepard, L. A. (1993). Evaluating test validity. *Review of Research in Education, 19,* 405–450.

South Carolina Department of Education, Education Oversight Committee. (2006). *South Carolina School for the Deaf and Blind 2006 annual report card.* URL: http://ssl.sc.gov/SchoolReportCards/.

Thurlow, M. L., & Wiley, H. I. (2004). *Almost there in public reporting of assessment results for students with disabilities* (Technical Report No. 39). Minneapolis, MN: University of Minnesota, National Center on Educational Outcomes.

Wiley, H. I., Thurlow, M. L., & Klein, J. A. (2005). *Steady progress: State public reporting practices for students with disabilities after the first year of NCLB (2002–2003)* (Technical Report No. 40). Minneapolis, MN: University of Minnesota, National Center on Educational Outcomes. Retrieved September 28, 2005, from http://education.umn.edu/NCEO/OnlinePubs/Technical40.htm.

Winter, P., & La Marca, P. (2001). *Combining information from multiple measures of student achievement for school-level decision-making: An overview of issues and approaches.* Washington, DC: Council of Chief State School Officers.

Part Two: *Case Studies from Selected States*

7

One State's Perspective on the Appropriate Inclusion of Deaf Students in Large-Scale Assessments

Courtney Foster

The State Assessment Office in South Carolina's Department of Education provides opportunities for continuous, expert feedback and decision making in matters related to content areas on tests and to the testing needs of special student populations. The Students With Disabilities Unit is therefore routinely asked to review test items and test forms for issues of universal design and content access, to oversee the development of customized materials, and to provide guidance for the accommodations needed during statewide assessments. Whatever success we have had at including deaf students in our statewide assessments may be attributable to our acceptance of the continuous need for adjustments in the accommodations offered and in the tests themselves.

Beginning in 1986, basic skills were at the forefront of the South Carolina assessment system. The Basic Skills Achievement Program (BSAP) was used to monitor the basic skills of students in Grades 3–8. It was also administered to students in Grade 10; passing this test was then a requirement for a high school diploma. The BSAP was divided into three subtests: reading, math, and writing. At that time (long before the Individuals With Disabilities Education Act Amendments of 1997), students who were not on a diploma track, as decided by their IEP team, did not participate in the BSAP. However, many students with disabilities were seeking a high school diploma, so accommodations and customized test forms were developed to meet their needs. A special review form was developed so experts in deaf education could list items they considered biased against students who are deaf. In addition, other materials such as videotapes of test administration content in sign language were developed for students who needed them to demonstrate content-area knowledge.

Starting with the graduating class of 2006, the South Carolina High School Assessment Program (HSAP) replaced the BSAP as the test that must be passed to be eligible for the state diploma. The HSAP has two subtests, English language arts and mathematics, administered in a student's second year of high school enrollment. HSAP was developed to meet both state and federal requirements. South Carolina state law mandates that all public school students pass an exit examination as one requirement for receiving a high school diploma. The No Child Left Behind Act (NCLB) of 2001 requires that states assess public high school students' academic achievement in reading, language arts, and mathematics at least once during their high school career.

With the NCLB and the reauthorization of IDEA (the Individuals With Disabilities Education Improvement Act of 2004), a student must participate in a statewide assessment (with appropriate accommodations if needed) or in an alternate assessment. There are many reasons beyond legal requirements for including students with disabilities in statewide assessment systems, including providing access to the general curriculum, fostering inclusive policy decisions, and setting high academic expectations for all students. Moreover, the participation of students with disabilities in large-scale assessments gives educators much-needed information about these students' achievement levels (McDonnell, McLaughlin, & Morrison, 1997). Although South Carolina has maintained its practice of making sure that students with disabilities participate in statewide assessments, we have explored various options for testing these students validly and fairly. And like many other states, we have more statewide assessments today than in the past. In addition to the HSAP, we have the Palmetto Achievement Challenge Tests (PACT) that assesses English language arts, mathematics, science, and social studies in Grades 3–8 and the End of Course Examination Program (EOCEP) that enables end-of-course assessments in Algebra I, Math for the Technologies II, English I, Physical Science, as well as U.S. History and the Constitution.

Statewide assessments are based on the South Carolina academic standards. The standards were developed as required by the Education Accountability Act (EAA) of 1998 and are reviewed and revised on a cyclical basis. Scores are used for school accountability purposes, as required by state legislation (EAA) and to meet the Adequate Yearly Progress requirements of federal legislation (NCLB). Test items are written to align with these academic standards, and they undergo a series of reviews and edits before appearing on a test form. When including students with disabilities in large-scale assessments, it is important to remember that one size does not fit all. We provide several customized forms of the tests, including Braille, large-print, and loose-leaf. As mentioned earlier, we also provide forms of the tests that are specifically reviewed for bias against students who are deaf.

In addition to developing test forms, we provide guidance to schools on accommodations for students with disabilities, publish these guidelines in our test administration manuals (TAMs), and post the TAMs to our Web site. We stress that the accommodations used in testing should be the same as those used during routine instruction. We allow accommodations with respect to timing, setting, scheduling, presentation, and response options. Moreover, there are some specific accommodations that are available for students who are deaf.

This chapter will provide details about the procedures that South Carolina follows in developing test items, reviewing test items, and providing accommodations for testing students who are deaf. Discussion will describe the processes used in the South Carolina state assessment system. These processes are dependent on staff resources and can be time-consuming. Planning for and monitoring these processes is ongoing as new information and research is made available. We carry out these tasks because our belief is that students with disabilities work toward the same academic goals as their nondisabled peers and therefore are included in an accountability system that guides educational policy.

ITEM DEVELOPMENT AND TEST CONSTRUCTION

Academic Content Standards

The philosophy of South Carolina's Department of Education is that items on statewide assessments should represent the breadth of content that students are expected to have learned by a particular grade level, provide items with a range of difficulty, and address appropriate taxonomic levels. Academic content standards for each content area are reviewed on a 5-year cycle. Starting with the most recent cyclical review of the social studies standards in 2005, and the English language arts and math standards in 2006, all content area standards are being revised using the new edition of Bloom's taxonomy developed by Lorin Anderson and others (Anderson & Krathwohl, 2001). The intent of this revision is to ensure that all of the standards across all content areas are written in the same style and that they describe clearly the specific behavior (skill, knowledge) to be developed in the curriculum. The standards are the foundation on which the assessment items are specifically written.

Test Item Specifications

In addition to the academic content standards, there are other specifications for the development of test items. South Carolina has general requirements for any item that appears on our statewide assessments. Some of our routine specifications for test items are to make sure that they are

- congruent with the knowledge and skills specified in the South Carolina Academic Standards;
- representative of an appropriate level of difficulty for the intended examinees as well as a broad range of skills and content;
- written at a level of reading skill appropriate to the examinees;
- free of repetitive wording that could be placed in the stem;
- reasonably parallel in structure and length;
- written in such a way that all answer options are grammatically consistent with the stem;
- not dependent on any other items for the correct answer (does not apply to items with multiple steps);
- free of clues to the answer for any other items;
- free of bias with respect to race, gender, ethnicity, socioeconomic status,

culture, and geographic region and free of content that would be offensive to any cultural, religious, or ethnic group;

- concise, presenting only necessary information (no extraneous information); and
- clear, using positive wording (with rare exceptions) and avoiding confusing language.

Item Review

At various stages in its development, each item goes through a series of edits and revisions both by internal assessment staff members and by experts in the field. The entire review process is built on the principles of universal design. The internal review involves three specific rounds of item revisions by staff members who are expert in both subject area content and special education. The first round of "raw items" (provided by our test contractor) is routed to the content experts in our office. In this round, the content experts review each item and its alignment with specific content standards. Edits to each item are made if needed. The second and third rounds of item review are similar and involve the continued refinement of each item.

The Students With Disabilities Unit is involved with each stage of the internal item review, considering issues with any item that could limit any specific group of students from accessing the content of the test. We do this review so the various customized forms will represent the standards that will be assessed and so all test forms will be comparable. In other words, we want to make sure that items are fair to the student populations that participate in South Carolina statewide assessments and to make sure that each test form represents the depth and breadth of the content to be assessed. A checklist was developed to guide our review process, a sample of which can be found in Appendix 7A of this chapter.

Besides the internal reviews by experts in subject area content and in students with disabilities, external reviews are conducted by teachers, who provide feedback on test items before their appearance on any test forms. Meetings of both a Test Content Review Committee and a Test Bias and Sensitivity Review Committee are held with each new set of items. These review committees are made up of teachers (in each of the various content areas), individuals in business and service organizations within the state, and experts on students with diverse needs (students with various disabilities, students with English as a second or other language, etc.). Each external reviewer must sign a test security affidavit to keep the contents of any test item and the discussion thereof confidential. Committee members look at each item with respect to their particular area of expertise and make recommendations with respect to items, including their relationship to the academic content standards and to instruction, the item format, the wording of individual items, or some combination. Only then do items appear on a test form.

In addition to the review committees, other committees meet each summer specifically to address issues with respect to testing students with disabilities in statewide assessment. One of these, the Sign Language Committee, provides feedback on issues with respect to deaf students with each administration. This committee consists of teachers with expertise in both deaf education and English for Speakers of Other Languages (ESOL), teachers who themselves are deaf, community advocacy groups, district personnel, and parents. Based on the feedback received from these committees, changes have been made to our procedures, our test development, and our materials. These committees are vital to the continued success of our assessment program in that they provide the voice from the field.

Once the revisions are complete, the item is added to a field-test form. Additional edits may be made to field-test forms with respect to formatting, etc., which completes the review process. Considering the many editing opportunities each item goes through, communication about item expectations with external reviewers and test contractors is crucial.

Item review is particularly critical in ensuring that deaf students have access to the content of the assessment. Often, deaf students who read and understand written material in the classroom, including course textbooks, magazines, and newspapers, can nevertheless be hindered by the vocabulary in some test items. The vocabulary in many assessments is generally not found in everyday conversation or written material. Sophisticated item format or content such as that found in long and complex sentences may make an item more difficult, and the student may need more time than is allowed in a standard administration to process the content (Mounty, 2001). Other important item features need to be kept in mind when developing a test form. These include the specific language used in the item (whether the language is construct relevant) and the issues of the inaccessibility of a particular standard for deaf students. A few examples of these issues follow.

As stated before, there could be an issue of the format of the item. Consider Example 7.1.

Example 7.1. Clarity in the Format of the Item
According to the article, which of the following is not a specific reason for having a hobby?

In this item, it may help that the word *not* is underlined to allow it to stand out to emphasize this item in a negative way. Although the negative wording in items is avoided to the extent possible, setting those negative terms apart will help focus the student's attention on the intent of the item.

Another issue is the specific language used in the item, language that may not be directly related to the construct. Consider Example 7.2.

Example 7.2. Problematic Language in the Item
According to the article, why did the author state, ". . . it was a lean, mean machine"?

Students who are deaf may have difficulty understanding words with multiple meanings. In asking the question "Why did the author state," the word *state* has several meanings. Instead, the item could be written as "Why does the author *say*." The construct being tested here—the interpretation of English idioms—is unchanged by the word *say*. However, it may be the construct itself that poses the problem. Look at the example again. This item is testing the interpretation of an

English idiom. Idioms are often particularly difficult for deaf students because these students do not hear them spoken in ordinary conversation and generally learn about their meaning through explicit instruction. They also experience similar difficulties with standards that rely on hearing (rhyming, references to sounds such as pitch or tone, etc.). However, these constructs must be tested because they are part of the statewide curriculum standards. An item that tests the same construct but in a way that is unbiased for this population and that is of the same level of difficulty may need to replace the existing item. Item substitutions are made on rare occasions, at the most one or two items across all grades and test forms for each administration. The item bank we use to develop tests has both the psychometric properties of each item and the related construct that the item measures. If an item was used on a previous test, we also have a "flag" on that item to inform us that the item was substituted for a specific population on a test form. Although ensuring accurate documentation of such substitutions is time consuming, substituting an item with another comparable item from a previously developed test is much less cumbersome than inventing a new item during the process to develop the test form.

ACCOMMODATIONS: BEYOND TEST CONSTRUCTION

For some students with disabilities, participation in state assessments is facilitated by the use of accommodations. Accommodations can range from something as simple as a grip on a pencil to the use of an interpreter to sign directions for a student during the test. South Carolina school districts, in conjunction with guidance from the state, must ensure that procedures are in place to accommodate the needs of students with documented disabilities in statewide and districtwide assessments. Participation in assessment goes hand in hand with access to the general education curriculum. Decisions with respect to the methods of assessing students with disabilities must be made on an individual basis by a student's IEP team or 504 accommodation plan team and must be documented by that team.

An administration manual is developed for each assessment administered by the state of South Carolina. The manuals include a section that outlines the specific procedures for the use of accommodations for a particular assessment. These manuals are provided to the testing coordinator of each school district, each school level testing coordinator, and all test administrators each year before test administration.[1] IEP teams are encouraged to be familiar with these manuals and to review them as part of the decision-making process each year.

Accommodations are generally conceptualized as fitting within one of the following categories: setting, timing, scheduling, response options, and presentation. If the team recommends an accommodation, there should be (a) evidence that the student is generally instructed and assessed with the same accommodation

1. These manuals are available on the South Carolina Department of Education's Web site at http://ed.sc.gov/agency/offices/assessment/publications/manuals2.html.

and (b) supporting data that indicate that the student consistently performs better with the accommodation during routine instruction and assessment. South Carolina provides for accommodations in all of these categories. Test accommodations do not provide an advantage for the student; rather, they help the student compensate for the effects of his or her disability and help to make certain that the tests are equitable for all students. Brief descriptions of these accommodation categories from our state administration guidelines are discussed briefly.

Setting

Setting accommodations are typically changes in the place where the assessment is given. The student may be administered the assessment individually or in a setting appropriate to his or her individual needs, for example, in a separate location or a study carrel. The student may also need another accommodation such as a signed administration that will require a separate location. The key purpose in accommodations related to the setting is to eliminate any possible distraction for a student. In a typical classroom, distraction may not be controlled to the extent that it can in a separate, distraction-free room.

Timing

Timing accommodations are changes in the duration of the testing. These may include changes in how much time is allowed for a particular test or how the test administration time is organized. If extended time for a test is recommended, then the teacher should have data demonstrating how much longer than other students the student typically takes to complete a test. Although South Carolina statewide assessments are not timed, test administrators must plan for students who are likely to take longer than the usual administration time.

Scheduling

Scheduling accommodations are changes that affect *when* the testing occurs. The assessment could be scheduled at a particular time of the day—for example, in the afternoon rather than in the morning. Scheduling accommodations may be appropriate when a student requires frequent extended breaks because of fatigue, low tolerance for frustration, the effects of medication, or a medical condition itself. This type of accommodation could involve scheduling the assessment for short sessions over several days or for several short sessions in one day. Scheduling testing over several sessions may be a consideration for a signed administration, not only to avoid student fatigue but also to avoid interpreter fatigue.

Response Options

Response accommodations are changes in the way that the student provides his or her answers during the assessment. For example, students may mark answers in the test booklet (for those tests with separate answer documents) or use a word processor to type their responses. On rare occasions, when a student is not physically able to write his or her responses, a scribe is used to record that student's responses to test items. (For more on using scribes, see Bello, Costello, and Recane as well as Fischgrund, this volume.)

Presentation

Presentation accommodations are changes in how the assessment is given to a student—for example, special test forms such as large print or braille and test forms reviewed (and appropriately modified) for bias against students who are deaf. Teachers may sign, cue, or communicate through a sign language interpreter any directions or other information that is normally read aloud to students. The signed administration of mathematics, science, and social studies tests are also presentation accommodations. For purposes of testing in South Carolina, a signed administration for a deaf student is considered analogous to an oral administration for a blind student, both of which are presentation accommodations.

Special Requests

There are times when students need additional support beyond what the guidelines specify. To get approval to use a particular support during testing, schools use a Special Request form. This form and supporting IEP documentation are provided to South Carolina Department of Education staff members. Decisions are then made as to the appropriateness of the request (e.g., Does the support change the construct of what is measured?), and written feedback is given to the schools to provide additional guidance or security measures needed for test administration. An example of this form can be found in Appendix 7B of this chapter.

Customized Materials for Deaf Students

South Carolina makes provisions for those accommodations that are generally recommended for students who are deaf. One of these, the use of interpreters as an accommodation, does not have a wealth of research to guide its use. There is some research to indicate that translating a test could relate to changes to item difficulty (i.e., signed items might become easier *or* more difficult than the original English version). There may be issues in the standardization of a test such as those related to an interpreter's skill level or whether guidance in the administration of the test is provided (Clapper, Morse, Thurlow, & Thompson, 2006).

To support the use of interpreters during statewide assessment, South Carolina makes provisions for other customized materials. These additional materials include a signed administration script (Pidgin Signed English or Signed Exact English) and the signed administration videotapes (American Sign Language, Pidgin Signed English, or Signed Exact English). These additional customized materials help to maintain the standardized administration of the test. The signed script is available in Grades 3–8 in all subject areas, and the videotapes are available in Grades 3–8 and Grade 10 in all subject areas.

The script provides directions for test administrators (TAs)[2] with respect to the

2. *Test administrator* is a broad term used to refer to the student's teacher, an educational interpreter, an oral transliterator, or a cueing transliterator, depending on the student's individual needs.

appropriate sign to use for some terms and specifies when to use conceptual signs or when to fingerspell certain words in the questions and in the answer choices. The script follows the order of the test items and includes what the TA should say (sign). At present, South Carolina makes provisions for TAs to review the sign language scripts two days before the test administration to prepare for administration and to verify that the signed words will be understood by the student. This review must take place at school with no students present and with adherence to all of the test security guidelines.

Producing a sign language script takes some time and expertise. Each item on every statewide assessment must be reviewed to provide sign language guidance to the TA for administering the test. The challenge we face is making sure that no assistance (cueing) is given in answering any test item through sign language interpretation and, at the same time, making sure that students who are deaf have the same access and understanding of what they are expected to do on any given test. When reviewing test items for the script, careful attention must be paid to those items for which using a sign may actually cue the answer to the question. If there is a cueing issue, the TA is instructed to fingerspell the particular word (or words) to avoid duplicate sign usage in the item and the answer choices. In signing the English language arts test (theoretically a modified test administration) there may be many instances wherein cueing could occur. Example 7.3, taken from the HSAP prototype assessment, provides an example of an item that poses issues related to cueing:

Example 7.3. An Example Illustrating an Item Requiring TA Guidance to Avoid Cueing

1. Look at the thesaurus entry.
   revolutionary *adj.* 1. disobedient 2. fanatical 3. innovative 4. resistant
   Which word **best** fits the meaning of *revolutionary* as it refers to Christiaan Barnard's historic work?
   a) word 1
   b) word 2
   c) word 3
   d) word 4
   (South Carolina Department of Education, 2006a)

For this item, the script would need to have directions for the TA to sign the words *look at the thesaurus entry* and the word *revolutionary.* Then, the TA would be directed to fingerspell *disobedient, fanatical, innovative,* and *resistant.* In this way, the construct is not changed and the answer choice is not cued during signing.

For subjects other than English language arts, preparing a script is often more challenging in that the potential for cueing can be quite subtle. Consider Example 7.4, which is an example from the PACT release items:

Example 7.4. A Second Example Illustrating an Item Requiring TA Guidance to Avoid Cueing

2. Scribes in ancient Sumer belonged to one of the upper classes of society. With which of the following tasks were scribes involved?

(a) working with metals to make jewelry
(b) healing the sick with medical herbs
(c) recording information on clay tablets
(d) cultivating crops using wooden tools
(South Carolina Department of Education, 2006b)

In this example, the word *scribes*, which uses the sign PERSON WHO WRITES, and the answer "(c) recording information on clay tablets" use similar hand positions, thus providing a cue, albeit subtle, to the correct answer. In this instance, interpreters would be directed to fingerspell the word *scribes* in the item and then to sign the answer choices.

A similar process in producing the signed script is followed when producing the sign language videotapes. The sign language videotapes include the signed test directions, questions, and some answer choices for the student. The videotape "administers" the test to the student, and the student may operate the videotape at his or her own pace. The videotapes provide additional assurance of a standardized administration because they replace the variety of TAs with a consistent source of administration. Some specifications for our sign language videotapes are as follows:

- The educational interpreter must be familiar with South Carolina regional signs and content terminology.
- The educational interpreter should
    - Monitor his or her hand placement, especially not covering mouth with hands when signing
    - Use facial expressions as needed when signing
    - Wear dark clothes—typically black, dark blue, or other plain, dark colors
    - Use a plain background that contrasts with what the signer is wearing
    - Sign test questions slowly
- The educational interpreter must pause at appropriate intervals to provide the student an opportunity to access graphic material provided in print or tactile formats (have interpreter sign to "pause tape" while the student reviews the graphic).
- The educational interpreter must have skills in presenting various types of test materials. For example, someone familiar with mathematical symbols is needed to correctly read and to communicate the higher-level math formulas and equations.
- There must be an indicator on the tape after each item to pause to allow time for students to answer the question (have the interpreter sign this indicator on the tape, and put wording on the screen to pause the tape to answer the question).

- Question numbers should appear on the screen before the question being signed so students can keep their place.
- The format of the videotape must follow the test format as much as possible. Any deviations from the print version of the test must be outlined in the TA's notes and be packaged with the videotapes.

The TA notes provide additional information with respect to specific items that may require special instructions during administration. For example, there may be directions from the videotape directing students to raise their hand and ask their teacher about certain words in graphs, charts, etc.—specific words, but not detailed content. The TA can use the TA notes to identify the items to which this direction may apply. Another example would be a table included on a test, and the signing of the words in that table would prove disorganized (column words versus row words). The educational interpreter on the videotape instructs the students to raise their hands and have their teachers assist them with the words in the table (if needed), and the TA notes direct the TAs that, for this item, they can sign words to individual students if needed. An example of the TA notes appears in Appendix 7C of this chapter.

In addition to the scripts and videotapes provided for test administration, teachers receive guidance on administration procedures and on preparation for testing. This guidance provides additional assurance of a standardized test administration. Guidance from the statewide assessment programs comes in two forms: specific administrative guidelines in preparing for the assessment and step-by-step procedures to use during the assessment. An example of an administrative procedure from our TAM for a signed test administration includes the following (see Example 7.5):

Example 7.5. Administrative Procedure From the TAM for a Signed Test Administration

1. Begin by signing the administration directions from the Test Administration Manual. The TA will be directed when to begin the videotape.
2. The videotape will be the "administrator" of the entire test. If a student does not understand a word, the student should first try to fingerspell the unfamiliar word for the TA. The TA can verify whether the student's fingerspelled word is correct. If the student did not spell the correct word, the TA may fingerspell the word, but not the phrase of the entire passage.
3. Students will work at their own pace and may replay passages and/or questions as needed. These may be repeated as many times as is necessary.
4. While some conversation involving the student(s) and the TA is expected, discussion concerning interpretation of any test item content is not permitted. Do not converse with the student(s) about any test questions. Remind students that they may replay the instructions, passages, or test questions as needed.

Resources for Customized Materials for Deaf Students

As with other development processes discussed earlier, the internal review of the videotapes and script is a time-consuming process. We receive the script and the videotapes from our test contractors and review these materials on a schedule that necessarily includes the review of other test forms and materials. We try to maintain a variety of resources to assist us with this process. In some cases, test contractors provide expertise in the area of disabilities, for example, an expert in deaf education, sign language interpretation, or both. During the review process, the expert makes recommendations about specific signs to use for certain concepts in the test. We review the script and videotapes with respect to those recommendations, and where there may be cueing issues, we recommend fingerspelling the particular word or words in the script or videotape.

We also rely on the expertise and collaboration outside the Office of Assessment. In the South Carolina Department of Education, the Office of Exceptional Children has staff members who specialize in the education of deaf students. These individuals provide feedback on the potential problems of any test item, on the quality of customized materials, and on the instructions and guidance given to teachers for purposes of test administration. We also have a specific Sign Language Committee that provides feedback as to the quality of those materials. Teachers who serve on this committee are currently in the classroom and provide the test administrator's perspective on the quality and use of the test materials. Most recently, our committee alerted us to the fact that some of the signs used on the videotapes were not the same signs that were used in the classroom, despite some of our best efforts to ensure regional sign use. As a result, we consulted with our test contractors to ensure the use of an interpreter from South Carolina on all videotapes.

Another valuable resource was the *Signs for Instruction: Reference Manual of Preferred South Carolina Signs*, a manual produced for teachers in 1987 (Lewis, 1987). This manual provided illustrations of signs to teachers to ensure standardization across the state as to how various academic concepts are taught in the classroom. The manual provides terminology for specific subject areas and academic concepts that are part of classroom instruction. Since 1987 however, we, like all states, have gone through many changes, particularly moving to a system with a standards-based curriculum and standards-based assessment. We found that this manual, although a comprehensive and valuable resource, missed pertinent subject area terminology taught in classrooms today, particularly those terms used in science, mathematics, and social studies. During spring 2006, staff members from both the Office of Assessment and the Office of Exceptional Children met and compared the conceptual signs recommended in this manual with the academic concepts that were represented on the state curriculum standards and statewide assessments. During this process, we determined that this manual needed revision to include those important terminologies.

The process of revising a document of this magnitude, including editing and reviewing its content, printing numerous copies, and finally distributing them to the classroom would take an extraordinary amount of time. We decided that the revision of this document should therefore be available "live" online, which will allow us to update and add terminology online with minimal work in the future. In January 2007, the online manual was made available to South Carolina teachers. Teachers can download the information and use it for classroom instruction. For assessment purposes, this information can be shared with test contractors for the production of sign language videotapes. This system began with 7,500 words with accompanying signs and in a few months increased to more than 24,000 words and signs. Teachers have been asked to provide regular input if they find that a sign is not available for a particular academic concept being taught. This way, we are able to continuously add terminology and related signs to the online system.

Looking to the future when materials will be customized in pace with technology, a pilot study is being planned to use DVDs as opposed to videotapes. The DVD will be used by means of a computer (with headphones as needed). Students will watch an interpreter on the computer screen and then answer the questions in their test booklet. As many as 15 students could be tested in a computer lab at the same time, as compared with being limited to testing 5 students individually because of the demands of a signed administration. School personnel may also find planning for the administration easier because by using computer labs, they will not have to supply multiple TV/VCRs for each classroom.

DVDs may also provide for more flexible test administration for students and teachers. Presently, students have to manually stop the videotape to answer each question. The DVD will work similarly to a music CD in that each question will be a separate track. It will automatically stop at the end of the track. That way, students can devote their full attention to the signer and the question and not to the logistics of operating a TV/VCR. Students will have the same ability to replay a question at any time. Also, using a computer to watch a DVD may be more familiar to the student and less stigmatizing than using bulkier videotape equipment.

REFLECTIONS FROM THE FIELD

One aspect of assessment that staff members have focused on in recent years is the monitoring of IEPs and 504 plans to ensure that documentation of the accommodations that are used during assessment are also a part of the student's routine instruction. Some research shows a concern that students are offered many accommodations, perhaps more than they need, as a result of teachers' knowledge of available assessment accommodations (Fuchs, Fuchs, Eaton, Hamlett, & Karns, 2000). As part of South Carolina's efforts to ensure that students are receiving appropriate assessment accommodations, we have developed an assessment monitoring system.

Monitoring takes place during various statewide test administration periods and involves a series of steps. First, our contractor provides a list of schools and the number of customized materials ordered for testing along with student names. From those lists, schools are chosen at random and are scheduled by department staff members for an unannounced on-site visit. Before the visit, the online IEP system gives staff members an opportunity to review IEPs for information on the student's routine instructional and assessment accommodations. During the visit, staff members are able to see that accommodations are implemented appropriately. It is easy to forget that on the other end of the item review and test development process is a student, but monitoring has given us the opportunity to see for ourselves whether the accommodations being used seem to be working well or whether there are issues or concerns that need to be addressed. In turn, monitoring reports help drive our policies and guidance about statewide assessment. Monitoring has also given us an opportunity to provide detailed information to our Office of Exceptional Children to assist them in planning professional development.

Another purpose for monitoring during assessment is to ensure that the materials used by students are of the highest quality and that the guidance given to teachers is clear. Monitoring provides the chance to sit down and talk with teachers and students about assessment and solicit their feedback to improve assessment materials. Examples of our monitoring forms—the IEP review form, the teacher interview form, and the student interview form—are found in Appendix 7B of this chapter.

During teacher interviews, we find that their biggest concern is whether students will be able to access the information that is presented to them on the assessment. Teachers are passionately concerned about the success of their students. However, our most important stakeholders are the students. During a recent monitoring visit, a high school student was interviewed about his experience during statewide testing. The student used a videotape during the assessment. Some excerpts from this interview follow.

> Yeah . . . [I used] the ASL one. It is hard sometimes, doesn't look right because you're not going to watch TV to take a test. The videotape was OK. I knew most of the words [signs]. . . . The one thing that is hard is that I have to go somewhere else to take the test . . . where there is a TV and stuff. I go to all the classes [with his peers] but I am [it is] different during testing.
>
> . . . You have to stop and rewind for the questions sometimes. So you have to be very close to the TV. And also there is someone there in case you need to know a word. There is a lot of stuff going on! [referring to all the staff and equipment for the test]
>
> . . . [when asked about the possibility of using a DVD] I think I could take a test with a computer. I work on computers all the days [all the time] at school. Other friends [students] could be in there like a classroom. It would be like a regular computer time. (Student interview conducted by Courtney Foster, April 2006)

Through the years, South Carolina has learned a great deal about testing students with disabilities, from research, from stakeholders, and from our own experiences. Also, there is ongoing research into new assessment methodologies and accommodations. Sometimes, it appears that we are consistently in a learn-as-you-go process. There are, however, some constant program elements that may provide some sense of stability in the ever-changing world of large-scale assessment.

One of those elements is communication. Communication with contractors and stakeholders during both preassessment and postassessment is critical. It is imperative that the state define precisely what it is that it will need from a contractor for statewide assessments. Specifications on how tests are to be developed are crucial to each contract that a state may have with vendors. It is vital for outside consultants to understand the state's specific testing policies and use of accommodations and customized materials.

Communication after test administration is just as important. States should make sure that after each test administration they review the development and production of test forms and adjust the procedures as needed. States should also include outside expertise in the decisions made and the development of statewide assessments. Even if there are special education professionals in-house, programs responsible for testing should seek outside expertise across the state. Experts may include teachers and school administrators as well as parents and community advocates. For example, the recommendation to provide a screen on the videotape that says "pause tape now" after each item so the student will have time to answer the question was made by a classroom teacher. The opportunity for input into a system developed by outside companies leads to a better understanding of the system by stakeholders and more "buy in" among officials in schools and districts.

Another element is flexibility with respect to time management. Preparing for the administration of a large-scale assessment takes a considerable amount of time. Developing and producing test forms, meeting with various stakeholder committees, providing guidance to state educators, and looking at student data is, in fact, a continuous cycle. It requires a team effort both within and outside the assessment office. It is critical that any production and development of test items and forms not be done in isolation. Test developers must continually solicit and respond to concerns and recommendations from the field. As states receive stakeholder feedback and engage in the best practices from the field, there will be more issues to address, thus requiring considerable time and effort on the part of assessment staff.

Research is changing the way we think about assessing students with disabilities. The specifications for developing customized materials for large-scale administration in 2001, for example, had almost doubled for 2006. Because research is ongoing, a third element is the ability to provide a means to accommodate in-depth studies of the state's large-scale assessment program. Having that planned research agenda may lead to empirical documentation of statewide, large-scale assessment practices. Reading research and implementing strategies is good, but to yield optimal effect on state practices, a state-specific research agenda will provide the information best-suited for local practice. South Carolina consistently engages in research opportunities and continues to develop its research agenda. For example, we have used confirmatory factor analysis with structural equation modeling to study whether the underlying factor structure of the PACT 2005 science test is equivalent for students who were administered the test in a regular or accommodated form. Recently, we repeated this procedure with the English language arts and the mathematics test of the PACT 2006 and PACT 2007. The long-term plan is to build on this agenda and to study item-specific information in accordance with various student disabilities to determine the construct stability and validity of our assessments for all students.

In an effort to assist South Carolina with its research efforts, we secured external funding through various federal grant opportunities. The Modifications, Accommodations, Reports and Standards (MARS) grant project will provide the means to continue with the research of the factor structure of accommodated versus non-accommodated forms. Several Enhanced Assessment Grants provided South Carolina the opportunity to look at different item formats. In 2005, the Achieving Accurate Results for Diverse Learners (AARDL) project studied how different item formats might benefit English language learners and students with disabilities on large-scale academic assessments. The Adding Value to Accommodations Decision Making (AVAD) project (2006) continues research from the AARDL project and will develop computer-based, access-enhanced science test item prototypes targeting students with disabilities and English language learners. In 2007, South Carolina received both an Enhanced Assessment Grant, Operationalizing Alternate Assessment for Science Inquiry Skills (OAASIS) and a General Supervision Enhancement Grant, Targeting Research to Investigate Alternate Assessment Development (TRIAAD). Both of these grants will focus on the development of an alternate assessment based on modified achievement standards. South Carolina continues to develop, implement, and research the various aspects of its large-scale assessments. We will continue to be in the midst of changing policies and new research from the field to guide our assessment programs. We will continue to have more questions than answers and will continue our own research, hoping to find the answers. We will continue to solicit feedback from stakeholders to improve our assessment programs. Most importantly, we will continue to keep the individual student in mind when making decisions for our state.

REFERENCES

Anderson, L. W., & Krathwohl, D. R. (Eds.). (2001). *A taxonomy for learning, teaching, and assessing: A revision of Bloom's taxonomy of educational objectives.* New York: Longman.

Clapper, A. T., Morse, A. B., Thurlow, M. L., & Thompson, S. J. (2006). How to develop state guidelines for access assistants: Scribes, readers, and sign language interpreters. Minneapolis: University of Minnesota, National Center on Educational Outcomes.

Education Accountability Act of 1998, South Carolina Code of Laws, §§ 58–18-100 *et seq.*

Fuchs, L.S., Fuchs, D., Eaton, S., Hamlett, C. L., & Karns, K. (2000). Supplementing teachers' judgments of mathematics test accommodations with objective data sources [Electronic version]. *School Psychology Review, 29,* 65–85.

Individuals With Disabilities Education Act Amendments of 1997, Pub. L. No. 105–17, 20 U.S.C. § 1400 *et seq.*

Individuals With Disabilities Education Improvement Act of 2004, Pub. L. No. 108-446, Part B. (2004).

Lewis, M. (1987). *Signs for instruction: Reference manual of preferred South Carolina signs.* Columbia: South Carolina Department of Education.

McDonnell, L., McLaughlin, M., & Morison, P. (1997). *Educating one and all: Students with disabilities and standards-based reform.* Washington, DC: National Academies Press.

Mounty, J. L. (2001). Standardized testing: Considerations for testing deaf and hard-of-hearing candidates. Washington, DC: Gallaudet University, National Task Force on Equity in Testing Deaf Persons. Retrieved April 7, 2008, from http://gri.gallaudet.edu/TestEquity/stantest.html

No Child Left Behind Act of 2001, Pub. L. No. 107-110, 115 Stat.1425 (2002).

South Carolina Department of Education. (2006a). HSAP prototype assessments. Retrieved April 7, 2008, from http://ed.sc.gov/agency/offices/assessment/programs/hsap/hsapprototypeassessments.html

South Carolina Department of Education. (2006b). PACT release items. Retrieved April 7, 2008, from http://ed.sc.gov/agency/offices/assessment/pact/PACTReleaseItems.html

APPENDIX 7A
REVIEW PROCESS GUIDELINES FOR STUDENTS WITH DISABILITIES (OPERATIONAL AND FIELD TESTS)

New Items (Best opportunity to look at items [Universal Design])

- ✔ Review all graphics and pictures (Can graphic be stated in words for Braille form?)
- ✔ Review for reading load of math, science, and social studies items (simplify language when appropriate)
- ✔ Rewrite items with content personnel (review changes for the validity of the construct)
- ✔ Flag items that cannot be changed for the item bank
- ✔ Review format and layout of items during field test proofs

Test Maps (Preliminary item inclusion list)

- ✔ Identify items that may be biased against students who are deaf or hard or hearing or who may be blind or visually impaired
- ✔ Review items for graphics and reading load
- ✔ Provide comments and recommendations to content personnel and test contractor with respect to cautions and changes for Braille, large-print, and sign language test forms
- ✔ Review recommendations with Braille and deaf education experts
- ✔ Mark any item that needs to be substituted (item cannot be edited) and proceed with customized form format

1st and 2nd Proofs (Customized form production)

- ✔ Review comments and any item substitutions for Braille, large-print, and sign language forms and recommend comparable items
- ✔ Focus on layout of test with passages, graphics, etc. on customized form
- ✔ Work within state specifications for ancillary customized materials (i.e., regional signs used on videotape)
- ✔ Have experts with regional sign language terminology work with contractors to produce videotapes for sign language administration

- ✔ Review ancillary customized materials (oral administration scripts and CDs, sign language videotapes, TA notes, and scripts) (state consultants)

Blueline and Print (Recommendations and follow-up)

- ✔ Check all recommendations from previous reviews
- ✔ Give approval to print

APPENDIX 7B
INTERVIEW FORMS

School Test Coordinator Interview Form

School ____

District ____

STC ____

Were there any problems with the customized materials (such as late arrivals, incorrect materials, etc.)?

How many students in this school are receiving an accommodated test administration?

Describe how you organize the special administrations in this school (rooms, staff, materials)?

What other information would you like to share? Comments or concerns?

IEP Review Form

Primary Disability ____

Grade _____ **General Ed** _____ **Self-Contained** _____ **Resource** _____

List accommodations specified in the IEP.

Present levels of performance that are related to the level of instruction that the student is receiving and that contain objective data used as a basis for IEP decisions on instructional supports and accommodations. YES NO

Participation in Statewide Testing addresses what accommodations the student will use on state assessments. YES NO

Accommodations to Regular Education addresses accommodations used to access the general education curriculum. YES NO

The above three pieces of information should align. Any discrepancies noted (give details)?

Teacher Interview Form

Teacher ____

Customized Form (if applicable) ______________________________

How is this student accommodated in the general education classroom?

Were there any issues with the administration (scheduling, staff, materials, etc.)?

What did the IEP team consider when deciding on testing accommodations for this student?

Any other comments?

Student Interview Form

Teacher ________________________ **Grade** _________

Student ____

Tell me about the test (easy/hard, enough time, could follow directions, etc.)?

State the specific accommodation that the student used. Ask: Do you think that (insert accommodation) helped you with this test? Why?

Do you get the same (insert accommodation) in all/some of your classes?

Any other comments?

APPENDIX 7C
TEST ADMINISTRATOR NOTES FOR THE SIGN LANGUAGE VIDEOTAPE ADMINISTRATION

Mathematics

1. You must sign to all students the directions on pages 40–41 of the TAM. The videotape includes the directions beginning on page 42 of the TAM. You may re-sign those directions to students, if needed.

2. For certain test items, students are instructed to stop the videotape and raise their hands if they have any questions. As a TA, you may provide additional assistance to individual students (if needed) with words in graphs, tables, matrices, and other stimuli, as outlined in the table below. Otherwise, no additional assistance can be given.

Item Number	Additional Assistance
Multiple-choice Item 4	TA may read words in the diagram.
Multiple-choice Item 10	TA may read words in the chart.
Multiple-choice Item 16	TA may read words in the diagram.
Multiple-choice Item 22	TA may read words in the graph.
Multiple-choice Item 25	TA may read words in the matrix.
Multiple-choice Item 33	TA may read words in the steps.
Multiple-choice Item 35	TA may read words in the table.
Multiple-choice Item 40	TA may read words in the graph.
Multiple-choice Item 45	TA may read words in the table.
Multiple-choice Item 47	TA may read words in the box.
Multiple-choice Item 50	TA may read words in the chart.
Multiple-choice Item 55	TA may read words in the expression.
Multiple-choice Item 59	TA may read words in the chart.
Constructed Response Item 64	TA may read words in the graph.
Constructed Response Item 66	TA may read words in the diagram.

This form is for template purposes only. These notes do not reflect any secure assessment currently in use.

8 High-Stakes Testing of Deaf Students in North Carolina

Jana Lollis

Increasingly, states are requiring that deaf students pass high-stakes tests to receive a high school diploma. Moreover, the design and production of these tests are unlikely to include careful consideration of the unique assessment needs of deaf students. This failure to attend to assessment concerns for special populations is certainly the case in North Carolina. This chapter provides background on the North Carolina case and reports on a study that explores the issues raised by specifically considering deaf students in the test validation process.

In North Carolina, students must pass the North Carolina Competency Tests of Reading and Mathematics, also referred to as the Eighth Grade End-of-Grade (EOG) Test, to receive a high school diploma. The North Carolina Competency Tests were originally developed for the general population of eighth grade students. However, beginning in 1997, all English-as-a-Second-Language (ESL) students and students with disabilities, populations not considered when the state's competency tests were developed, have been required to pass this test to receive their high school diploma.

Because this testing program has tremendous effect for deaf students, many of whom read well below the eighth grade level, I chose to study the validity of the North Carolina Competency Test of Reading for use with deaf students. This study was necessary because no evidence was found to indicate that anyone familiar with deaf students was involved in the initial construction or validation of the test. To research the validity of this test, I worked with experts in the field of deaf education and reading to study and replicate as closely as possible the procedure for the initial development of the test. In this chapter, I first examine the construction and implementation of high-stakes tests in North Carolina. Second, I report results of a replication study conducted with educators of deaf students serving as reviewers of the reading competency test to determine whether it would have been judged appropriate for use with deaf high school students by these North Carolina reading and deaf education specialists (Lollis, 2002).

HISTORY OF HIGH-STAKES TESTS IN NORTH CAROLINA

In 1994, North Carolina initiated its EOG testing program for Grades 3–8. The tests were established for two purposes. The first purpose was to ensure that all students who graduated in North Carolina with a high school diploma had passed a minimum competency test in reading and mathematics. The second purpose of the testing program was to test students' knowledge in reading and mathematics at the end of Grades 3–8 to ensure that students were mastering the core competencies as established by the statewide curriculum known as the *Standard Course of Study* (North Carolina Department of Public Instruction, 1996, p. 1). These purposes raise two issues for deaf test-takers: valid measurement and opportunity to learn. The issue about valid measurement can be stated as two research questions. Are deaf students exposed to the same curricula as their hearing counterparts? Can the testing program results be interpreted to mean the same thing for both deaf and hearing students? This study did not address the opportunity-to-learn issue, but instead focused on the validation of the test for use with deaf students.

In 1995, the North Carolina State Board of Education mandated that all high school students pass the mathematics and reading portions of the Eighth Grade EOG Test as a requirement for obtaining a high school diploma. If the students did not pass the reading and math EOG tests at the end of eighth grade, they were required to continue to take these tests during their high school years until they passed. In high school, the same tests were called the North Carolina Competency Tests of Reading and Mathematics.

Beginning in 1997, students with disabilities and ESL students were required to take and pass the reading and math competency tests along with their nondisabled peers to obtain a high school diploma. Specific to this discussion, during the 2004–2005 school year, of the 106,179 eighth-grade students who took the eighth grade EOG reading test, 137 were eighth-grade deaf students (North Carolina Department of Public Instruction, 2005). Students who fail either the mathematics or reading tests at the end of their eighth-grade year are permitted to take the previously failed tests again twice a year during their high school years. Students who attend summer school may also elect to take the test a third time. Because there are only a few forms of each test, many students, including deaf students, may end up taking the same form of the test multiple times.

INITIAL CONSTRUCTION OF THE NORTH CAROLINA READING TEST

The North Carolina Competency Test of Reading, Form M, consisted of 10 passages and 68 questions. Of the 10 passages, 4 were "literary" (i.e., poetry, fiction, biographies, plays, essays), 4 were "content based" (i.e., science, social studies, art, health, and mathematics), and 2 were "consumer/human interest" (i.e., recipes, directions, forms, projects, brochures, and short informational pieces relevant to the students) (North Carolina Department of Public Instruction, 1996). Each multiple-choice test item contained a what-where-why question and four options consisting of the correct answer and three distractors.

The North Carolina Department of Public Instruction began test construction in 1991 with the selection of 100 reading passages. A frame was written for each passage to serve as an introduction, to stimulate reader interest, and to assist in comprehension. Readability indices of the passages were computed using the Fry (1968) Readability Formula and the Degrees of Reading Power Index. These two indices reported difficulty levels as grade-level equivalents (e.g., difficulty appropriate for an eighth-grade level). The literary and consumer/human interest passages were computed to have eighth-grade reading difficulty whereas the content-based passages were computed to be ninth-grade level of difficulty (North Carolina Department of Public Instruction, 1996). The questions North Carolina Department of Public Instruction used in its initial analyses of the passages were also used in this study.

The test items were constructed by first choosing test item writers. The second step was to write the pool of items. Classroom teachers were used to write the items because it was thought that their classroom experiences would ensure instructional validity (North Carolina Department of Public Instruction, 1996). The third step in the process was to have the pool of items analyzed by curriculum specialists and classroom teachers to ensure that the test items were valid representations of the objectives for which they were written. The fourth step involved a team of reviewers revising and rewriting items based on feedback from the curriculum specialists and classroom teachers. The fifth step of the process involved writing additional test items and passages as they were needed (North Carolina Department of Public Instruction, 1996). The sixth and final step involved a team who classified the items based on the difficulty level and thinking skills level (North Carolina Department of Public Instruction, 1996).

After the test passages and items were completed, the first part of the field testing was conducted during the winter of 1992. In May 1992, a representative sample of students was selected to take the reading field test forms. Schools included in the field testing were "representative of the state based on geographic location and ethnic/racial characteristics of the student population" (North Carolina Department of Public Instruction, 1996, p. 19). There was no specific knowledge of deaf students being involved at this point. (When the office of testing was contacted about whether or not deaf students were included in the initial field testing, the response was that sampling was intended to be representative of all students.) After the field testing was completed, several statistical analyses were performed, including differential item functioning (DIF), which is used to determine whether the pattern of responses reveals bias for particular subgroups. The subgroups tested for response biases were males/females and Blacks/Whites; no DIF analyses were performed for ESL/English-fluent, disabled/nondisabled, deaf/hearing, etc. If particular items had high statistical indices, then they were flagged and reviewed by individuals who either represented the particular minority groups or had experience with exceptional children and who had appropriate knowledge of the curriculum area. If an item was considered to be "biased," it was eliminated from the test item pool. Items were also evaluated based on their relevance to the curriculum and their quality.

STUDY OF THE NORTH CAROLINA READING TEST

The research question addressed in this study follows: Using the same approach originally used by North Carolina Department of Public Instruction to determine curricular validity for the North Carolina Competency Test of Reading, do judgments of experienced teachers of deaf students support that the North Carolina reading test possesses curricular validity for deaf students? Specifically, which items on Form M of the North Carolina Competency Test of Reading meet the criteria related to (a) North Carolina Department of Public Instruction item review questions and (b) issues specific to deaf education (e.g., cognitive, linguistic, or experiential variables known to differentially influence deaf and hearing students' performance)? This research was conducted in 2002.

Reviewers

Participants, referred to as reviewers for this study, consisted of eight experienced teachers of deaf students in two schools for deaf students in North Carolina. Four of the reviewers were hearing, and four were deaf. All were White females. Six of the reviewers were from the North Carolina School for the Deaf (NCSD) in Morganton, and two of the reviewers were from the Central North Carolina School for the Deaf (CNCSD) in Greensboro. Attempts were made to recruit teachers from mainstream programs and from the Eastern North Carolina School for the Deaf. The state director of the mainstream programs was contacted but declined to have any teachers in mainstream programs involved. Teachers at the Eastern North Carolina School for the Deaf were also contacted, but chose not to participate in the study. For these reasons, the participants came from only two schools for deaf students. All the individuals from NCSD and CNCSD who met the qualifications were contacted and were willing to participate in the study.

All of the participating reviewers had to satisfy certain qualifications. First, they had to have experience teaching English to deaf students who were required to pass a reading competency test similar to the test in this study to obtain their high school diploma. (The particular form of the reading test, Form M, used in this study is no longer in use.) Further, all of the reviewers had to be familiar with the North Carolina reading test, which was administered twice a year. All of these reviewers had at least 3 years' experience teaching English to deaf students, with five of them having more than 20 years' experience teaching deaf students. The eight reviewers together had a combined total of 159 years of experience teaching deaf students (an average of 20 years teaching deaf students per reviewer). Six out of eight teachers had master's degrees. Five of the teachers had degrees both in English and in deaf education.

Review of Test Passages and Items

Using questions based on initial construction of the reading test by the North Carolina Department of Public Instruction, the eight experienced teachers of deaf students judged the appropriateness of the 10 passages and 68 test items of the North Carolina reading test. The reviewers answered five questions for each passage and six questions for each test item. Reviewers made a yes-no decision for each question (i.e., determined whether the particular qualities in question were present or absent). If they responded no, they were asked to explain their response about the passages or test items.

To evaluate the passages, the reviewers used the following questions:

- Which of the following best describes how easy this passage is for deaf eighth-grade students (check one): ____ easy, ____ medium, ____ hard.
- Is this passage appropriate as a reading competency test for eighth-grade deaf students?
- Would this passage be interesting to my students to read?
- Structurally, does this passage have a distinct beginning, middle, and end?
- Is the frame (the introduction in italics) appropriate for the passage?

To evaluate the test items, the reviewers used the following statements, which have been identified as being (a) the same criteria used by the North Carolina Department of Public Instruction to evaluate test items, (b) new for this study, or (c) modified for this study from questions used by the North Carolina Department of Public Instruction:

- The skill tested in this item was taught during the 1999–2000 school year. (Same as North Carolina Department of Public Instruction.)
- This item is appropriate for the end-of-grade test. (Appropriateness is based on conceptual quality, language quality, format and graphics quality, and cultural bias.) (Same as North Carolina Department of Public Instruction.)
- Performance on this item is not affected by a student's hearing loss. (New for this study.)
- This item contains no content that will be more familiar to hearing students than to deaf students. (Modified from North Carolina Department of Public Instruction.)
- For deaf readers, differential performance on this item may be related to different familiarity compared with hearing readers with this question format. (New for this study.)
- This item contains no content or stereotyping that is offensive on the basis of gender, ethnicity, culture, or disability (i.e., hearing loss). (Modified from North Carolina Department of Public Instruction.)

Data Analysis

Data analysis consisted of tabulating responses and listing comments from the eight teacher reviewers. For each passage, results from the eight reviewers were used to determine: (a) the percentage of reviewers rating a passage to be easy, medium, or hard; (b) the number and percentage of No responses to each of the five questions about passages; (c) the total number and percentage of No responses to the six questions per test items; and (d) the total sum and percentages of No responses across passages and items. Finally, the total No responses for the passages and test items were combined for an overall assessment of each passage.

Reviewers' Judgments About the Passages

None of the reviewers rated any of the passages to be easy for deaf eighth graders. More than half of the reviewers judged that 6 out of the 10 passages were hard. Passage 1, a poem with dialect, was considered to be the most difficult passage on the test, with all of the reviewers rating it as hard for deaf eighth graders. Two passages (Passage 4: Earthquakes and Passage 9: How to) had near consensus with 88% rating them hard, followed by two passages (Passage 3: Myth and Passage 7: Music) rated as hard by 75% of the reviewers, and one passage (Passage 6: Food Label) rated as hard by a simple majority (57%) of the reviewers. More than half of the reviewers were in agreement that the remaining four passages rated a medium level of difficulty.

There are some relationships between the reviewers' judgment of passage difficulty and particular qualities of the passages. Five of the six passages that received an overall rating of hard were also identified by at least 50% of reviewers as being inappropriate for use with deaf students in the eighth grade. Each of the four passages identified by six or more teachers as being uninteresting to deaf students was also identified as being hard. The two passages identified by at least 50% of the reviewers as not having a distinct beginning, middle, and ending were also considered to be hard passages.

The passage that was judged to be most problematic, across all questions and passage categories, was Passage 7 (music), followed by Passage 1 (poem), Passage 6 (food labels), and Passage 9 (how to). Three of the four questions relating to Passage 7 (music) received more than 50% No responses from reviewers. Two of the four questions related to the remaining three passages were judged by at least 50% of the reviewers to be problematic.

A fairly high level of agreement was evident between reviewers' judgments of difficulty and difficulty calculated by the readability formulas for both the literary passages and the content passages. For the consumer passages, however, the reviewers' judgments and the formulas did not match as well as they did for the literary and content passages, largely because Passage 6 was judged to be highly problematic, and there were few other consumer passages to offset the issues with Passage 6.

Reviewers' Judgments About the Test Items

Problematic items were identified using a criterion of at least a 50% agreement among the eight raters. Of the 68 test items accompanying the passages on the North Carolina reading test, a total of seven test items were judged to be inappropriate (two literary items, five content items, and zero consumer items). The passage with the most negative responses for the test items was Passage 7 (music), with three test items having at least 50% negative responses.

Comments by Reviewers

The following comments are typical of the rationale reviewers gave for indicating a No response for the test items.

Literary Passages

For Test Item 3, a hearing reviewer commented, "Deaf students often have difficulty with questions presented using the negative." Another hearing reviewer observed that there was a "negative in the foil." A deaf reviewer indicated a problem with respect to the criterion *familiarity in content*, saying, "Hearing students would be more familiar" with the phrase used in the foil.

Test Item 15 had four comments, two of which mentioned critical thinking. One deaf reviewer said, "Critical thinking is involved" in answering this item. Another deaf reviewer commented, "The passage . . . involves critical thinking and cause/effect relationship." A hearing reviewer said this item is inappropriate because there is "unfamiliar syntax in the question." Another hearing reviewer, choosing another criterion (*performance is affected by hearing loss*) for the same test item stated, "It is unlikely that a deaf student would hear this story from a hearing parent or any adult. Storytelling very often with deaf kids?? It varies . . ."

The reviewers' comments suggest that their judgments may have been based on hearing status. That is, the reviewer may have been more lenient or more severe based on whether or not the reviewer was deaf or hearing. Deaf reviewers gave more negative marks for each of the six test item questions. For Test Item 3, equal numbers of deaf reviewers and hearing reviewers gave negative marks, but for Test Item 15, the negative marks came from three deaf reviewers and one hearing reviewer. From these comments, it appears that deaf reviewers may have some additional insight into the difficulties facing deaf readers, for example, the fact that answering certain items involves the use of critical thinking skills or a recognition of cause/effect relationships, both of which involve higher-level thinking skills.

Content Passages

With respect to test items for Passage 7 (music), a hearing reviewer chose the evaluation criterion *performance is affected by hearing loss* because "all items refer to music." Another hearing reviewer chose the criterion *familiarity of content* for these items saying, "again the obvious . . . some hard of hearing may cope better, but that would be difficult to determine." The third hearing reviewer picked the criteria *offensive content* and *stereotyping*, saying, "the obvious." The fourth hearing reviewer chose the criteria of *interest* and *beginning/middle/end* saying, "general background knowledge–hearing would probably have some familiarity with folk songs." Interestingly, most of the reviewers' comments about music were from the four hearing reviewers.

For Test Item 62, one hearing reviewer observed the two different spellings of an unusual proper noun ("misspelling?"). She also noted that a phrase used would be problematic for deaf students. A deaf reviewer noticed the same phrase and labeled it as an idiomatic expression. Because of this wording, she marked the criteria *inappropriate for testing* and *familiarity of content*. A third reviewer (second deaf) marked the criteria *inappropriate for testing* and *question format* and said, "This expression is not used/familiar to Deaf students." Another hearing reviewer said this test item was inappropriate because she noted the two different spellings of the unusual proper noun, one in the passage and one in the test item, which "could confuse students."

Test Item 8 had four comments from reviewers. Two of the responses from deaf reviewers dealt with inferencing—"requires inferencing and prior knowledge." A hearing reviewer noted the use of "negative in foils." That test foils should be free of negations was one of the criteria that North Carolina Department of Public Instruction stipulated in their development of the test. Another deaf reviewer marked the criteria *performance not affected by hearing loss* and *familiarity in content.* This reviewer said, "The question was too wordy."

Reviewers' comments about questions related to the content passages followed the same pattern as for the literary passages. That is, deaf reviewers gave more negative marks than the hearing reviewers. The only exception to this pattern was the criterion *performance not affected by hearing loss.* Unexpectedly, hearing reviewers gave more negative responses for hearing loss than the deaf reviewers.

Consumer Passages

For the consumer passages, none of the test items received 50% or more of No responses. Neither deaf nor hearing reviewers had problems with consumer test items, even though they did have problems with the passages.

Differences Between Hearing and Deaf Reviewers

When deaf and hearing reviewers' evaluations of overall difficulty of passages are compared, it is found that they assigned almost an equal number of negative responses to questions about the passages (hearing 45% versus deaf 55%). Differences appear, however, related to the test items. Specifically, deaf reviewers were twice as likely to assign negative responses to the test items as hearing reviewers (68% to 32%, or 253 No responses for the four deaf reviewers to 118 No responses for the same number of hearing reviewers).

One primary difference between deaf and hearing reviewers in their analysis of the test items is that deaf reviewers appear to recognize more readily the fact that certain items required the use of critical thinking and inferencing skills. The deaf reviewers made 18 comments about critical thinking skills compared with only 1 comment by a hearing reviewer.

Another major difference between deaf and hearing reviewers related to comments concerning items that related to sound. That is, hearing reviewers made 16 sound-related comments compared with deaf reviewers, who made 3 sound-related comments. It seems logical that the hearing reviewers would be more aware than deaf reviewers of items that were affected by sound, although in the passages, they were equal in their comments about sound.

SUMMARY OF FINDINGS

Reviewer judgment ranked passage difficulty in basically the same order as the grade levels derived from the readability formulas. None of the reviewers rated any of the passages as easy for deaf eighth graders. At least half of the teachers judged six out of the ten passages to be hard. Of those six passages, however, only two had formula-calculated difficulty levels above eighth grade. Two test items in the literary passages and five items in the content passages received negative responses from at least 50% of the reviewers. When the number of negative responses with respect to the test items was examined in terms of hearing and deaf reviewers, the deaf reviewers assigned more than twice as many No responses as their hearing peers. Another finding was that the reviewers' judgments indicated that much of the content in the test was not addressed in the curriculum.

IMPLICATIONS

Keeping in mind the limitations of this study, a major finding is that many of the passages and test items on Form M of the North Carolina Competency Test of Reading are problematic and possibly inappropriate for deaf students, which is based on the No responses of reviewers, who are all experienced teachers of deaf students, as well as their comments about passages and items. This finding has important implications for future North Carolina test development, reading instruction and curriculum of deaf students, current use of test results, and research.

Implications for Test Development

Findings from this study have implications with respect to future North Carolina test development or reading tests developed by other states that are used with high-stakes consequences. First, it would seem prudent for North Carolina Department of Public Instruction test developers who plan to use the North Carolina Competency Test of Reading with deaf students to consider the input of individuals who are familiar with deaf students when constructing future tests. Further, in light of the finding that deaf reviewers assigned twice as many negative responses as their hearing counterparts for the quality indicators and item validity indicators, test developers should give serious consideration to including reviewers who are deaf themselves and who have the necessary qualifications pertaining to teaching reading or English language arts to students who are deaf. Having reviewers familiar with deafness involved in test construction would likely eliminate the observed problems related to sound or music as the content basis for reading passages, which are judged inappropriate for deaf students.

A similar study was conducted in New York in which educators of deaf students reviewed the New York Language Arts Test (Martin, 2004). Martin was permitted to use student responses to the test for direct comparison with the reviewers' evaluation, which was not the case for Lollis (2002). Martin found that the students' results on the test validated the judgments of the reviewers. For example, passages that reviewers rated as difficult were the same passages on which the students' responses indicated that they struggled more. This finding is consistent with the indirect evidence on accurate teacher judgment reported by LaSasso (1982), who asked experienced teachers to rank the order of difficulty of four passages graded by the Fry and Dale-Chall formulas,[1] which were written between third- and sixth-grade reading levels, and found that teachers' rankings corresponded to the formula-determined rankings. The Martin (2004) finding is also consistent with the findings of Lollis (2002) presented above. The methods used by Lollis (2002) and Martin (2004) could be used not only with other state-mandated tests but also with other special populations such as ESL students to determine the appropriateness of state tests for a variety of identified populations.

Implications for Instruction and Curriculum

The Lollis finding that indicated that much of the content was not addressed in the curriculum suggests a possible lack of alignment between the reading curriculum experienced in schools for the deaf and the reading test. People may question the quality of the teachers or the schools, but a careful examination of the curricula of North Carolina for students in eighth grade and above will show that only minor portions of the language arts curricula deal with specific reading skills for students still learning to read (North Carolina Department of Public Instruction, 2004). The general assumption obviously is that students have finished learning to read by the end of eighth grade, which is not the case for many deaf students.

Questions concerning the quantity and quality of explicit reading instruction in the schools serving deaf students may also be raised. The North Carolina schools for the deaf are expected to follow the statewide curricula and, therefore, do not have in place a curriculum dealing specifically with deaf students and their special language and reading needs. Also, educators of deaf students are often not given the same access to teacher training and current research in the area of reading that their counterparts in regular education would have. Reading curricula for deaf students need to explicitly address test-taking skills because many deaf students lack those skills. Deaf students at all instructional levels need regular exposure to and systematic practice in taking the different kinds of tests that their hearing peers take.

Moreover, the reviewers' judgment that many of the questions on the North Carolina test require critical thinking skills, including inferencing (which they implied would be skills lacking among some deaf students), supports the curricular need for explicit instruction in higher-level thinking skills at all instructional levels (e.g., the Instrument Enrichment curriculum). Inferencing and other critical thinking skills are vital for fluent reading and test-taking abilities. Although some instruction for deaf students has successfully incorporated some form of thinking skills curriculum into the schools, a greater priority needs to be given to this aspect of instruction. Given these needs, there is plenty of room for improvement when it comes to deaf students' opportunity to learn. Both curriculum and instruction may be inadequate relative to the expectations embedded in the North Carolina Competency Test of Reading.

---

1. The Dale-Chall Readability Formula, in addition to using average sentence length, factors in the number of unfamiliar words to compute reading levels.

Implications for Use of Test Results for Deaf Students

Because of the high-stakes nature of the North Carolina Competency Test of Reading, it is incumbent on teachers and program administrators to understand the limitations of the test for deaf students and to advocate for alternative types of reading assessment such as portfolios. The Standards for Educational and Psychological Testing state that students' futures are not to be decided on the basis of a single test, even with numerous administrations of that one test (American Educational Research Association, American Psychological Association, & National Council on Measurement in Education, 1999). The use of multiple measures such as portfolios and other alternative assessments would permit a more accurate assessment of deaf students' reading abilities, thereby lessening the possibility that test bias might occur because of lack of exposure to content or language. The finding that reviewers found many passages and items on Form M to be problematic also suggests that care should be exercised by all when interpreting a North Carolina deaf student's performance on the North Carolina reading test. However, it is not clear whether the problem is failure to measure the intended construct (i.e., the results are an artifact of poor test design) or inadequate opportunities for students to learn before being required to take the test.

Implications for Research

Findings from this study also have implications for future research. At least two analyses of student responses to items are needed. First, the finding that many of the test items on Form M of the North Carolina Competency Test of Reading are judged by experienced teachers of deaf students to be problematic for deaf students raises concern that some test items on the test may be biased against deaf students, though the test items, for the most part, were generally considered to be appropriate for use on a reading test. The interpretation of this finding may be clarified by applying the same statistical procedure used by the North Carolina Department of Public Instruction in the original test construction to determine whether individual test items were biased, namely, the Mantel-Haenszel DIF procedure (Mantel & Haenszel, 1959). The procedure used in the state's investigation of differences attributed to race in performance on individual test items, statistically controlling for comparable overall test performance, also can be used in the study of deaf-hearing performance differences. The Mantel-Haenszel DIF statistics, which typically serve as the basis for rejecting items for inclusion in the test development process, are an important additional measure for judging the appropriateness of individual test items for deaf students. Findings from the Lollis (2002) study would be strengthened if there were a relationship between test items found to have large Mantel-Haenszel DIF indices for deaf students and test items that were identified by reviewers in this study as being problematic for deaf students.

Second, it would also be helpful to analyze distractor responses to determine whether deaf students exhibit a distribution of responses on specific items different from hearing students. Differences in distractor response selection might suggest that deaf students are using different test-taking strategies (e.g., visual matching or position of distractor) to select responses to questions.

In addition, research is needed to determine the optimum qualifications of test reviewers. In the present study (Lollis, 2002), discrepancies were found in ratings assigned by deaf and hearing reviewers. In the absence of corroborating statistical data such as that provided by the Mantel-Haenszel procedure, it cannot be determined which group is more accurate. On the one hand, it could be that deaf reviewers are more apt to be strict about the appropriateness of test passages and items for deaf students; it could also be that these differences indicate an understanding on the part of deaf reviewers that hearing reviewers may not have. On the other hand, hearing reviewers are more likely to identify which items are affected by sound, and given the review procedures used, these items are likely to be changed on high-stakes tests because of an identified bias. Further research is needed to determine the meaning and value of the different tendencies of deaf and hearing reviewers.

Beyond the traditional development of assessment instruments reviewed here, research is needed on the use of alternative assessments with deaf students. The use of alternative assessments is increasing, and their specific use with deaf students for reading needs to be studied. Because alternative assessments can be linked to state-established standards, the instructional practices relating to these alternate standards also should be investigated.

CONCLUSION

If states continue requiring deaf students to pass high-stakes tests to receive a high school diploma, they will have to confront the lack of research that supports current practices. The design and production of these tests too often fail to consider the unique assessment needs of deaf students. As described here, this failure to attend to assessment concerns for special populations occurred in North Carolina. Whether in North Carolina or any other state, responsible test development must include a validation process that attends to the needs and circumstances of all identified special populations. Otherwise, high school diplomas may be denied to qualified students, which is neither the expressed intent of the state's assessment and accountability system nor an example of equal protection under the law.

REFERENCES

American Educational Research Association, American Psychological Association, & National Council on Measurement in Education. (1999). *Standards for educational and psychological testing.* Washington, DC: American Psychological Association.

Fry, E. (1968). A readability formula that saves time. *Journal of Reading, 11,* 513–516, 575–578.

LaSasso, C. (1982). The effectiveness of teacher judgment in determining relative text difficulty for prelingually, profoundly deaf students. *Teaching English to the Deaf, 7,* 25–28.

Lollis, J. L. (2002). *The appropriateness of the North Carolina state-mandated reading competency test as a criterion for high school graduation for deaf students.* Unpublished doctoral dissertation, Gallaudet University, Washington, DC.

Mantel, N., & Haenszel, W. (1959). Statistical aspects of the analysis of data from retrospective studies of disease. *Journal of the National Cancer Institute, 22,* 719–748.

Martin, P. (2004). *An examination of the appropriateness of The New York State English Language Arts Grade 8 Test for deaf students.* Unpublished doctoral dissertation, Gallaudet University, Washington, DC.

North Carolina Department of Public Instruction. (1996). *Technical Report 1.* Raleigh, NC: Author.

North Carolina Department of Public Instruction. (2004). Standard course of study: English language arts. Retrieved April 9, 2008, from http://www.ncpublicschools.org/curriculum/languagearts/scos/2004/

North Carolina Department of Public Instruction. (2005). *The North Carolina state testing results ("The green book.").* Retrieved April 9, 2008, from http://www.ncpublicschools.org/docs/accountability/testing/reports/green/gb0405.pdf

9

Implications and Complications of Including Deaf Students In Statewide Assessments in Illinois

Michael Jones

The Illinois School for the Deaf (ISD) began its involvement in statewide assessment issues in 1992 when the Illinois State Board of Education (ISBE) created a task force of 30 stakeholders to determine how all students in special education and bilingual programs could participate in the newly created Illinois Goal Assessment Program (IGAP). Largely because of my position as director of the Evaluation Center at ISD, I was selected to participate on the task force to represent the views of educators in the state who worked with deaf students.

A PERIOD OF DOUBTS AND CONCERNS

After attending several task force meetings, it became clear to me that discussions were generally based on the presumption that all students with disabilities should be required to take the IGAP. At that time, this concept was new to me, and I was frankly surprised that such a requirement was being proposed. I, along with two members serving on behalf of bilingual programs, presented the minority view that the state tests might not be appropriate for some students. The topics of IGAP, assessment, and participation were all talked about in general, vague, and philosophical terms. I suggested that the committee might want to do something concrete such as actually look at the IGAP tests to determine appropriateness for our student populations.

Because my recommendation was not supported, I met with the manager of the Student Assessment Section at ISBE early in 1993 and reviewed the tests under his supervision. We discussed normative data for deaf students taking the Stanford Achievement Test as analyzed by the Gallaudet Research Institute on reading comprehension and math computation (Allen, 1986), and we talked about the Illinois tests and the effects a profound hearing loss can have on the acquisition of English. When the manager realized that 17-year-old deaf students had a mean reading comprehension at the third-grade level, he readily understood that deaf students would be unfairly penalized on the IGAP because of their limited fluency in English. He had a background in linguistics and was well-aware of the problems encountered when assessing student knowledge in a language the students did not know well. It took him only a few minutes to conclude that the IGAP was not appropriate for students who were deaf.

When I returned to my office at ISD, I decided to put some of our discussion on paper, with additional supporting data. I wanted to document the issues so the information could be shared with the task force at large. The letter is as follows:

Dear Dr. B:

The information that follows was taken from the first two student files on my desk after I returned from our meeting last Friday. I have written brief summaries about the students and have included written language samples of their work. These will demonstrate the effects a congenital, profound hearing loss can have on the acquisition of English and the related skills of reading and writing.

File Number 1:

This uncorrected language sample was written by a profoundly deaf, young man who is 15.5 years of age. He is a *serious* student who has scored in the superior range, up to 133 Performance IQ (WISC-R), on each of his last four reevaluations. On the WISC-R Verbal Scale, he scores in the mild deficit range—IQ of 70—due to the English-based test. As an 8th grader he took the Stanford Advanced II level in math and scored above grade level on Math Computation. However, the reading test he took was at the Intermediate I level and he earned a grade equivalent of 3.2. His teachers report he works well independently and grasps academic material easily. He is fluent in American Sign Language and understands abstract discussions.

Written Language Sample:

If I could make a new school rule, I want 30 minutes each class and not counting flex. I want period time 8:00 to 8:30, 8:30 to 9:00, 9:00 to 9:30, 9:30 to 10:00, 10:00 to10:30, 10:30 to 11:00 and end of period. I want to each 4 person is each class. If you not finished, can subtract 10 points 1 not 59%. If you are late, you took tardy slip, add 10 minutes after school. If you are trouble, you can go to after school, add 30 minutes I you are incomplete slip. you can play only home games, at dorm, 1 2 hours. If you finished at school at 11:00, and if you help extra unit, 12:pp to 2:00 The end.

File Number 2:

This boy is 12.5 and is in junior high school. He also displays superior intellectual functioning with a Performance IQ of 125. On the SAT Primary II Reading subtest he scored 3.1. Math Computation at the Intermediate II level was 8.4. His teacher described him as a motivated student, eager to accept challenging tasks. He is able to grasp concepts quickly. He is attentive to detail, able to transfer and apply information to multiple situations.

Written Language Sample:

Suppose I have Children Someday

I have children. I will be very happy. Because children is cute and happiest to me than make me In good mood fast. And I loves to play with children they was very cute.

Both of these boys read a little above the mean when compared to same-age deaf students in both the 1974 and 1983 norming samples analyzed by the Gallaudet Research Institute. These two students have much higher achievement in math computation than their peers in both Gallaudet norming samples. As we discussed, when we add the skill of reading to math—as in word problems—the scores of deaf students go down. Since reading is an "academic disability" for deaf students, a math test consisting of word problems will be discriminatory for that population. Since all the items on the IGAP math tests consist of word problems, they will not validly assess the deaf students' knowledge of math. The results will reflect the extent of their disability rather than whether or not they have mastered state goals and objectives.

After reviewing the GRI [Gallaudet Research Institute] data I shared with you, reflecting on our discussion of deafness and the IGAP, it seems to me the only deaf students who can take the IGAP and not be penalized on the basis of their disability are those few who can read at grade level. This means that of the 320 students at ISD, we would test one elementary student, four in junior high, and four in high school—assuming each one of these nine students is in the appropriate grade scheduled for IGAP testing.

If we decide it is nondiscriminatory and appropriate for these nine students to take the IGAP, we need to address the relevance of participating since an $n = 9$ yields insufficient data to determine a school's accountability.

In order to find out how well schools are preparing deaf students, it appears we will have to use teacher-made, alternative assessments, portfolios, etc. If we want to compare programs to identify what works best, then we may need a standardized instrument which will permit objective comparisons.

At the next meeting of the task force, I reported on my meeting with the manager of the Student Assessment Section and distributed copies of the letter with the Gallaudet Research Institute supporting data on norming samples and academic achievement of deaf students. At the final spring meeting of the task force, the manager of the Department of Special Education at ISBE announced that few, if any, deaf students would take the IGAP. They were the only disability group excluded from participating in the state tests.

CHANGING TIMES BRING A MANDATE FOR INCLUSION

The 1997 reauthorization of the Individuals With Disabilities Education Act (IDEA) strengthened federal insistence that states include all disabled students in state assessments. The effects were not immediately felt at ISD, but in 1999, at my insistence, ISD's curriculum coordinator and I were reluctantly permitted by ISBE to review all subject-level tests for the new Illinois Standards Achievement Test (ISAT). We discovered that some items on the third-grade reading test required the ability to hear to answer the questions. We met with the same manager of the Student Assessment Section whom I had advised in 1993, and I recommended that these discriminatory items dealing with phonics be removed from the test. We also questioned the rationale for including deaf students in the ISAT. I reminded the manager about the Gallaudet Research Institute's Stanford achievement data that I had used in 1993 to exclude deaf students from participating in the IGAP. I requested, once again, that our students be exempted from taking the ISAT. On this occasion, however, the ISBE manager stated that all students were mandated to take the tests; a slot was reserved for every student in the state. There were to be no exceptions.

We broached the subject of out-of-level testing, which had been standard practice when administering the Stanford to deaf students, but the manager responded that all students would be tested at grade level. We countered that when English is used to assess performance with students who are deaf, the results most often greatly underestimate the students' knowledge. We described the reading, writing, and language problems associated with assessment and deafness, but to no avail. Politically, times had changed, and so had the directives being issued by this manager of the Student Assessment Section of ISBE.

Once it was clear that all deaf students in Illinois would be required to take the state tests, the issues for educators of these students quickly became how to ensure that there would be appropriate accommodations for each student. A list of accommodations was reviewed at the students' Individualized Education Program (IEP) meetings and appropriate ones were selected. In general, any accommodation that is routinely used in a student's classroom is considered appropriate for the state tests. Teachers can sign directions, modify the language of directions, sign the tests (except the reading test), modify testing time, and use overhead transparencies and other assistive devices. The first year we administered the state tests, IEP teams decided that most of our students might benefit from extended time. However, it turned out that most students completed the tests quickly, not because the tests were easy for them but because the complexity of English vocabulary, syntax, and morphology was such that they could not read at grade level. Subsequent discussions with the students suggested that they were selecting answers uncertainly, without fully understanding the text.

The Illinois Learning Standards (ILS) were developed to set uniform, high expectations for student learning. Illinois offers five statewide assessments to measure student progress in meeting the ILS. The following descriptions are of the assessments for the 2006–07 school year:

- The ISAT measures reading and mathematics in Grades 3–8. Science is assessed in Grades 4 and 7, and writing in Grades 5 and 8.
- The Prairie State Achievement Examination (PSAE) consists of two days of testing for students in Grade 11. Students take the ACT on Day 1. On Day 2, they are assessed in science (ISBE developed), WorkKeys® Applied Mathematics, and WorkKeys® Reading for Information.
- ACCESS for ELLs® (Accessing Comprehension and Communication in English State-to-State for English Language Learners) assesses English proficiency in reading, writing, listening, and speaking for all Limited English Proficiency (LEP) students in Grades K–12. The ACCESS tests must be taken in addition to any ISAT or IMAGE tests that the students take.

- The Illinois Measure of Annual Growth in English (IMAGE) is given in Grades 3–8 and 11 to LEP students who have been enrolled in a state-approved bilingual education program (Transitional Bilingual Education or Transitional Program of Instruction) for 5 or fewer years and who are otherwise ineligible to participate in the ISAT.

- The Illinois Alternate Assessment (IAA) is for the small group of students with cognitive disabilities for whom all other state assessments are inappropriate. Reading, mathematics, and science are evaluated in Grades 3–8 and 11. Writing is assessed in Grades 5, 8, and 11. Data are collected and organized in portfolios.

Summer curriculum workshops were held, beginning in 2000, to align the school curricula with the ILS and ultimately to help prepare ISD students for the state tests. Educators were challenged to raise the bar and teach content at grade level. They also were encouraged to teach test-taking skills and use more performance assessments in class, which required the use of rubrics. Since 2000, each spring, two educators from the language arts department and two from math are hired to coordinate tutoring sessions in evenings. They meet with eleventh graders 4 hours a week for 8 weeks to prepare the students for the PSAE.

There are four performance levels on the ISAT and PSAE: Exceeds Standards, Meets Standards, Below Standards, and Academic Warning. Student performance is not tied to either grade promotion or graduation. However, students in Illinois are not permitted to graduate unless they have participated in the ACT/PSAE.

ADVOCATING FOR FAIRNESS IN THE ASSESSMENT OF DEAF STUDENTS

In the years since 1999, educators of deaf students in Illinois generally have come to support the inclusion of disabled students in the statewide testing process and embrace the principle of accountability. However, the consensus is that administering the ISAT and PSAE to most deaf students at grade level does not yield valid information with respect to their progress toward the ILS. For example, in 2002 when ISD received ISAT and PSAE results for 35% of our students who took the tests, of the164 subtests administered to these students, only 11% of the scores were at the Meets Standards level, and 89% were either Below Standards or at the Academic Warning level. These students were not able to demonstrate achievement at the same rate as hearing peers because of English language deficits related to their disability. Plus, it is crucial to remember that 45.4% of deaf students in Illinois (Gallaudet Research Institute, 2003) had an additional disability, which further compromised their performance on state tests designed for and validated with nondisabled students.

When the new Illinois test instruments were used in 1999, new assessment issues for deaf students were identified: (a) the ISAT and PSAE were appropriate for only a select few students at the top of their classes, (b) the IAA was an appropriate measure of performance for the small group of deaf students who had cognitive deficits and multiple disabilities, and (c) the remaining students who were in between, estimated at 90%, were the ones being "left behind" without an appropriate state measure of how they were learning and meeting standards. (Many deaf educators refer to this majority of their students as the "gap kids.") These students, many of whom have additional disabilities, began their assessment sessions with the best of intentions. I believe they performed to the best of their ability. But the state tests were designed for a completely different student population, and it is unrealistic to expect students who have never heard the English language to compete as equals on English-based tests with students whose native language is English.

A logistical problem arose when receiving schools were not able to get score reports for the students in their programs. ISD routinely requests copies of student scores from 150 home schools annually. Unfortunately, the largest percentage of reports we ever received in one year was 35%. After receiving a stream of complaints about this reporting problem from supervisors of schools for the deaf in the state, ISBE addressed the issue by requiring that sending schools assign each student a unique student information number. For various reasons, however, sending schools have failed to assign numbers for students at receiving schools. Consequently, schools for the deaf receive even fewer score reports now than before.

Illinois is fortunate to have a strong group of supervisors and educators for deaf students, and we have been vocal in advocating for appropriate, valid state tests for our student population. We have a passion for what happens to our children. In the spring of 2000, a joint subcommittee of the Illinois Supervisors of Programs for Hard of Hearing/Deaf Individuals (ISHI) and the Illinois Teachers of Hard of Hearing/Deaf Individuals (ITHI) sent a summary of their deliberations to the deputy superintendent of ISBE, stating their commitment to accountability and having students progress toward the state standards. Recognizing the importance of valid and appropriate assessment, the committee offered to work with ISBE toward these goals.

ISBE responded that they believed the IAA, a portfolio type assessment, was appropriate for some of our students. However, most deaf students would have to take the ISAT, which prohibited out-of-level testing. The subcommittee of deaf educators wanted ISBE to add a criterion to the state's list for determining whether deaf students were capable of taking the ISAT. They specifically requested a criterion based on the student's competency in English. ISBE agreed the idea needed "closer examination," but nothing ever came of it. In 1995, I reviewed the reading comprehension levels of all ISD students who participated in the Stanford norming project and found that 89% scored below grade level. More than two thirds of the students were four to seven grade equivalents lower than their hearing peers. Because reading levels are significantly depressed for deaf students, when tested at grade level, all the ISAT results mean is that the students cannot read at grade level.

Another problem area relates to the quality of the signed presentation of classroom content by interpreters for deaf students in public schools. In a study of educational interpreters, Schick, Williams, and Bolster (1999) found that less than half in their sample "performed at a level considered minimally acceptable." Interpreting skills in their study were assessed with the Educational Interpreter Performance Assessment (EIPA). In 2002–2003, ISHI conducted a pilot study of the EIPA to see how well it would evaluate interpreter performance and identify training topics for professional development. Fifty educational interpreters representing 11 programs in Illinois were evaluated with the EIPA. Subjects were intentionally selected to represent a wide range of interpreting skill to see whether the EIPA was effective in identifying training needs for staff members at various skill levels. There are five EIPA levels:

1. Beginner–Not an appropriate level for interpreting in the classroom.
2. Advanced Beginner–Interpreted messages contain serious deficiencies. A person at Level 2 requires serious mentoring to be recommended for interpreting in the classroom.
3. Intermediate–Needs additional training and supervision. A person with intermediate skills can interpret basic content in the classroom, but will have great difficulty communicating all information as well as accurately expressing complex information.
4. Advanced Intermediate–Is limited in complex situations. A person with Level 4 skills can convey most of the content presented in the classroom, but in some complex situations may experience difficulty in accurately interpreting information.
5. Advanced–Complex messages are interpreted clearly. A person with Advanced skills can accurately interpret most classroom interaction.

The results of the ISHI study indicated that the EIPA was effective in identifying areas that needed to be targeted for professional development of educational interpreters in the state. The results on the levels earned through the EIPA evaluation cannot be generalized statewide to all Illinois educational interpreters because we intentionally selected a broad range of skills among the volunteers. However, the EIPA levels that were assigned did reflect the abilities of the 50 interpreters in the sample. How did they do? Only one interpreter received a Level 5, Advanced rating. Seventy-nine percent earned a Level 3 or below, which meant that the students for whom they had interpreted did not have access to the same amount and quality of instruction as their hearing peers. In other words, deaf students in numerous public school programs are being served by unskilled signers rather than by highly qualified interpreters, and the students' educational achievement suffers. These children are needlessly being left behind.

These data underscore how discriminatory the high-stakes testing process can be for students who are deaf. First, the students are tested in a language that is foreign to them. Because they cannot hear the English language, most struggle (even through adulthood) trying to learn to read and write even at elementary levels. Remember that reading and writing at grade level are often difficult tasks for hearing students in public schools, and their native language is English. (Imagine how much lower their scores might be if they had never heard English spoken.)

Second, deaf students must take high-stakes tests at grade level, which means they cannot demonstrate what they have learned because they cannot read the tests. I am a test supervisor for the ACT and PSAE given to eleventh graders at ISD. Students attend a special session 2 weeks before the tests to complete identifying information and nontest portions of the ACT. In April 2005, approximately 90% of the students had serious difficulty completing the Student Profile Section and the Interest Inventory (ACT Assessment, 2004) because they could not read the information. They knew the answers to all the items when supervisors signed the questions, but the students were unable to independently complete the *nontest* items! The first word that threw the group off was *Gender,* which was clearly a reading problem and not one of not knowing the information. Students were directed to consider whether "they liked the activity, did not like it, or were indifferent to it." Most students did not understand the English word *indifferent.* The following list describes several more instances in which other interest inventory items were misunderstood:

- "4. Conduct a meeting"—Students did not realize that *conduct* was a verb. They thought it was a noun referring to their behavior in a meeting.
- "18. Run a lawn mower"—*Run* is an action related to people and animals, not an inanimate object. Test supervisors interpreted this item as "mowing the grass."
- "22. Present information before a group"—*Present* was understood as a noun and meant *gift* to the students.
- "35. Balance a checkbook"—Students were unfamiliar with this usage of the English word *balance.*
- "54. Engrave lettering or designs on a trophy or plaque"—Students were unfamiliar with the English words *engrave, lettering* (thought it meant the noun *letter*), *designs, trophy,* and *plaque.* However, they all understood this item easily when it was signed.
- "69. Teach people a new hobby"—Students did not know the English word *hobby.*
- "88. Conduct a door-to-door opinion poll"—Students misunderstood *conduct* as "behavior" and were confused by the term *door-to-door.* The words *opinion* and *poll* were not known by the students. They understood this item easily, however, when it was translated into American Sign Language (ASL).

The students, of course, knew the answers to all 90 items as long as each one was signed in ASL. These examples clearly demonstrate that even when students know the answers, valid assessment of most deaf students cannot be done by presenting items in written English.

Third, few educational interpreters have advanced skills, which means that many deaf students in public schools are missing significant amounts of crucial instruction. Policymakers need to be aware that it is not fair to deaf students to provide them with poor interpreters and then require the students to compete on high-stakes tests with hearing peers when the deaf students have access to maybe only half of the content presented in their classes.

Another fairness issue deals with the mandated reporting of test results to the public. ISD and the other large programs for deaf students in Illinois do not receive report cards on Adequate Yearly Progress (AYP), which will be an issue for us once ISBE figures out an efficient reporting system. The only negative effect that state tests have had on our programs so far has come from districts that publicly blame their inability to meet standards on their students with disabilities. I was involved in one case where the superintendent of a school district was quoted in a newspaper as saying that students at ISD were responsible for his district's failure to make AYP. I immediately called the president of the district's school board and reported that the superintendent's remarks were unethical. Before the ISATs were even given that year, the superintendent had requested a list of ISD students from his district that would take the ISAT. I personally sent him a copy of the following data: Grade 3, 1 student; Grade 4, 3 students; Grade 5, 1 student; Grade 6, 0 students; Grade 7, 3 students; Grade 8, 4 students.

Thus, the superintendent knew our numbers had been insignificant compared with the 1,616 other students in Grades 3–8 in the school district when he made his statement to the press. I informed the president of the school board that if anyone in the school district made a statement like that again, I planned to present my information to the public. The parents of ISD students were embarrassed and had to shoulder public blame just because of the situational ethics of the superintendent.

THE SEARCH FOR MORE APPROPRIATE ASSESSMENT TOOLS AND PRACTICES

In 2001, I served on a steering committee established by Office of Special Education Programs (OSEP) at the U.S. Department of Education (USDOE). This committee consisted of 45 stakeholders who evaluated ISBE's compliance with IDEA. My section of the comprehensive OSEP report was on the assessment of all special education students in Illinois. After reviewing the state data and interviewing staff members in the ISBE assessment section, my recommendation was that better assessment practices needed to be followed in assessing each disability area and that appropriate assessment tools needed to be developed for each one.

Every recommendation included in the comprehensive, final OSEP report had to be voted on and accepted by every member of the steering committee present at that meeting. After discussion, if one person disagreed with the recommendation, it was removed from the report. The recommendation on addressing the prevailing, unfair testing practices for most students in special education in the state was unanimously supported. While policymakers deal with data and ideas, educators and service providers deal with the students. Not one person on the steering committee was against assessment or accountability. All supported good assessment practices that would validly measure student learning and progress toward state goals. The consensus at the time was that the Illinois tests discriminated against our students with disabilities.

The steering committee made other recommendations, including the following:

- ISBE should convene a task force of stakeholders to begin writing performance indicators. These were to be designed and aligned with the different disability groups the students represented.
- Students with disabilities should participate in statewide assessment programs *only* if the test instrument is valid and nondiscriminatory for the student with disabilities.

In the last meeting with OSEP and ISBE representatives, I stressed that the basic premise of IDEA dealt with the *individualization* of educational programs. However, when it came to assessment, the federal and state mantra was "one size fits all." A plea was made to address this inequity at the federal level so all students in special education could be assessed appropriately to see whether they were learning and meeting standards. The concluding statement in my report asserted, "One cannot assume a statewide assessment designed for and validated with nondisabled students is appropriate for students with disabilities, even when administered with special procedures and accommodations."

Unfortunately, the steering committee's comprehensive Illinois report, which spanned 17 months of work, was looked on with disfavor by both OSEP and ISBE, even though committee members were trained by both agencies on how to assess ISBE's compliance with IDEA. The agencies convened a small, new committee and in less than a month distributed a new document and Illinois plan. Three members of the original steering committee addressed this situation with ISBE and OSEP, but we were not successful in having our final report with our recommendations be the official report submitted.

Connie Nagy, a high school math teacher at ISD, and I served on a panel at the national conference on high stakes testing at Gallaudet University in November 2002.[1] We shared information on the IAA, ISAT, and PSAE as well as our testing experiences in Illinois. Returning home from the conference invigorated, I learned that the superintendent of ISBE was working with a newly appointed committee to review the state's assessment plan. I wrote the superintendent explaining that Illinois had the opportunity to be a national leader in showing how assessment could be improved for students who are deaf. Also, I shared several points presented at the Gallaudet conference by Dr. James Popham:

1. High Stakes Testing: Are Deaf and Hard of Hearing Children Being Left Behind? A national conference held at Gallaudet University, Kellogg Conference Center, Washington, DC, November 15–16, 2002.

- Our tests must make instruction better. This approach results in truly meaningful assessment.
- We need standards-based assessment that actually tests what is taught.
- It is in our best interests to do what is right for the children.
- Children in special education classes have a tougher life.
- Implementing the regular curriculum does not mean administering regular assessment for these students.

In the last paragraph of my letter to the superintendent, I took the opportunity to present an example of gross inequity in testing practices in the state. (Sometimes, persistence pays off.)

I am currently assisting ISBE by serving on the committee that is developing the new teacher certification test in the area of deaf education. At our meeting two weeks ago, I asked the National Education Standards moderator what grade level the Illinois tests are being written at, and was surprised to find out it was the 8th grade. This means our students with severe and profound disabilities in Illinois are being held to higher testing standards than our college and university graduates who do not have disabilities.

TAKING ACTION

Illinois State Representative Jim Watson, 97th District, began his close relationship with supervisors of deaf education programs in 2003 when he was approached about shortcomings in the statewide testing process for our deaf students. Representative Watson and ISHI members attended a two-day meeting on assessment at ISD in September. ISBE sent two representatives. The Gallaudet Research Institute played an important role by sending Dr. Carol Traxler, Senior Research Scientist, and Sue Hotto, Research Associate, to provide an overview of the national picture on assessment of deaf students and to describe Gallaudet Research Institute's surveys and services. They reported that all states were struggling with assessment of deaf students. However, some states such as California are experiencing serious problems because they are tying high school graduation to a passing score on the state test (see Moore, this volume). Most disabled students are unable to meet the standard and, as a result, cannot qualify for jobs that require a high school diploma. Employment in some jobs that have always been accessible to them are now no longer available. In addition, the students cannot access some local postsecondary education programs because they lack a diploma.

Major concerns expressed over the two days were that the Illinois tests lack validity with deaf students, the tests must be administered at grade level, and the tests do not allow our students to demonstrate what they have learned in school. Even with accommodations, most students are not able to score at the Meets Standards level. The point was made that good assessment protocol promotes multiple measures, but Illinois does not make provisions for these.

All participants supported accountability and the promotion of higher standards. However, the question of how to find a way to validly assess student progress that the state would find acceptable remained unanswered. Quite a bit of time was devoted to the problems of programs trying to get copies of student scores because all score reports were sent to home schools.

Representative Watson listened to supervisors describe their personal experiences with the Illinois testing and reporting system and responded that he was almost speechless at the incredible state of affairs. We expressed a plea for assistance because this situation was a political problem that required a political solution. Participants then developed an action plan for the state:

Illinois Assessment Action Plan for Students Who Are Deaf

Vision Statement

Students who are deaf will have the opportunity to demonstrate their progress toward meeting the Illinois Learning Standards via valid and reliable assessments.

Outcome 1: Federal and state legislators and policymakers will understand that hearing loss precludes normal accessibility to spoken language, typically limiting linguistic competence in English.

Outcome 2: Deaf students will have the opportunity to demonstrate they meet the Illinois Learning Standards through a valid assessment.

Outcome 3: Students who are deaf will have access to the general curriculum.

Outcome 4:: The federal regulations implementing NCLB will not restrict the percentage of deaf students who may be held to alternate assessment standards, thereby allowing each deaf student to be assessed with valid and appropriate tests.

Outcome 5: In order for assessment to inform instruction, duplicate state assessment score reports for individual students will go to the receiving school (i.e., the school providing instruction).

Outcome 6: There will be a data system that allows assessment information to be reported with respect to educationally relevant variables.

Outcome 7: Federal and state law will allow deaf students to take a specified alternate assessment if the student's lack of English proficiency as determined by an English language proficiency test would keep the student from understanding the regular state test, even with accommodations.

Each outcome was accompanied by a needs statement, activities, responsible parties, timeline, and an evaluation component. Participants expressed that the two-day meeting was outstanding, and the Illinois Action Plan has had a positive effect in the state. I developed an *Impact of Deafness Kit* for Outcome 1 to educate policymakers about hearing loss. Written materials were kept to a maximum of one page per topic. The kits included the following materials:

- An audiogram with graphics of what is heard at various levels of intensity and frequency
- A 6-minute audiotaped spelling test given at three levels of simulated hearing loss
- Written materials on language acquisition and hearing loss

- Written materials on the effect of hearing loss on reading and writing English
- Assessment data on deaf students
- Data on characteristics of deaf students and performance on the ACT
- A copy of the fall 2003 newsletter *Research at Gallaudet* on the high-stakes testing conference at Gallaudet in 2002

Representative Watson was the first person to see the *Impact of Deafness Kit*. He came to my office where I showed him the audiogram with overlaid pictures and explained the printed classification guide on the degree of severity of hearing losses (slight, mild, moderate, severe, and profound). Next, I administered a spelling test developed by Sound Hearing, which simulates a severe, moderate, and mild high frequency hearing loss. Because policymakers have hectic schedules with limited amounts of time for appointments, I played only the 6-minute test portion of the tape. Representative Watson was clearly frustrated by the experience. The test begins with 10 spelling words presented with a severe high frequency loss. No one gets any of these words right, but one's expectation is that subsequent tests on the same words will be easier because they simulate a moderate and then finally a mild hearing loss. (The highest score I have recorded on this test was three correct items earned by U.S. Representative Ray LaHood's office manager.) What everyone learns from this experience is (a) a little hearing loss is a big thing, and (b) the majority of students we serve have profound hearing losses that are much worse than those demonstrated on the spelling tests.

Representative Watson ordered 30 kits, which he then shared with colleagues at the state capitol. The superintendent of ISD, the ISBE consultant for deaf students, and I distributed another five kits during several meetings with policymakers from different departments at ISBE. The most significant effect at ISBE occurred when the consultant administered the spelling test to the manager of the Department of Special Education and his assistant. Immediately after the test was completed, the manager ordered the consultant to develop a new state policy whereby placement for all deaf students was to be driven by the student's personal communication needs. He further stated his intent to make Illinois the national leader on this issue! The consultant left the office dazed. (The manager of the Department of Special Education and I had been on different sides of contested issues, especially the OSEP report. Thus, the manager's sensitivity and response to the needs of deaf students were especially significant.) True to his word, the directive was issued to all district superintendents, directors of special education, and other interested parties on June 10, 2005.[2]

A summary of the two-day ISHI assessment meeting and a description of the *Impact of Deafness Kit* was published in the ITHI newsletter, which was distributed

2. This document is available on the Internet at http://www.isbe.net/spec-ed/pdfs/hearing_impaired_guidance.pdf.

to members statewide. Teachers and supervisors ordered kits for personal use with policymakers they knew.

To try to effect change at the federal level, U.S. Representative Ray LaHood visited the ISD campus in January 2004 to meet with Joan Forney, ISD superintendent, and me on our concerns related to unfair assessment practices and federal legislation, which of course, drives the state plans. It took me fewer than 20 minutes to go through the *Impact of Deafness Kit.* After taking the spelling test and seeing the data in the kit, Representative LaHood decided to arrange a meeting so our concerns could be shared with Secretary Rod Paige at the USDOE. Superintendent Forney and I thought a positive step forward would be for the USDOE to issue policy guidance to all states recommending (a) that each review their own state test and remove items that were discriminatory for students with disabilities and (b) that multiple measures be permitted for assessing students with disabilities. Representative LaHood took his *Impact of Deafness Kit* with him as well as the one I had addressed to President Bush. We all knew the president had no time for a spelling test, but I told Representative LaHood to tell the president that I was a native Texan and that we think big!

Superintendent Forney, Jan-Marie Fernandez, principal of Mantua Elementary School in Fairfax County, Virginia, and Barbara Raimondo, government relations liaison for the Conference of Educational Administrators of Schools and Programs for the Deaf went to Washington, DC, and met with Dr. Troy Justesen, (Secretary Paige was not available) and two USDOE staff members in May 2004 to address assessment issues. They reviewed the negative effect deafness has on the development of English and, consequently, on academic achievement for deaf students. The group "seemed" to agree that current testing methods were not appropriate for all of our students. Dr. Justesen reported that the USDOE was involved in a 5-year research study to improve testing for students. They are looking at universal design. However, the project is directed at nondisabled students. Superintendent Forney, in her summary letter to Dr. Justesen after the meeting, suggested that policy guidance be sent to the states to promote the use of universal design on state tests and multiple measures. The thinking was that these requests were reasonable and would not be too difficult for USDOE to accomplish. Though some of us have doubts about the value of universal design for deaf students because of its English bias, permitting multiple assessment measures for students with disabilities would be one step closer to valid assessment of these students.

ISD discovered phonics-related items on the third-grade reading test during the 2004 ISAT administration. When brought to the attention of ISBE, they reported they could not do anything about it. The state was unable to identify which scores belonged to deaf students so the students' test scores could not be adjusted. ISHI and ITHI members were upset with the unfair and discriminatory test practices. In addition, the state's immediate responses to our concerns seemed insensitive. When Representative Watson heard about this situation, he asked ISD to arrange a meeting with the manager of the assessment section at ISBE. Over the next few months, Representative Watson, Superintendent Forney, and I had several meetings with ISBE policymakers, including the senior director for state contracts at Harcourt who had just been awarded the Illinois contract beginning in 2006. We provided input to Harcourt on assessment issues relative to the Illinois deaf student population. Harcourt reported they had norms for deaf students on the items ISBE wanted to use for the 2006 Illinois test. (which meant they were SAT-10 items). I mentioned that in the previous week, the Gallaudet Research Institute had only grade equivalents because the norms were not yet available from Harcourt. Neither ISBE nor the contract division at Harcourt were aware of that fact. Working closely with the Gallaudet Research Institute on the norming project and having more current information than Harcourt on the norms added to ISD's credibility. (In my follow-up e-mail to the manager of the assessment section, I reported that Harcourt and Gallaudet had too few deaf students participating in the norming, which meant that they could not run individual percentiles at this time. Norms were to be published within a five-percentile range.) Later in the meeting, I showed Harcourt and ISBE several minutes of a videotaped, accommodated version of a state test administered in ASL. Everyone was impressed with the signed test that was produced by Data Recognition Corporation in Minnesota. My suggestion to do a pilot study with a sign-accommodated test in Illinois was responded to by Harcourt as something that might be doable. They had received a federal grant for research and development and this type of project could be funded by it. My follow-up communication with Harcourt on this topic, however, was met with little enthusiasm.

The manager of the assessment section at ISBE and Representative Watson were invited to ISD to speak at the October 2004 meeting of ISHI. The ISBE manager announced plans for an accommodated test for deaf third graders! Our persistence had paid off. The state intended to print a separate reading test for our third graders, which would not have discriminatory items on phonics. The supervisors applauded this announcement as a step in the right direction, but still expressed dissatisfaction with the unfairness of the tests for our student population. The senior director for state contracts at Harcourt was also present at the meeting so he could hear firsthand statewide concerns relative to the inequities of testing deaf students.

I reported to Representative LaHood that ISBE agreed to remove prejudicial items from the third-grade reading test. With this minor success in hand at the state level, we once again urged Representative LaHood to request that the USDOE distribute policy guidance to state departments of education to review and remove discriminatory items from their tests and to permit the use of multiple measures when assessing students in special education.

RECOMMENDATIONS FROM DEAF STUDENTS

I was one of three test supervisors for the 2005 ACT/PSAE tests at ISD. Because I was finishing this chapter at that time, I took notes on student behavior for both days. Thirty-six eleventh graders were tested and only one student was an inactive participant. The other students appeared to work to the best of their ability. Each one completed all the subtests within the allotted time frames, except for the English test where only one-half of the students finished on time. Even though most of the students were unable to read the tests, they approached the tasks responsibly.

Immediately on completion of the final subtest, I took the opportunity to briefly describe this book on assessment. I mentioned other ways to assess knowledge and described my experience consulting on the ASL-accommodated version of the South Carolina tests (see Foster, this volume). I asked the students what they wanted me to indicate in this chapter that would clarify the best way and the worst ways to assess their knowledge. Six students wanted me to share their written comments with you, the readers of this chapter. All wished for their full names to be printed along with the statements, and permission was received from parents when appropriate. Try to guess the students' IQs and achievement levels in reading and math while reading these unedited statements.

Gabriela Cernas. "I think that when kids deaf take act test and its hard for them because they don't know how reading english and reading. That probably the kids got low score from act test. If the kids deaf take act test for ASL with one person and they will got high score. I just guess."

Bregitt Jimenez. "Act test provided ASL in it, will help us so much because deaf people, we, get first lanuage is ASL. None of us had first lanuage beside ASL. We will have increase of confients to have ASL test."

Max Nemirovsky. "I truely believe that ASL interpreting into ACT will impact our scores. It would help deaf kids understand more clearly and have a higher chance of having a future. This wold be a great opporunity for us and the other deaf people too."

Dmitry Rossoshansky. "Hearing kids different Deaf kids. Most of Deaf people have been struggled reading and need more time reading. My opinion is ASL video tape will help Deaf people to answer question faster. Hearing people's first language is English while Deaf people is ASL. I definitely Deaf students will get high score as if we do have ASL video tape."

Becky Sommer. "I felt that deaf students should have a chance of success because hearing students have greater chance of success. We should give the deaf students more time on test such as ACT/PSAE because they read and understand slower than hearing students. No deaf students would misunderstand ASL."

Makisha Velez. "I think ACT should have ASL because deaf people would be understand and answer it. Some deaf people have difficult to read english. So they perfer to read asl."

Table 9.1. Time Taken by Deaf Students on Six Tests in the 2007 ACT/PSAE

Test	Time Allowed	Actual Time Taken	Mean
ACT Reading	35 minutes	27 minutes (100%)	
ACT Science	35 minutes	20 minutes (79%)	16 minutes, 30 seconds
		27 minutes (100%)	
ACT Writing	30 minutes	21 minutes (79%)	15 minutes, 48 seconds
		24 minutes (24%)	
PSAE Science	45 minutes	28 minutes (84%)	23 minutes, 12 seconds
		31 minutes (95%)	
		36 minutes (100%)	
PSAE Math	45 minutes	30 minutes (79%)	24 minutes, 22 seconds
		35 minutes (100%)	
PSAE Reading for Information	45 minutes	29 minutes (79%)	24 minutes, 34 seconds
		37 minutes (100%)	

Two of these students have *superior* Performance IQs. The others are average to high average. The best reader has an average IQ and a 9.4 grade equivalent on reading comprehension, which is outstanding for a deaf student, but still two grades below grade level. The others have reading scores in the *second- and third-grade range*. The students have much higher scores on math procedures: two students test at pre-High School equivalent; two students test at Grade 9 equivalent; one student tests at Grade 8 equivalent; one student tests at Grade 5 equivalent.

The comments of these six students share common themes. On the topic of English-based tests, their comments can be summarized as follows:

- Deaf students struggle with English, which results in low scores.
- English is the first language of hearing students.
- Hearing students have a greater chance of success on these tests.
- Deaf students need more time to read the tests.

On the topic of videotaped, ASL-accommodated tests, their comments can be summarized as follows:

- ASL is the first language of deaf students and they would not misunderstand the tests.
- They will get higher scores. This form of accommodation would provide a great opportunity to demonstrate what they know and increase their chances for a better future.

During the administration of the 2007 ACT/PSAE for 19 "average" deaf students, I recalled (after the first two tests) that several top students in the 2005 group had recommended extended time because "deaf students read slower." Thus, I timed the 2007 students on the remaining six tests (see Table 9.1).

The means given for the five tests indicate that the students used on average only 52% of the time allotted. What is particularly shocking about this finding is that nine nonreaders (students with cognitive and multiple disabilities) were not even in this group. They were tested separately.

I think Gabriela Cernas hit the nail on the head when she said, "I just guess." The data on the ACT Profile Table support her statement. Deaf students with multiple educational disabilities, including mental retardation, score as well on the ACT as deaf students with Performance IQs in the superior range.

Gabriela, Bregitt, Max, Dmitry, Becky, and Makisha are all fluent in ASL. When they sign, there are no inappropriate pauses to think of vocabulary, spelling, or syntax. Communication among the students is naturally paced and automatic, just like it is with hearing students. Ideas flow freely; knowledge is shared, discussed, and debated. With their mastery of ASL vocabulary, syntax, morphology, and pragmatics, each one can be sophisticated and eloquent in their language use. If we truly want to use a standardized instrument to assess what these students know, then that instrument must use their language. That approach is the best way I know of to get information from the students.

REFERENCES

ACT Assessment. (2004). Taking the ACT assessment for state testing: Spring 2005. Iowa City: Author.

Allen, T. E. (1986). Patterns of academic achievement among hearing impaired students: 1974 and 1983. In A. N. Schildroth & M. A. Karchmer (Eds.), *Deaf children in America* (pp. 161–206). San Diego, CA: College-Hill Press.

Gallaudet Research Institute. (2003). *Regional and national summary report of data from the 2001–2002 Annual Survey of Deaf and Hard of Hearing Children and Youth.* Washington, DC: Gallaudet Research Institute, Gallaudet University.

Individuals With Disabilities Education Improvement Act Reauthorization of 1997, Pub. L. No. 105–17, 20 U.S.C. § 1400 *et seq.*

Schick, B., Williams, K., & Bolster, L. (1999). Skill levels of educational interpreters working in public schools. *Journal of Deaf Studies and Deaf Education, 4*(2), 144–155.

10

Testing, Accountability, and Equity for Deaf Students in Delaware

Ed Bosso

It is 6:30 a.m. on the first day of the Delaware Student Testing Program (DSTP) at the Delaware School for the Deaf (DSD), and the atmosphere is already tense. Will enough staff members be present to administer the test with appropriate accommodations? If one key staff member assigned to administer the test is absent, then the entire schedule and staffing assignments for the test administration will be affected. The DSTP, which includes writing, reading, and mathematics during this spring session, is a high-stakes test that has consequences not only for individual students but also for the school.

Teachers and administrators have been working tirelessly to finalize logistical preparations for testing in Grades 2 through 10. Faculty meetings have taken place to review security and test administration protocols and procedures, training has been conducted for staff members who will be involved in test administration. The "DSD DSTP Help Desk" is staffed and ready to support teachers who will administer the test, primarily with translation of test directions and test items. Schedules have been carefully crafted and reviewed multiple times to ensure appropriate staffing for the test administration and adequate instruction for students who are not involved in this particular test session.

At 7:20 a.m., secondary students arrive and gather in assembly for some last-minute instructions and a positive message about performance on the test. Some students make comments about not wanting to attend mandatory summer school if they do not score well while others worry about receiving a diploma. Indeed, the stakes are high!

Joey, a 14-year-old boy who came to the school from a local school district a few months ago, sits quietly in the corner of the assembly as the principal frantically waves his arms from the stage, gesturing to students in ways that are not easily understandable to Joey. Joey was identified as having a hearing loss when he was age 4 and was fitted with hearing aids and placed in his local school district where he has been "educated" for the past 10 years. He is currently in the ninth grade but reads on a second-grade level and has minimal writing skills. In essence, Joey has "failed" his way into DSD. Joey will participate in the ninth-grade assessment with accommodations because he does not meet the criteria established for the alternate assessment.

Mike, an eighth-grade student seated next to Joey, is worried about meeting the standard on the test to avoid mandatory summer school. He has been a student at DSD since age 5. Mike's parents have remained involved in his education and have learned basic communication skills in sign language. Most of Mike's deeper linguistic competence has come from his peers and teachers. He is currently performing on a sixth-grade level across all content areas, and today, he will take the eighth-grade test with some accommodations.

On the other side of the room, Julia wonders whether all of her hard work and effort will earn her a diploma with distinction. Julia is a 16-year-old sophomore who has been a part of the DSD program since she was an infant. She has had early and ongoing access to meaningful language and communication, which has fostered her linguistic and cognitive development and has set the foundation for lifelong learning and academic success. She will participate in the tenth-grade assessment and will likely exceed the standard in all areas.

Although the preceding student information is contrived, it mirrors the reality not only at DSD but also in schools and programs for deaf students across the country. The issues and challenges described here and throughout the chapter are based on real, everyday experiences associated with testing and accountability at DSD. These profiles clearly illustrate the diversity of deaf students served and some of the challenges that educators face related to curriculum access, instructional strategies, and assessment.

Rigorous standards for achievement, high expectations for all children, and closing the achievement gap with fair and equitable measures of progress are goals shared by educational leaders, parents, and community members, including those involved with the education of deaf children. Discussion in this chapter about some of the unique challenges confronted when educating and assessing deaf students in the age of heightened accountability should not be interpreted as, or used as, arguments against having high standards of accountability. In fact, efforts to find ways to ensure equitable inclusion of deaf students within assessment and accountability models are a strong indication of a commitment to high expectations for learning and standards of achievement.

Too often, an inordinate amount of time and energy are expended on articulating and admiring the problem rather than seeking solutions. This chapter will identify challenges and problems related to equity and fair access to assessments for deaf children, but more important, it will explore possible actions and solutions.

BACKGROUND

During the past two decades, there has been an unprecedented push for educational reform in the United States for all students. This push for standards-based educational reform has resulted in the creation of national and local academic standards, curriculum alignment, and the development and administration of standardized assessments for all students. Many states have initiated accountability systems to monitor progress and to hold students, schools, and districts accountable. The reauthorization in 2001 of the federal Elementary and Secondary Education Act (ESEA) of 1965 as the No Child Left Behind Act (NCLB) of 2001 has rapidly increased the push for reform and, despite controversy and local protest, appears to be a catalyst in closing the achievement gap.

In 1998, approximately 4 years before NCLB was signed into law by President George W. Bush, the Educational Accountability Act was passed in Delaware and set in motion a plan for student and school accountability based on performance results from the DSTP. Although there have been a number of changes and amendments to the original legislation, the state of Delaware remains poised to hold students, educators and schools accountable. Performance on the DSTP dictates local school accountability ratings accompanied by rewards and sanctions, guidelines for promotion and retention, mandatory summer school, and diploma options for students.

Testing is conducted on an annual basis in reading, math, and writing for students in Grades 2 through 10, with retesting in Grades 11 and 12 as necessary. Science and social studies are assessed in Grades 4, 6, 8, and 11. Meeting the standard in these areas may eventually be tied to diploma requirements.

Promotion, retention, and mandatory summer school based on DSTP test scores went into effect in 2002. Students can score in one of five categories on the DSTP based on established cut scores: 5—distinguished, 4—exceeds the standard, 3—meets the standard, 2—below the standard, and 1—well below the standard. Students scoring a 1 are required to attend summer school and be retested to be considered for promotion. Students scoring a 2 may be promoted to the next grade provided they have an Individual Improvement Plan (IIP). The Individualized Education Program (IEP) can serve as the IIP for students in special education as long as it addresses areas of need identified by the DSTP.

DSD is not exempt from school or student accountability. Students with disabilities, including deaf students, must participate in the DSTP or the Delaware Alternate Portfolio Assessment (DAPA). In Delaware, school staff members may consider providing accommodations during the DSTP, according to the *Delaware Student Testing Program Guidelines for Inclusion of Students with Disabilities and English Language Learners,* prepared by the Delaware Department of Education (Delaware Department of Education, 2006). These accommodations may be used *only* if students are eligible for services under the Individuals With Disabilities Education Act or Section 504 of the Rehabilitation Act of 1973, have an IEP or 504 Plan, and have an instructional program that includes accommodations, assistive devices, or both in the teaching process.

ACCOUNTABILITY AT THE DELAWARE SCHOOL FOR THE DEAF

DSD is administered by the Christina School District and complies with all local and state requirements. The school district has established performance targets that set the expectation for *all* students in the district, including students at DSD, to make aggressive progress toward meeting standards in reading, writing, math, science, and social studies as measured by performance on the DSTP. Again, the issue is not with high expectations and accountability but with equitable access to fair assessments with appropriate accommodations.

The education of deaf children at DSD presents some unique challenges and circumstances that are *not* generally confronted by other public schools. Although all schools face the challenges of educating students from diverse backgrounds who arrive at school with varying degrees of readiness, DSD encounters student demographic variables unlike other public schools in Delaware. The composition of students at DSD includes students who come to school without competence in a first language; students who lack access to world knowledge and incidental learning; students who learn English as a second language; students with multiple disabilities; and students who face equity issues related to testing, accommodations, and accountability. Other complicating factors include the age of identification and early intervention services, as well as age of enrollment into an "appropriate" program that provides for language and communication access. Each of the aforementioned issues must be given consideration in terms of the resulting effect on equity with respect to education, assessment, and school accountability.

Early language access. Approximately 90% of all deaf children are born to hearing parents—parents who do not possess proficiency in the language most accessible to deaf children: American Sign Language (ASL). At DSD, approximately 97% of our students are born to hearing parents. Improving student achievement, therefore, involves addressing the language learning needs of our students and parents, as well as addressing the complex and diverse instructional needs of children who lack competence in any one language. The age at which students are identified with a hearing loss and receive early intervention services also has a significant effect. Students who are identified and receive services before the age of 6 months have more successful outcomes (Yoshignaga-Itano, 2000).

Access to world knowledge. Given the lack of early access to language and learning, the acquisition of world knowledge is negatively affected. Language is the cornerstone for education. Lack of free and unrestricted access to language from birth (during the critical period for language acquisition and brain development) results in a weak foundation for learning and irreparable damage to maximum educational development. It is also important to note that because the majority of DSD's students have hearing families, their access to world knowledge is often limited because the primary language used in these homes is spoken English and is therefore not accessible to the deaf child.

Age of enrollment. With each year that passes in which students do not have maximum opportunities for language acquisition and learning, the task of educating these students becomes significantly more complicated. Students enroll at DSD for a variety of reasons and at various ages, depending on individual circumstances and needs. All too often, students simply "fail" their way into DSD after years of opportunity have been wasted. Although the school accountability formulas may address the movement of students from one school to another, it is impossible for any formula to account for multiple years of language deprivation and restricted access to world knowledge and incidental learning. For example, the scores on the Grade 3 DSTP test for a student who comes to DSD at the age of 8 can be distributed between the sending and receiving school so each school is accountable for the student's results. But regardless of the equitable distribution of performance scores in this case, DSD remains accountable for the student's performance in subsequent years and absorbs the lasting effect of the damage (often irreparable) done during the first 8 years when language access and learning were restricted. The educational effect multiplies exponentially as the age of enrollment increases.

Students with multiple disabilities. Although the special education system in the state of Delaware does not allow for dual classification of students, DSD has a significant number of students—approximately 58%—who have multiple disabilities. Nationally, as many as 48% of deaf students have additional disabilities (Gallaudet Research Institute, 2005). These multiple disabilities are often compounded by language acquisition deficits and related learning needs, which have a significant effect on instruction and assessment.

Equity issues. Assessment of deaf children at the Delaware School for the Deaf involves equity issues with respect to test development, test administration, and availability of appropriate testing accommodations. Test items can be biased against deaf students, particularly with phonics- or sound-based items. The administration of the DSTP and the availability of appropriate accommodations that address the unique language-learning needs of deaf students present another set of challenges. Appropriate accommodations that ensure equal access to the test and to the opportunity for students to demonstrate what they know without interference from their disability are difficult to administer and, in some cases, do not exist.

TEST DEVELOPMENT

Test developers do not typically consider students with low-incidence disabilities when designing and developing tests, which often leads to inappropriate items surfacing on the test. The most cited examples among professionals in deaf education are phonics-based questions. Other items have an auditorily based context and are sometimes outside of the normal life experiences of deaf children. For example, a writing prompt that surfaced on a DSTP test asked students to describe "the sights and *sounds* of a typical day at the beach." Other examples have included references to music. One could arguably say that these experiences should be at least familiar to deaf students through information gained in conversations and through printed material. However, sometimes, the simple mention of sound-based phenomena within an item can be enough to stymie a response from the student.

The lack of "world knowledge" exhibited by deaf students who have not had early access to language magnifies the challenges when these students must understand and respond to decontextualized information. In addition, certain test items present difficulties in terms of the manner in which they are written; some early efforts in Delaware focused on simplifying the language of test items to counter these difficulties. Fortunately, in Delaware, teachers are afforded the opportunity to be involved in the development of test items that measure progress toward the standards. A second opportunity to assess the effectiveness of particular test items before they are introduced on an actual test happens during field testing.

Every item on the DSTP has been reviewed by the DSTP Bias Review Committee. The function of this committee it to review each developed item for any bias in one or more of the following areas: sexism, sex stereotypes, racial or cultural stereotypes, blindness and visual impairment, deafness and hearing loss, special education, objectionable stereotypes, and historical distortions.

The committee is composed of teachers and individuals with extensive knowledge and experience in these areas. The committee also reviews items for accommodations needed for blind and visually impaired students as well as deaf students. In cases when an item cannot be modified or is not appropriate for a blind student, it will be removed from the Braille version of the test, and the scoring will be adjusted.

After items are written and before the submission of the test items to the test publishing company for inclusion in a field test, they are submitted for review to the Bias Review Committee. Any item that is judged to contain bias is returned to the Delaware Department of Education content specialist with a description of the bias identified. The item may be revised to eliminate the bias and then be resubmitted to the Bias Review Committee for another review before field testing occurs with Delaware students.

The opportunity for bias review is not always an option with standardized formative assessments such as the Measures of Academic Progress assessment by Northwest Evaluation Association that is used at the local level. There are not high-stakes consequences attached to these local assessments in terms of mandatory summer school and diploma requirements; however, the fact that items with bias are present on the formative assessment prevents students from showing what they know and could present an opportunity to discuss strategies for addressing the item and moving forward with the remainder of the test.

TEST ADMINISTRATION AND GUIDELINES FOR INCLUSION OF STUDENTS WITH DISABILITIES

Students with disabilities may be administered the test under various conditions in Delaware as outlined in guidelines published by the Delaware Department of Education. The following descriptions are excerpted directly from the *2005–2006 DSTP Guidelines for Inclusion of Students with Disabilities and Students with Limited English Proficiency* (Delaware Department of Education, 2005):

Testing Condition 1: Students may be tested under regular conditions. Note that students may elect to test under regular conditions even if accommodations are being used in the classroom.

Testing Condition 2: Students may test with accommodations that do not change the construct being assessed. Such accommodations do not interfere with the comparability of student scores to the scores of students testing under standard conditions. The scores for students testing with these accommodations are aggregable (will be included) in the calculations of the results presented in the State Summary. Students will receive an individual score report.

Testing Condition 3: Students may test with accommodations that change the construct being assessed (for example, reading aloud the reading passages in the reading comprehension test – accommodation 46). Such accommodations interfere with the comparability of student scores to the scores of students testing under standard conditions (i.e., testing conditions 1 and 2).The scores for students testing with these accommodations are non-aggregable and will not be included (not aggregated) in the calculations of the results presented in the State Summary Report; however, students will receive an individual score report.

Testing Condition 4: Students with disabilities may participate in the Delaware Alternate Portfolio Assessment (DAPA) if they meet the criteria. The scores for students testing with this assessment are aggregable (will be included) in the calculations of the DAPA results presented in the State Summary. Students will receive an individual score report.

Testing Condition 5: The grade 4, 6, 8, or 11 SD/LEP student may be exempted from the science and social studies tests if he or she meets the criteria. Students who are both SD and LEP (SD/LEP) in grades 2–10 may receive special flexibility for the DSTP reading and writing tests using the criteria.

Testing Condition 6: SD/LEP students who meet the criteria outlined on page 24 may take an alternate assessment for LEP students (if available) in place of the DSTP reading and writing.

At the Delaware School for the Deaf, students primarily fall under testing conditions 1 through 4 with a very small percentage in the category described in testing condition 1. Approximately 10% of students participated in the alternate portfolio assessment (DAPA) in 2005–2006, which is described in testing condition 4.

WHY TESTING ACCOMMODATIONS?

Students learn differently and certainly bring different strengths to tasks in which they are asked to demonstrate what they know. However, systems tend to impose uniform conditions and materials in test situations that can prevent students from fully demonstrating their abilities. During instruction, accommodations can help students learn what we expect them to know as well as give students options for demonstrating that knowledge and skill. During assessments, accommodations assist us in measuring a student's skills and abilities, not the student's disability. In short, testing accommodations are intended to allow a student the opportunity to "show what he or she knows" both in the instructional setting and on assessments.

This provision exists within the Individuals With Disabilities Education Improvement Act of 2004 (IDEA 2004) but is implemented in varying degrees from state to state. In Delaware, testing accommodations are reviewed on an annual basis, and all changes are published annually by the Delaware Department of Education in the *DSTP Guidelines for Inclusion of Students with Disabilities and Students with Limited English Proficiency* (Delaware Department of Education, 2005).

The National Center on Education Outcomes Web site includes the following description of testing accommodations:

> Accommodations are changes in testing materials or procedures that enable students to participate in assessments in a way that allows abilities to be assessed rather than disabilities. They are provided to "level the playing field." Without accommodations, the assessment may not accurately measure the student's knowledge and skills. Accommodations are generally grouped into the following categories: presentation (e.g., repeat directions, read aloud, large print, Braille, etc.); equipment and material (e.g., calculator, amplification equipment, manipulatives, etc.); response (e.g., mark answers in book, scribe records response, point, etc.); setting (e.g., study carrel, student's home, separate room, etc.); timing/scheduling (e.g., extended time, frequent breaks, etc.). (Lehr & Thurlow, 2003)

CHALLENGES WITH TESTING ACCOMMODATIONS

Theoretically, testing accommodations should provide access and equity for deaf students. Phrases like "level the playing field" would indicate that students would have equal access to assessments and the opportunity to "show what they know." However, there are some challenges that exist with respect to testing accommodations. The following areas represent some of the challenges and issues related to the provision of accommodations during instruction and assessment.

Decision-making process with respect to accommodations. The IEP team is responsible for making decisions about participation in assessments and for making decisions about which accommodations are appropriate for which students. However, there is often not consistency with respect to selecting accommodations to be used during instruction and assessment, and it is not clear whether the selection is always based on need. A lack of clear guidelines for making decisions with respect to accommodations may lead to "over-accommodating" students. Table 10.1 shows the average number of accommodations made for DSD students on a reading test.

Feasibility of accommodations. Appropriate accommodations that ensure equal access to the test and the opportunity for students to demonstrate what they know without interference from their disability are difficult to effectively implement and, in some cases, simply do not currently exist. For example, the following accommodation (see Example 10.1), excerpted from the *2005 DSTP Guidelines for Inclusion,* (Delaware Department of Education, 2004), is nearly impossible to effectively implement given the resource demands associated with this accommodation.

Table 10.1. Accommodations per DSD Student on the DSTP Reading Test, March 2004

Grade	Number of Students Tested	Average Number of Accommodations per Student
3	$n = 4$	11.2
4	$n = 9$	12.9
5	$n = 6$	9.5
6	$n = 7$	9.6
7	$n = 3$	11.0
8	$n = 13$	7.7
9	$n = 6$	8.7
10	$n = 14$	8.2
	$\mathbf{n = 62}$	

Example 10.1. DSTP Test Accommodation

Accommodations for Interaction or Processing During the Test

13. For the writing test, permitting deaf students to videotape their first draft in American Sign Language and use the videotape as a tool for writing the second and final draft of the paper. Students must be tested individually.

Although this accommodation has great potential, it currently requires resources such as videotaping equipment, a television/VCR for playback, and additional faculty and staff members for students to be tested individually, which make it nearly impossible to implement.

Intense demands on local resources. The demands on local resources can be extreme when providing accommodations in testing situations. Appropriate implementation of accommodations requires extensive time for preparation before the test, professional development to build capacity and maximize consistency, the delivery of timely technical assistance to faculty and staff members who are administering the test during the official test dates, and a disproportionate number of faculty and staff members for test administration. Table 10.2 shows the number of staff members required to administer a reading test with accommodations for Grades 3 though 10 at DSD.

CHALLENGES WITH TEST ADMINISTRATION

Challenges with test administration include logistical issues such as adequate time for training and preparation as well as scheduling and time constraints that interrupt the flow of the testing sessions. Additionally, the need to ensure sufficient

Table 10.2. Number of DSD Staff Members Required for Test Administration of the DSTP Reading Test, March 2004

Grade	Number of Students Tested	Number of Staff Members Required to Administer Test With Accommodations
3	$n = 4$	4
4	$n = 9$	8
5	$n = 6$	3
6	$n = 7$	5
7	$n = 3$	2
8	$n = 13$	8
9	$n = 6$	5
10	$n = 14$	8
	$\mathbf{n = 62}$	**43**

numbers of available and qualified faculty and staff members affects administration. All of the aforementioned issues certainly influence the validity of the test and resulting outcomes.

One of the allowable accommodations in Delaware includes signing test directions and portions of the test. It is necessary to receive testing materials in advance to adequately prepare staff members to provide this accommodation; however, test security restrictions often limit how much in advance of the actual testing dates the materials can be received. In addition to training faculty and staff members to *sign* directions, questions, and passages, adequate time and staff resources are needed to make transparencies of the test items so students have a visual referent when the test is being signed. Although technological advances such as document cameras (e.g., ELMO cameras) would seem to make transparencies and overhead projectors obsolete, the transparencies and overhead projector have often proven to be the most reliable in high-stakes testing situations.

In addition to identifying adequate numbers of qualified faculty and staff members and providing time for preparation and training, an inordinate amount of time is required to develop a schedule for testing that takes into consideration matching the appropriate faculty and staff members to meet student needs and effectively administer the required testing accommodations. Scheduling for testing sessions often begins 3 to 4 weeks in advance of the official testing dates. Administering the test with accommodations in Grades 2 through 10 within the state-mandated testing window is a challenge that requires special permission from the Delaware Department of Education to modify the predetermined schedule for test administration.

The actual preparation and training for test administration is a complex issue that brings to "center stage" staff language competence (in both ASL and English).

In many situations, faculty and staff members do not demonstrate the necessary competence in both languages to administer the test, which most certainly leads to a wide variation in the presentation of test items to students. For those faculty and staff members who do possess competence, there is the issue of translation skills. Fluency or competence in both languages does not automatically mean that an individual has the skill and ability to translate items from one language to another. Assuming a person has language competence and the necessary skills to translate questions, there still are situations in which an appropriate translation from English to ASL may provide an unfair advantage to the test taker by providing too much visual information. For example, when providing an accurate translation from English to ASL of a math item that asks a student to identify the parallel lines in a diagram, the sign for the word *parallel* would provide the student with the answer. The degree of complexity in the situation increases when students are given different forms of the test booklet; thus, the translation of the test items to a group of students at a particular grade level is compounded further, unless arrangements can be made to provide students with the same form of the test booklet.

Perhaps the most difficult accommodation to provide with consistency and accuracy is scribing. On-demand scribing presents some very unique and complex challenges, including those of translating from one language to another (in this case, from ASL to English); making decisions with respect to selection of vocabulary and sentence structure at appropriate age and grade levels; determining when and how to interrupt a student for clarification to request repetition of a phrase or a fingerspelled word; determining when to stop a student's dictation to actually scribe the answer; and self-monitoring for facial expressions that may unintentionally provide feedback to the student. One solution would be to videotape the student's signed responses and employ a team later on to complete the English transcription. But this approach, though it appears to be very fair and reasonable, would bring into question the feasibility of routinely devoting so many resources to this task.

RECOMMENDATIONS FOR ADDRESSING THE CHALLENGES OF PROVIDING ACCOMMODATIONS

The discussion with respect to accommodations for instruction and assessment should be frequent and should occur at various levels within the educational system. In Delaware, these discussions occur at the state, local, and building level on at least an annual basis. At the building level, the first order of business related to accommodations is to discuss the decision-making process. We have approached this task in a number of ways—the most common format being discussion during faculty meetings and professional development days, accompanied by written information. Information includes general guidelines for making decisions. The following excerpt describes one such process:

When Making Decisions About Accommodations . . .

- Think about what happens during instruction.
- Think about the student as a learner.

- Determine how a student can demonstrate the knowledge and skills being evaluated.
- Consider the test constructs.
- Identify the minimal accommodations needed for the student to learn and/ or demonstrate knowledge and skills in area being assessed.

Additionally, DSD provides ongoing training related to making decisions about accommodations during instruction and test administration. Faculty and staff members have worked collaboratively with school administration to develop technical assistance documents such as the "DSD Accommodations Tip Sheet" (see Example 10.2), which provides lists of commonly used accommodations and indicates for which students these accommodations might be appropriate.

Example 10.2. Sample DSD Accommodations Tip Sheet

Description of Accommodation	Comments
Reading, re-reading or providing signed assistance of test questions, multiple choice options and writing prompts . . . (____ **all allowable items or** ____ **items requested by student)**	• Most DSD students should have this accommodation.
Presenting instructions, test questions, and individual via an overhead projector and transparencies.	• Students who will have test administered using overhead projector and transparencies should have this accommodation. • Most students will have this accommodation.
For written responses, deaf student records a videotape as an organizational or prewriting tool . . .	• Can be used if being regularly used as part of classroom instruction. **Note:** equipment and time limitations are prohibitive to the implementation of this accommodation at this time.
For the writing test, using an electronic dictionary or thesaurus phrase whenever dictionary or thesaurus use is permitted for other students. Teacher (test administrator) may be used as a resource for spelling whenever dictionary or thesaurus use is permitted for other students.	• Almost all students should have this accommodation unless achieving close to grade level. • NOT for science, social studies or math (writing and text-based responses on reading test ONLY) • Thesaurus must be used by administrator when this accommodation is implemented during testing.
For written responses, student dictates to a test administrator following the scribing protocol. Responses can	**Use for all tests except reading and writing.** • Used for students on content area

be signed or verbal and can be done through audio or videotaping.	portions of the test where written English competency level may prevent students from "showing what they know."
Reading or signing passages or texts for the reading test (or using cued speech or oral interpreter) . . . . (____ **all allowable items or** ____ **items requested by student)**	• Used if compensatory necessity/lifelong need (documented reading disability) • Can be used when students' reading ability is significantly below grade level and must be used as part of instruction (opportunities for practice) **Note:** Involve Test Coordinator/Administrator before proceeding with this accommodation.
This student is in a functional life skills curriculum and is to be included in the Delaware Alternate Portfolio Assessment.	• Must be an IEP team decision and based on established criteria.

Source: From *Delaware Department of Education DSTP Guidelines for Inclusion.*

On a state level, DSD's role in shaping practices related to testing and accommodations for deaf students has involved participation in the following areas:

- DSTP Disability Task Force that makes recommendations with respect to allowable accommodations
- DSTP test item development
- Delaware Department of Education Bias Review Committee
- Research on the effect of testing accommodations
- Advocacy for accommodations that address the unique language learning needs of deaf students need to be investigated/researched

DESIGNING ACCOUNTABILITY FOR DEAF STUDENTS

Student demographic variables such as those mentioned earlier, combined with students' prior achievement and schooling experiences and instructional background variables, make for a very complex situation when attempting to design an equitable accountability model for deaf students. The general purposes of an accountability system, as outlined by Gong (2002), are as follows:

1. To identify and promote improved educational practices and results
2. To inform stakeholders of the condition of education at the school, district, and state levels and to identify areas in which improvement is needed and success is being achieved

3. To obtain the support of all stakeholders in making the changes needed to enable students to achieve at high levels
4. To inform policy decisions and actions by officials at the local, state and federal levels; by parents, students, members of the community; and by other interested individuals to improve academic performance where needed and reward it where appropriate

Unfortunately, when federal, state, and local entities design accountability systems, low-incidence disabilities such as deafness have not been a recognizable "blip" on the radar. Deaf students have not been given consideration in the development of standards and curriculum or in test design and item development. Therefore, solutions have been more reactive than proactive in nature.

Currently, DSD is working with the Delaware Department of Education to explore more appropriate and equitable ways to measure student progress, but our measures of progress are only as good as the instrument, so in Delaware, there is much work to be done. As short term solutions are investigated at the local level, DSD is working in collaboration with the Conference of Educational Administrators of Schools and Programs for the Deaf and other organizations to examine more viable long-term solutions for equitable accountability systems and models for appropriately measuring growth for a very diverse and changing student population. All of these efforts keep high expectations for achievement at the very core of the discussion. Equality and equity are very different, and too often, educational systems focus on equality when equity is the issue. The Christina School District's beliefs include the following statement: "Equity without excellence is tokenism and excellence without equity is privilege." Deaf students have a right to equity *and* excellence.

REFERENCES

Elementary and Secondary Education Act of 1965, Pub. L. No. *89-10, 20 U.S.C. 6301 et seq.*

Gallaudet Research Institute. (2005). *Regional and national summary report of data from the 2003–2004 Annual Survey of Deaf and Hard of Hearing Children and Youth.* Washington, DC: Gallaudet Research Institute, Gallaudet University.

Gong, B. (2002). Designing school accountability systems: Towards a framework and process. Washington, DC: Council of Chief State Officers.

Individuals With Disabilities Education Improvement Act of 2004, Pub. L. No. 108-446, 20 U.S.C. 1400 *et seq.*

Lehr, C., & Thurlow, M. (2003). *Putting it all together: Including students with disabilities in assessment and accountability systems* (Policy Directions No. 16). Minneapolis: University of Minnesota, National Center on Educational Outcomes. Retrieved on June 6, 2008, from http://education.umn.edu/NCEO/OnlinePubs/Policy16.htm.

No Child Left Behind Act of 2001, Pub. L. No. 107–110, 115 Stat.1425 (2002).

Yoshinaga-Itano, C. (2000). Development of audition and speech: Implications for early intervention with infants who are deaf or hard of hearing. *The Volta Review, 100,* 213–234.

Yoshinaga-Itano, C., Sedey, A., Coulter, D., & Mehl, A. (1998). Language of early- and later identified children with hearing loss. *Pediatrics 102* (5), 1161–1171.

11

Participating in the Massachusetts Comprehensive Assessment System

Michael Bello,
Patrick Costello,
and Suzanne Recane

The national lexicon of education has changed in recent years. Assessment-driven instruction, on-demand testing, accountability, high-stakes testing, testing accommodations, alternate testing, authentic assessment tools, and competency determination are now terms that dominate our school discussions. The federal education laws, No Child Left Behind Act of 2001 and the Individuals With Disabilities Education Act of 1990 and its various reauthorized forms mandate that every student be educated using the "general curriculum," be instructed in a standards-based, research-proven instructional pedagogy, and participate in annual assessments. The world of education has changed, and Massachusetts has been in the forefront of the current trend.

In 1993, Massachusetts passed educational reform legislation that provided large funding increases for public schools. In return for the funding increases, the legislation mandated school accountability as proven through a comprehensive testing program. As a result, a standards-based set of curriculum guidelines, *The Massachusetts Curriculum Frameworks* (http://www.doe.mass.edu/frameworks/current.html) were developed in all content areas, and a comprehensive system of assessment aligned with the curriculum frameworks, the Massachusetts Comprehensive Assessment System [MCAS] (http://www.doe.mass.edu/mcas/about1.html) was implemented with high-stakes criteria for high school graduation. Only publicly funded students are tested, and every student is held accountable. Starting with the class of 2003, all graduates have been required to demonstrate competency in English language arts and in mathematics to graduate. All students, including special education students, are included in the testing program. Starting in 2010, a passing score in science and technology/engineering will be required for graduation, and in 2012, a passing score in history and social science, focusing on U.S. history, will be required.

Initially, those of us involved in the education of deaf students resisted the changes. We argued that the testing program would not be fair. We contended, as did many other educators, that one test could not be used for all children to determine competency and that, like all previously developed written tests, this one would not allow deaf students to validly demonstrate their knowledge. However, it became apparent early in the change process that nothing, including legal challenge, was going to stop the testing movement, and it also became apparent to those of us at The Learning Center for Deaf Children (TLC) that we did not have enough time to resist the changes and to simultaneously prepare our school and students for the new requirements. If we wanted our students to graduate, we needed to be "on board" with the changes, and we had lots of work to do.

TLC decided that it would work cooperatively within the newly established MCAS assessment system. We decided that the new requirements would provide a significant opportunity to educate the decision makers at the state Department of Education level about the issues involved in fair and equitable assessment for deaf individuals. After several years of experience, we have seen many beneficial aspects of the higher standards and the strict accountability system for our students. Expectations have been raised, and deaf students have benefited; however, the issue of how deaf students can validly demonstrate their actual knowledge and achievement continues to be a problem.

At the onset of the new legislation, TLC began the process of aligning the school's curriculum with the Massachusetts Curriculum Frameworks. By 1999, when the first testing began, the school's curriculum was fully aligned in all content areas. From the beginning, it became apparent to our teachers and administrators that adhering to a rigorous, grade-appropriate curriculum for every student was the best way to "raise the achievement bar." Students participated in the appropriate grade curriculum standards regardless of their achievement level. Even though we had always prided ourselves on providing a challenging level of education, it was apparent that in some instances we were not. The accountability system did, indeed, expedite improvements in our schoolwide curriculum.

However, our efforts to explain the assessment needs of deaf students were just beginning. From the start, we arranged to have faculty participate in statewide MCAS implementation committees and working groups. Our faculty was represented in content institutes, assessment development committees, test scoring workshops, alternate assessment committees, bias review consultations, and state special education advisory committees. Our goal was to have TLC representation on all state committees open to our participation. This goal proved to be a valuable strategy in our state, where there had been little or no expertise in the Department of Education with respect to deaf student issues.

In the next two sections of this chapter, we will discuss our experiences and the challenges involved with test administration and the provision of accommodations. We discuss several specific testing accommodations used with deaf test takers and our experiences with the MCAS Alternate Assessment, our state's alternate method through which students can demonstrate standards-based achievement when the on-demand test is not appropriate. In some cases, our efforts have been effective and have helped our students validly demonstrate their knowledge. In all cases, the effort has proven to be costly in lost teaching time, additional expense, and hours of additional labor. We describe here in this chapter what has worked and ask the lingering questions that need to be answered for deaf students to participate in a fair assessment environment.

MCAS TEST ADMINISTRATION AND ACCOMMODATIONS

Administering high-stakes tests is challenging for all schools, and our school is no exception. State policies on the implementation of testing accommodations follow federal guidance, which mandates that the student's Individualized Education Program (IEP) team may decide the specific accommodation (or accommodations) to be used as long as the chosen accommodation is used as part of routine daily instruction. Our state Department of Education provides a comprehensive list of approved accommodations (see Massachusetts Department of Elementary and Secondary Education, 2008). Additional accommodation requests that are not on the approved list must be submitted for review and approval by the Department of Education on an individual basis. As a result, the level and number of individualized accommodation requests is significant.

It should be noted that MCAS testing is conducted during specific periods of time, and a large number of tests must be administered during a relatively short period of time. This challenge is the single most complicating issue in test administration and in the providing of accommodations. The providing of a simple accommodation such as interpreting the instructions of a test requires that a large number of teachers interpret with many small groups of students. The staff resources required to provide fair testing throughout the school year is enormous, and the disruption to the normal instructional day is significant.

When American Sign Language (ASL) interpretation is provided as an accommodation, TLC uses a team of a deaf person and a hearing person to administer the test. Students are tested in small groups to provide quality test administration. Providing a sufficient number of teams to cover all testing needs is difficult. We are allowed only 4 days lead time to review the secure test items and prepare for administering the test in ASL. It is difficult to manage the daily instructional needs of our school while providing faculty time to prepare for and conduct test administration.

In addition, there are many complex questions with respect to the use of ASL interpretation as an accommodation. Our school routinely uses ASL accommodations in the exam areas of mathematics, science, and history and social science. For those tests that are signed in ASL, our teams struggle with several complicating factors. The first factor to consider is the choice of signs to be used when interpreting a given question. We realized early in our MCAS experience that there was often a lack of consistency in the signs used within our own school. Faculty needed time to discuss sign options and arrive at a consensus on appropriate sign choices for test items.

An additional frequent discussion point is deciding whether or not to fingerspell or use the ASL sign for a concept. For example, if a math question involves the concept of reflection and the student must respond to a prompt involving reflection in a multiple choice format, the interpretation options are to fingerspell the word *reflection* or to sign REFLECTION. Signing REFLECTION may inadvertently be providing additional information and support for the student. However, because that concept may be best described in the classroom with the sign, fingerspelling the word *reflection* on the test would mean that the instructional language used routinely for the student is not used during test administration. Although we have put added importance on using fingerspelling when teaching math concepts to provide our students with the necessary practice in identifying key math concepts with the appropriate English word, the question of whether to fingerspell or sign is a constant point of discussion when our faculty prepares to interpret MCAS exams.

A major concern when providing ASL interpretation on the MCAS is the ability of the signer to provide a consistent tone and level of interpretation when students ask for a question to be repeated several times. Our interpreting teams work closely to maintain the quality of their interpretation, including attention to consistency in tone and sign choice. It is quite tiring to interpret questions repeatedly without inadvertently making changes in delivery. Our faculty struggle to interpret each question with absolute consistency regardless of the number of repetitions requested.

The question of whether to interpret the reading texts in the English language arts MCAS is another area of heated debate. The accommodation to sign the reading test was developed as a parallel accommodation to the read-aloud accommodation provided for hearing students. Using "read aloud" or sign language interpreted ("sign aloud") accommodations was originally intended for use with a very small number of students (see Massachusetts Department of Elementary and Secondary Education, 2008, to review the accommodations guidelines). The Massachusetts Department of Elementary and Secondary Education is currently analyzing the frequency and rationale for use of the read-aloud and sign language interpretation for the reading tests by various programs. Members of the IEP team often debate whether or not such an accommodation should be used. If our goal is for assessment to ultimately drive instructional decisions, how will the interpretation of reading test material affect reading instruction for deaf students?

An important new development in the area of ASL accommodations is the use of media presentation format for test items. One Massachusetts school for the deaf received permission to make a videotape of their faculty interpreting the MCAS exam. The next year, TLC was granted permission to make an iMovie digital-video version of our faculty signing the tenth-grade math exam. The use of the computerized video technology was very effective. Students were able to have an individual copy of their ASL-interpreted MCAS exam on a desktop computer, which they could then control for speed of delivery. Additionally, our students could repeat an ASL interpreted question over and over without having to ask in front of their peers for a question to be repeated. Finally, some students who experienced difficulty with the level of complexity of questions were observed viewing the interpretation of a question on the computer over and over at a decreased rate of speed. The students were very excited with the use of the media format and improved passing rates matched their excitement.

Unfortunately, the state Department of Education decided that allowing schools to make their own ASL-interpreted video or DVD of secure test items was not an allowable process. TLC (is now) worked with the Massachusetts Department of Elementary and Secondary Education and other programs and schools for the deaf on the development of a single, universally used, statewide pilot of an ASL interpreted version of the tenth-grade math MCAS. The already complex issues of sign language accommodations are now being considered on the state level. Now, consistency of sign choice among different educational programs is a major consideration. Creating a product that will work for students in all types of settings, using a variety of sign systems, is a complex task. The state has created a tenth-grade math MCAS video/DVD version for the last 3 years. The logistics, cost and implementation considerations of this type of project are significant. However, from the information collected during the piloting of the video and computer-based video DVD at TLC and another school in Massachusetts and feedback from students using the state-produced 10th grade math MCAS on video and DVD, the potentially positive outcomes far outweigh any complicated design and implementation issues. This media-based option is needed for the other MCAS exams, especially for the science and technology/engineering content area. How may a state level test that is developed annually best be accommodated through the use of media presentation format in an effective manner for deaf students across the state of Massachusetts? How might test materials in a media presentation format be supported financially, and how can state and schools work together to best facilitate this goal?

Accommodations that are often used in the classroom are sometimes difficult to provide in a testing situation. For example, how do we best deal with the issue of the lack of an ASL-English word-for-word dictionary when students are completing their English language arts long composition? May we use an accommodation sometimes referred to as a "human dictionary," which involves providing students with a direct sign-to-word response on request? If so, what should the protocol be for this accommodation? We have found that some classroom-based accommodations, although used routinely in the classroom, become highly complex areas of discussion when considered for implementation on a high-stakes assessment exam not designed for deaf students. Our school would like to see formal research partnerships between educators and researchers in the field of deaf education that focus on developing a better understanding of the effect of accommodations for high-stakes testing and on identifying best practices for deaf students to validly demonstrate their knowledge on high-stakes tests.

One of the most controversial accommodations that has been used in the state by several of the schools and programs is a technique called "scribing." This accommodation was intended to be used with an extremely small number of students who could not write for themselves. A student with a physical disability would talk, and an assistant or a teacher would write what was said. Another example in which scribing may be used, cited when the accommodation was under development, is when a student breaks his or her arm during the test administration schedule and needs to have another person write his or her responses. Because scribing was listed as a possible accommodation, some schools and programs for the deaf determined that an interpreter could scribe a student's ASL answers into written English.

Obvious questions arose from the use of this accommodation. What was the skill level of the interpreter? How did the interpreter determine the level of linguistic complexity and what word choices were selected? Is it possible to scribe from ASL to English in an on-demand schedule in one day? And the ultimate question: Is this product really the student's work or that of his or her interpreter? After much discussion and heated dialogue among state educators of the deaf, the state Department of Education now advises IEP teams to consider alternatives to the use of a scribe for students who are deaf and taking the ELA Composition test. One suggestion is to permit a deaf student to sign his or her draft composition onto video and then transcribe the sign composition into written English while viewing the video (p. 17 of the participation guidelines).

In summary, our school continues to grapple with important questions when providing accommodations when administering the MCAS exams. Our questions include the following:

- When should fingerspelling be used or not used when interpreting MCAS exams?
- How can we logistically manage quality MCAS administration duties while continuing to provide quality daily instruction to students who are not taking the MCAS test?
- If our goal is for assessment to ultimately drive instructional decisions, how does the interpretation of reading test material affect reading instruction for deaf students?
- How may a state-level test that is developed annually best be accommodated through the use of media presentation format in an effective manner for deaf students across the state of Massachusetts?
- How might test materials in a media presentation format be supported financially and how can state and schools work together to best facilitate this goal?
- How might educators and researchers in the field of deaf education develop and execute quality research on the effect of accommodations and test construction to best understand the most effective ways to provide deaf students the ability to validly demonstrate their knowledge on high stakes exams?

As we continue to confront the challenges of administering high-stakes testing, questions are analyzed and responded to and new test administration questions arise. In addition, the need for increased state and federal commitment and financial support for the educational and vocational needs of deaf students leaving high school without a diploma continues to be another area of concern. Although these concerns are outside the focus of this chapter, they drive our focus on advocating for the best possible assessment procedures. In our next section, we will examine another route students may take in their attempts to validly demonstrate their knowledge for state and federal school accountability assessments.

MCAS ALTERNATE ASSESSMENT PORTFOLIOS

In 1999, the Massachusetts Department of Elementary and Secondary Education started working proactively to develop guidelines for participation of students with disabilities in MCAS and to create the MCAS Alternate Assessment. Committed to including all students with disabilities in the statewide assessment system, the Massachusetts Department of Elementary and Secondary Education convened a statewide MCAS Alternate Assessment Advisory Committee, a group composed of regular education and special education teachers, public school superintendents and administrators, college and university faculty members from teacher training programs, special education representatives from publicly funded private schools, parents of students with special needs, and educational legal advocates and lawyers.

Massachusetts Department of Elementary and Secondary Education staff members, along with program consultants from Measured Progress (a standards-based assessment development company), the Inclusive Large Scale Standards and Assessment group from the University of Kentucky, and the Institute for Community Inclusion, coordinated the efforts of the MCAS Alternate Assessment project, facilitating the statewide advisory committee meetings and tasks. The purpose of this committee was to advise on the development of participation guidelines for all students with disabilities in statewide testing, comment on the development of test accommodations guidelines, assist in the creation of printed resources to provide access to the state curriculum frameworks for all learners, and assist in the development of the parameters and requirements for an alternate assessment process for MCAS. TLC's curriculum coordinator joined this committee and provided feedback from our school and from other educational programs for the deaf. After the initial piloting of MCAS exams, an ad hoc committee of educational administrators, teachers, and interpreters from various programs and schools for the deaf throughout Massachusetts started having informal meetings to discuss statewide testing developments and provide comments to the state-level advisory committee.

One of the first tasks completed by the MCAS Alternate Assessment Advisory Committee was the development of resource guides for each content area of the statewide curriculum frameworks assessed through MCAS. At first, this task was a controversial aspect of the committee's work. Parent and legal advocates were clearly concerned that any resource guides or additional printed guides on the curriculum frameworks might be viewed as separate sets of standards for students with IEPs. However, with consistent commitment to following the intent of each standard, the resource guides were developed and became an important tool for

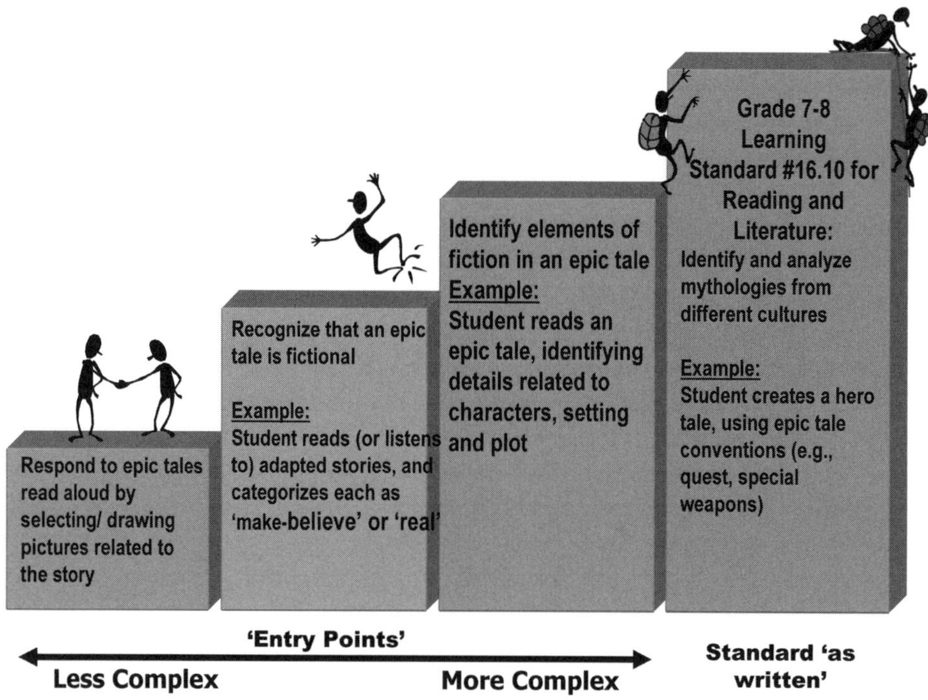

Figure 11.1. Access to the general curriculum: A continuum of learning (ELA—Reading and Literature).

teachers to understand the essence of each standard. It also provided clarity on how to bring each student to the standards that their grade-level peers were responsible to achieve in a manner that allowed for scaffolded instruction according to the individual needs of the student.[1]

With the use of these resource guides, teachers of students with significant special needs, who previously felt that the statewide curriculum frameworks and standards did not reflect their students' educational needs, were now able to bring their students to the standards in a meaningful manner. For the content areas of English language arts, mathematics, science/technology and engineering, and history and social science, a separate resource guide provides the standards as written. It also provides a summary of the standard, labeled as "the essence" of the standard, and entry points for the teacher to consider using to give students access to the grade-level standard in a manner that meets the students' academic abilities.

Figure 11.1 is an example of the professional development presentation slides that the Massachusetts Department of Elementary and Secondary Education uses to help teachers and administrators understand how to bring all students to the

1. Current revisions of the resource guides can be viewed at http://www.doe.mass.edu/mcas/alt/samples.html.

standards in a meaningful manner. Teachers are provided guidance on how to bring students to "entry points" or "access skills" for the standards. An entry point is an activity or task that gives the student an opportunity to experience the essence of the standard at his or her ability level. An access skill refers to the social skills, communication skills, motor skills, or some combination that a student may be working to develop independent of the instructional activity but that would further enable the student to benefit from the instructional activity. The resource guides have become instrumental in helping teachers understand how they can make meaningful instructional design decisions with the standards as a foundation but with attention to the student's individual needs and with the highest of expectations.

The participation guidelines developed with the advice of the MCAS Alternate Assessment Committee are discussed in earlier sections of this chapter. An IEP team is not permitted to waive a student on an IEP from the statewide MCAS process. The issue of which accommodations are to be considered acceptable evolved throughout the process of developing the guidelines. Accommodations that are routinely administered to a student during the regular academic day would be considered appropriate for the MCAS testing situation, with approval of the Massachusetts Department of Elementary and Secondary Education. The issue of accommodations continues to be a point of discussion for the statewide MCAS Alternate Assessment Advisory Committee, which continues to meet periodically every year.

The MCAS Alternate Assessment is most often considered to be the process used for students with significant cognitive disabilities. However, the reality of testing all students does mean that "all students" may include students who are cognitively able but working with unique learning needs. Students requiring therapeutic support, students with learning disabilities, students who were not provided necessary linguistic or educational support (or both) in their earlier academic years, and other "unique" learners are often not able to validly demonstrate their knowledge on a paper-and-pencil test on a given day, even with accommodations. From the beginning of the development of the MCAS Alternate Assessment, the needs of this relatively small number of unique learners were considered along with those of students who had significant cognitive disabilities that were traditionally considered in need of an alternate testing process. Our school believed, from the very onset of the MCAS Alternate Assessment, that this portfolio-based system—developed to meet the alternate assessment expectations—would be an important option for deaf students with additional learning and behavioral needs. The MCAS Alternate Assessment portfolio can and has been used to determine whether a student has earned the competency determination, which is the current label used by the state of Massachusetts for what was traditionally referred to as a diploma. For a publicly funded student to receive a diploma or competency determination, the student must pass the required MCAS exams and satisfy all local high school course and credit requirements. The MCAS Alternate Assessment has become a very important choice within the MCAS process for a significant number of our students.

The general process that is used for the MCAS Alternate Assessment portfolio involves collecting student work throughout the academic year by following a system of requirements outlined by the state Department of Education. Teachers are provided an extensive manual with specific instructions for identifying the standards to be worked on with the student, the forms needed to document student work, and a scoring rubric used to score the completed MCAS Alternate Assessment portfolio. The resource guides are also part of the educator's manual for the MCAS Alternate Assessment.

The Massachusetts Department of Elementary and Secondary Education has made a strong commitment to professional development for Massachusetts teachers and administrators. Introductory workshops on the MCAS Alternate Assessment are provided each fall. Follow-up trainings are offered throughout the school year to provide teachers additional support as they lead their students in the compilation of their portfolios. MCAS Alternate Assessment portfolios are due the first week in May and are then scored by teams of teachers, administrators, and other licensed school support personnel at a MCAS Alternate Assessment scoring institute in July. Our school has sent several teachers and supervisory staff members to these scoring institutes. They report that the scoring institute is an important professional development experience and an ideal way to get a sense of how other schools are meeting the challenge of the MCAS Alternate Assessment portfolio requirements.

Important developments have occurred since our presentation at the 2002 conference on high-stakes testing at Gallaudet University.[2] One area of change is in the length of time during which student work may be collected for portfolio items from specifically identified grade and content areas of the MCAS Alternate Assessment. For example, in Grades 5 and 8, the science portfolios require coverage of three strands, chosen from earth and space science, life science (biology), physical science (chemistry and physics), and technology/engineering. Rarely are three strands covered in a typical school year. Students are therefore permitted to collect their work for their science portfolio for 2 years, with submission happening in Grade 5 or 8.

The high school MCAS Alternate Assessment portfolios are also allowed to include information from more than one academic year. High school students may submit a portfolio for competency determination for a diploma or submit a noncompetency portfolio to demonstrate academic progress. The requirements for the high school competency portfolios have evolved over the last several years. Students may start gathering their work for their MCAS Alternate Assessment competency portfolios starting in the ninth grade. Students are also allowed to submit their competency portfolios for multiple reviews.

When a student's MCAS Alternate Assessment competency portfolio is scored,

---

2. The conference, High Stakes Testing: Are Deaf and Hard of Hearing Children Being Left Behind?, was held at Gallaudet University Kellogg Conference Center, Washington, DC, November 15–16, 2002.

each requirement is scored individually and feedback is provided. If a student has passed an individual component, then he or she may resubmit the portfolio with the passing information and updated student work that was developed with attention to the feedback provided on previously submitted work. This development has been extremely important for many students in our school. Students who previously felt that they were not able to pass the MCAS requirement have gained confidence and much-needed motivation to continue striving to meet the standards required for competency. The Massachusetts Department of Elementary and Secondary Education permits students to submit portfolios knowing that a student is building his or her case for competency. An incredible amount of teacher and staff support is required to provide the instructional time and supports that many learners need to meet the high standards. Students often must continue to work through multiple submissions. However, the unique learning needs of these particular students are best met through the MCAS Alternate Assessment portfolio route rather than through the on-demand, paper-and-pencil process of taking the MCAS exams.

The evolution of the competency portfolio process has had significant effects on our high school curriculum. Our English language arts and mathematics courses of study have been aligned to correspond to the MCAS Alternate Assessment portfolio requirements. For example, five comprehensive essays are required for the English language arts competency determination portfolios. The high school English curriculum has been restructured so all students may have the opportunity to work on these types of essays. Students who are most able to demonstrate their skills through the MCAS Alternate Assessment route have the opportunity and the curriculum-based structure to develop and refine their required five essays throughout their English language arts instruction. In addition, our high school math curriculum has also been revised to provide the hands-on, project-based assessment opportunities necessary to allow for adequate instruction, practice, and compilation of quality mathematics portfolio products. All students benefit from this restructuring of the curriculum and instructional approach. The content prepares students for the MCAS exam, and the products of the instruction align with the MCAS Alternate Assessment competency portfolio requirements. In addition, students who previously would have been placed in basic "consumer" mathematics courses have demonstrated personal strengths in areas of algebra and geometry that they might never have realized in the previous course offerings.

Another development that has affected the MCAS Alternate Assessment process in recent years is the requirement that all components of the MCAS Alternate Assessment portfolios, with the exception of the high school competency portfolios, must include data charts. Data charts are an important assessment component of instructional achievement for students with significant disabilities. A data chart demonstrating progress over time in multiple settings and situations provides a potentially richer snapshot of student achievement than a limited number of class activities. However, for unique learners who are working near or on grade-level standards, data charts are not always the best manner in which to demonstrate rich examples of student evidence. The emphasis on data charts has led our

Table 11.1. How Students Are Included in the Composite Performance Index for AYP

MCAS Test Index for Students Taking Standard MCAS Tests		MCAS Alt Index for Students with Significant Cognitive Disabilities Taking the MCAS Alternate Assessment (up to 1% of all assessed students)	
MCAS Scaled Score	Points Awarded	MCAS Alternate Assessment Score	Points Awarded
200–208 *Failing/Warning*—Low	0	Portfolio not submitted	0
210–218 *Failing/Warning*—High	25	Incomplete portfolio	25
220–228 *Needs Improvement*—Low	50	Awareness	50
230–238 *Needs Improvement*—High	75	Emerging	75
240–280 *Proficient/Advanced*	100	Progressing	100

Source: From the Massachusetts Department of Elementary and Secondary Education (2006).

school to more closely analyze assessment developments and refinements in the field of special education. This emphasis continues to be an area we need to analyze for best practice application.

Initially, because of the enormous teaching time commitment involved in compiling student portfolios, some IEP teams were reluctant to recommend the alternate test for many students. As a result, many students who could best demonstrate their skill through an MCAS Alternate Assessment portfolio were taking the on-demand test because it could be completed with less time and effort but, unfortunately, were failing it.

This issue was overcome with the introduction of the Adequate Yearly Progress (AYP) requirements. The state Department of Education developed a composite performance index for the MCAS Alternate Assessment that could be used to determine an AYP score for the most disabled students. Up to 1% of all assessed students can be included (see Table 11.1).

Even though these students could not achieve a passing score on the MCAS on-demand test, there is incentive for principals and administrators to use the MCAS Alternate Assessment portfolio with more students because the portfolio scoring results can favorably affect the overall AYP of the schools and districts. Now we are hopeful that the needs of the individual student, and not the ease of testing, become the driving force behind test administration decisions.

Our school continues to focus on important questions with respect to the MCAS Alternate Assessment portfolio:

- How can we provide our faculty with the necessary time and support needed to effectively work with students as they compile their highly time-consuming MCAS Alternate Assessment portfolios?
- How can we best collect data for the noncompetency MCAS Alternate Assessment portfolio data chart requirement when data charts may not necessarily provide the best "snapshot" of a student's accessing the standards?
- How can we provide sufficient time and focus for students working on the MCAS Alternate Assessment portfolio requirements for competency on the high school level without taking valuable time away from other important areas of study in the high school curriculum?

CONCLUSION

Standards-based curriculum reform and mandated student assessment has been beneficial in raising the expectations of all students, including deaf students. Our school's process of aligning to the high-stakes assessment requirements as mandated by federal and state guidelines has been and continues to be a highly complex, time-intensive journey. We are constantly juggling increased content expectations and assessment requirements, continuing to explore and develop effective instructional approaches to support students faced with rigorous content and assessment expectations, and striving to advocate for and deliver accessible test experiences for all students. Although we have experienced an increased understanding of how assessment can effectively affect instruction, the questions we continue to grapple with reveal the challenges inherent in enabling deaf students to validly demonstrate their knowledge through high-stakes assessment systems.

REFERENCES

Individuals With Disabilities Education Act of 1990, Pub. L. No. 101-476, 20 U.S.C. §§ 1400–1485.

Individuals With Disabilities Education Act Amendments of 1997, Pub. L. No. 105-17, 20 U.S.C. § 1400 *et seq.*

Individuals With Disabilities Education Improvement Act of 2004, Pub. L. No. 108-446, 20 U.S.C. 1400 *et seq.* Part B. (2004).

Massachusetts Department of Elementary and Secondary Education. (2006). *MCAS Alternate Assessment educator's manual.* Retrieved on June 5, 2008, from http://www.doe.mass.edu/mcas/alt/resources.html.

Massachusetts Department of Elementary and Secondary Education. (2008). *Requirements for the participation of students with disabilities in MCAS.* Retrieved April 10, 2008, from http://www.doe.mass.edu/mcas/participation/sped.pdf.

No Child Left Behind Act of 2001, Pub. L. No. 107-110, 115 Stat. 1425 (2002).

12
Marlon's Charge: A Journey Into the World of Assessment

Joseph E. Fischgrund

Thirteen-year-old Marlon stared at the fifth grade test booklet on his desk, then looked quizzically at the test proctor sitting before him. The proctor, sensing Marlon was unsure of himself, tried to remain neutral. "Ready?" the proctor signed, his eyebrows raised, indicating a question. Marlon's return look signaled uneasiness.

The passage on the statewide test was titled "Napoleon's Charge." Marlon carefully and accurately fingerspelled the first word. He had not seen it before, but there was something vaguely familiar about it. Perhaps it was the strange combination of the *e* and the *o*, a letter combination he had seen in many words on buildings in his native Haiti. But the word itself was mostly a curious string of letters related to sounds and a language he had never heard.

Marlon shaped the pointing finger of his right hand into a fingerspelled *x* and drew it downward across the palm of his left hand, making the sign for the word *charge*, as in charging the cost of something. How was he to know the multiple meanings of words spelled the same in this curious language?

The examiner thought, "Uh-oh, this is not a good start! He's already missed the basic premise of the story and he's just at the title." The story, it seemed, was about a boy who had a dog named Napoleon that had just charged through his new neighbor's carefully manicured garden and destroyed several plants. Ultimately, it became a story of redemption, as the boy made friends with his new neighbor despite the inauspicious beginning marked by Napoleon's headlong charge across the lawn.

"How in the world will Marlon's responses to this test indicate what he knows?" thought the test proctor, trying not to let his expression indicate his dismay. After all, Marlon's family had come from Haiti just 6 years ago, when Marlon was 7, looking not only for a better life in America but also for help for their deaf son. His father was a hard-working night porter at a major hotel chain, a job arranged for him by a cousin who had preceded him in emigrating to the United States. Not much English was required for the job, and it paid the family's bills. Marlon's mother worked during the day at a local nursing home where the pay was low but some medical benefits were provided. The parents' schedules conflicted nearly every day, so there was little time for them to communicate with each other and even less time to try to communicate with their deaf son. Relaxation came only on the one weekend a month when both parents were off at the same time. Still, this situation was better than the poverty and constant strife they had experienced in their native land.

Even more important to them, Marlon was safe, well taken care of, and in school. Every day, he got on a yellow bus and went to the school for deaf children about 45 minutes from his home. He seemed happy; he brought home books and papers from school, much of this material strange to his parents. On the few occasions they had visited his school, they had seen him signing animatedly with his friends. And Marlon's teacher, from what they understood, spoke glowingly of his academic progress and of his chance to go to a place called Gallaudet in the future. They were not quite sure what Gallaudet was, but the word had a French look to it, so perhaps it was okay.

The test proctor's thoughts were interrupted by Marlon's hand waving and a facial expression that clearly signaled he needed help. The proctor carefully explained, as he was allowed to do, the directions for the test, but when Marlon pointed to the word *Napoleon* and signed WHO? the proctor could sign back only that he would need to figure it out himself. Marlon proceeded to work diligently and completed the test. Not unexpectedly, his response to the open-ended question about how the title reflected something about the story was a disaster.

Watching Marlon struggle with "Napoleon's Charge," the test proctor thought, "Who is kidding whom about accountability and how in the name of Jerome Bruner could this test process have anything to do with the process of education?" The test proctor collected Marlon's papers, sealed them in the required envelope to give to the assessment coordinator, scribbled out a hall pass so Marlon could return to class, and—with the same sense of frustration and defeat that Marlon's expression so clearly indicated—walked slowly back to his office.

Like most American deaf students, Marlon was being put through this exercise by the notion that by giving the same test to all students in a particular educational system—including students with and without disabilities, students who can hear and students who cannot hear, students from remarkably different backgrounds and educational experiences—something can be determined about how much the students have learned and how well their teachers have taught them. In this way, the school itself can be held accountable for the success or failure of its students as measured by the test.

Under pressure from the mandates of the No Child Left Behind (NCLB) Act of 2001, all 50 of the United States now give statewide, standardized tests. And the stakes are indeed high. In some states, failure to pass the last test at the high school level means either that a diploma is denied or that a lesser diploma is granted. Schools routinely get their names in the newspaper for failing to meet specified goals, parents rail about alleged failure at school board meetings, administrators lose their jobs or are transferred to other schools, and the public's confidence in the educational system is shaken on a daily basis. In such an atmosphere, is it any wonder that fewer and fewer young people today want to become teachers?

And now, schools and programs for deaf students are obliged to administer tests designed for students in regular educational programs—tests written in a language in which the students have had limited experience or for some students, a language they have never heard. How have we arrived at this situation? What are its implications for deaf students, and are there indeed other ways in which we might assess what deaf children have learned and still hold their educational systems accountable in a rigorous manner? Or, has NCLB's charge through our educational systems left our educational gardens—places where students should be growing—in a shambles like those trampled by Napoleon?

ASSESSMENT, TESTING, ACCOUNTABILITY, AND EDUCATION

Everyone who is trained to be an educator in the United States is aware that the purpose of assessment is supposed to be to inform and improve instruction. How could anyone disagree with such a premise? How has it come to be that assessment in the United States is now, above all else, a measure of accountability?

It is easy enough to blame this situation on politicians, but the educational establishment—including policymakers and educators of deaf students—bears a great deal of responsibility for the accountability measures being taken by NCLB and the imposition of statewide, high-stakes tests. For too many years, educators focused almost solely on education as a process, denigrating the results of standardized tests. When parents would ask about their child's misspellings, they were told that those were not really misspellings at all but inventive phonetic spellings—all part of a warm and fuzzy process toward literacy. When parents complained that their child did not know his or her multiplication tables, they were told not to worry; their child was doing fine with math concepts. And when legislators and taxpayers demanded to know what had become of the literally billions of dollars spent on education in the United States, they were told that educators knew what they were doing, that their writing processes and new math and manipulatives would work out just fine. Besides, educators would add, standardized tests were unfair and even discriminatory. Although all standardized tests, by their very nature, are in fact discriminatory or contain bias, this fact is not an excuse to dismiss altogether meaningful qualitative assessments and rigorous measurements of educational outcomes and progress.

In deaf education, meaningful assessment was for many years almost nonexistent in many schools and programs. Since 1974, Stanford Achievement Tests, with their norms for deaf individuals, have become the staple of academic assessment in programs serving deaf children—especially in schools for the deaf. Screening tests are given, the test itself is administered, answer booklets are sent off to be scored, and results are received. However, even with the improvements in the reporting system that allow individual profiles to be generated and that have the potential to improve instruction, most school administrators will readily admit that this information rarely finds its way in a meaningful manner to teachers and that any potential to improve instruction is largely untapped or ignored.

One of the unintended, negative consequences of the Stanford testing and accompanying norms for deaf students is the widespread misunderstanding of the fact that the median reading level among deaf students of high school age is comparable with a third- or fourth-grade level for the population at large. As Marc Marschark recently pointed out, "The suggestion that deaf children leave secondary school [in the United States] reading at the level of a hearing 8- or 9-year-old is an overgeneralization. What we know is that 50% of deaf and hard of hearing children read *above* that level and 50% *below* that level" (Marschark, M., 2005). How or why we get such outcomes has yet to be fully explained, despite our penchant for testing.

So is it any wonder that we now find that assessment has come to mean testing, that testing is seen first and foremost as a measure of accountability, and that the true function of assessment—informing and improving instruction—is no longer even part of the conversation? Instructional improvement has now been replaced by discussions of test modification versus accommodation, pre- and post-intervention assessments, and evidence-based practices. The emphasis is now on attainment of scores or benchmarks, not on individual performance or progress. The ultimate irony in this turn of events is that the concept of Adequate Yearly Progress (AYP), which by definition means a process-oriented assessment taking place over some period of time, is in most states determined by a single, static reference point, namely, a score on a statewide standardized test.

Given this state of affairs, what can educators of deaf children do? How can we begin to respond?

ONE STATE'S RESPONSE: THE PENNSYLVANIA EXPERIENCE

In 2002, shortly after the passage of NCLB, the director of the Bureau of Special Education in the Pennsylvania Department of Education, Dr. Fran Warkomski, directed the statewide advisory committee on the education of deaf children to explore the implications of statewide high-stakes testing and the concept of AYP for deaf students. This still-active, statewide advisory committee, Educational Resources for Children With Hearing Loss (ERCHL) is made up of representatives of schools for the deaf, public school programs, parents of deaf children, Deaf community members, and state department of education staff members. Dr. Warkomski gave ERCHL two specific tasks. The first was to develop a set of test accommodations for deaf students broad enough to address the needs of students using the entire spectrum of communication modes. These accommodations would be described in the *Pennsylvania Guide to Accommodations* that was being prepared for the soon-to-be implemented Pennsylvania System of School Assessment (PSSA) tests. The second task was to explore the issue of how AYP could best be determined and measured for deaf children.

A subcommittee of ERCHL began gathering information about what was being done in other states, meeting with other stakeholders, meeting with the Pennsylvania Department of Education assessment staff members, and developing a response. Within less than a year, the subcommittee and ERCHL developed a comprehensive set of accommodations for the PSSA tests. These were originally published as a separate appendix to the more general statewide accommodation guidelines for students with disabilities. Later, they were integrated into the text of those guidelines. Among other things, the descriptions of accommodations specifically delineated guidelines for (a) the appropriate use of interpreters, including what could and could not be interpreted; (b) requirements that all assistive technology specified in the IEP be in place in the testing environment; and (c) the use of transcribers (or "scribes"; see chapters by Case, by Foster, and by Bello, Costello, & Recane, this volume) for open-ended passages, etc. These guidelines were available by the second year of the implementation of the PSSA and were of great assistance to school districts, special programs, schools for the deaf, and most important, deaf students who were taking the PSSA tests.

The development of recommendations to the Pennsylvania Department of Education related to the measurement of AYP for deaf students was a more challenging process. ERCHL was very fortunate to have the consulting services of two widely respected researchers—Dr. Michael Karchmer of the Gallaudet Research Institute and Dr. Marc Marshark of the National Technical Institute for the Deaf and Rochester Institute of Technology—as the committee addressed the complexities of measuring AYP for deaf students. After almost 2 years of work and deliberations, the ERCHL committee developed a document that was submitted for consideration by the Pennsylvania Department of Education. These recommendations are now under consideration by the Pennsylvania Department of Education and might also form the basis for reflection and action by other educators, parents, consumers, policymakers, and other interested stakeholders. An adapted and condensed version of that report, which could be considered for other state settings, is included in Appendix 12A at the end of this chapter.

SOME FINAL THOUGHTS AND RECOMMENDATIONS

The following are some suggestions and observations concerning how educators of deaf children can respond to assessment as an accountability trend. First and foremost, educators of children who are deaf need to stop the "not fair" whining about high-stakes assessment. Yes, giving the same tests to deaf children that are designed for large numbers of hearing children for what are essentially political purposes is indeed not fair. But repeating that over and over again will hardly change current practices. Because it does not appear that accountability by testing will go away anytime soon, ignoring it or decrying its existence are not helpful options.

What is unfair about the tests? Is it that they are based on the written form of a spoken language deaf students have never heard? If so, we must be able to articulate that position in specific ways by presenting examples of knowledge requirements that cannot be adequately responded to without having extensive auditory experience. These arguments need to be made on a state-by-state basis, with careful analysis of all test items, and presented to those responsible for test development (See Foster, this volume). Have tests that are given to deaf children in fact been checked for auditory bias in the items? Most tests are vetted to some extent to try to exclude cultural bias, but can a test really be vetted to exclude auditory bias? If so, how would that be done, and what resources would be required to accomplish such a task? (See chapters by Lollis and by Thurlow, Johnstone, Thompson, & Case, this volume.) If the tests are truly discriminatory, can this discrimination be demonstrated, and can the issue be addressed as a civil rights/disability rights bias issue?

As educators of deaf students, we need to be clear about what accommodations can really do. All statewide testing programs allow for accommodations. These range from having test proctors read and interpret only instructions to having them read and interpret questions in areas other than reading comprehension. In some states, where there are open-ended questions, students are allowed to dictate answers to a neutral recorder whereas, in other states, this practice is not accepted. Matters become even more complex because the issue of allowed accommodations for deaf students is decided on a state-by-state basis (see Case, this volume), often with little input by professional educators, Deaf individuals, or other knowledgeable people. Educators, consumers, parents, and researchers who are knowledgeable about and experienced in the use of accommodations should develop a set of national guidelines and standards for accommodations, taking into account the issues of communication background, age, use of sign language, use of auditory input, role of assistive technologies, etc. Furthermore, if we are to have any chance of meaningfully using the results of tests, it will be necessary to know what accommodations were provided, what the effect of those accommodations is, and whether those accommodations are truly such that the biases inherent to all tests are for the most part ameliorated.

In addition, we need to think very carefully about the notion of accommodations itself. Accommodations imply that there are set standards for all people and that those people with differences must find ways to prove that they, too, can attain those inviolate, universal standards. Is this assumption one that we really want to embrace? Just as communication through accommodations (e.g., interpreters, relay systems) is not nearly as desirable or effective as direct communication, is the assessment of what a child knows or has learned through accommodations—and especially accommodated communication—really acceptable? Shouldn't we be developing and implementing a validated, *direct* way for deaf children to demonstrate what they have learned rather than filtering that demonstration through someone else's (most often auditorily influenced) instrument, accommodated communication, or both?

We as educators also need to understand thoroughly the notion of test modifications as opposed to accommodations. It is possible that all tests for deaf children need to be modified. Modification is often taken to mean that standards are lowered, that content is watered down, and that a modified test does not test the child on exactly the same thing as all other children, thus making it a very different, unequal, and lesser measure of educational progress or achievement. In this case, however, the modifications that are necessary are changes to or elimination of all test items that are based on ability to hear (e.g., which two words sound the same) or on audionormative world views (e.g., asking someone to describe how they feel after a concert). In these cases, accommodations such as interpreting the question simply will not work, and thus, modifications are in order. These kinds of modifications do not lower standards; they, in fact, eliminate bias and allow students to demonstrate what they have learned. Accommodations try to take an uneven playing field and tilt it one way or another in the hope of finding true level, but in fact, the field itself remains unchanged and will always have a definite and disadvantaging slope. Modifications accept the fact that there may need to be a different playing field for deaf children—one that is not lesser but simply different—just as deaf children are different from hearing children.

New methods of test analysis and interpretation must be developed. For example, a way must be established to factor in a deaf student's communication and language history. It is now well established that all children—hearing and deaf—face some cognitive and educational difficulties if they do not have full access at a very early age to a rich language acquisition environment or are delayed in the acquisition of a first language (Hart & Risley, 1995). In the case of deaf children who are born deaf into hearing families, almost all are late in beginning the process of language acquisition (Marschark, Lang, & Albertini, 2002). For many, the acquisition process begins well into or even beyond the time frames generally identified as "critical periods" for language acquisition (Lennenberg, 1967). Can this reality be factored in as part of item and standards analysis so test results can be used relative to a child's language acquisition history?

All of these changes will call for a robust research agenda, an agenda that addresses issues such as what accommodations really do, what kinds of modifications would lead to more appropriate but not watered down assessments for deaf students, what methods of disaggregation and data analysis are appropriate for such a small number of students, what can be drawn from data that actually improves instruction, what effects bilingualism and bimodal language functioning have on testing and test taking, and a host of other issues. In developing and implementing this agenda, it will be critical to include not only individuals who are truly knowledgeable about and experienced in the education of deaf students but also, most important, deaf individuals themselves.

CONCLUSION

So, there is much to be done, and it will require concerted effort and strong leadership to implement the above recommendations and our much-needed research agenda. This leadership must include our schools, our universities, parents, our national and state organizations, and our Deaf community leaders. The tests are high stakes and for our students, the stakes are very high.

Meanwhile, Marlon will soon be taking the eighth-grade Pennsylvania statewide high-stakes test. He is a delightful young man and an eager student, and he has made not only adequate but also outstanding educational progress. Let us do more than hope that by the time he takes the eleventh-grade test, which may determine whether or not he receives a Pennsylvania high school diploma, we will have an assessment system that lets Marlon demonstrate how much he really has learned and knows, including who that Napoleon fellow really is.

REFERENCES

Marschark, M. (2005). Plenary Address, International Conference on Education of the Deaf, Mastricht, Netherlands.

National Association of the Deaf. (2002, January). NAD Position Statement on High Stakes Assessment and Accountability, January 2002. Silver Spring, MD: Author.

No Child Left Behind Act of 2001, Pub. L. No. 107-110, 115 Stat. 1425 (2002).

Hart, B. & Risely, T. *Meaningful Differences in the Everyday Experience of Young American Children.* Baltimore, MD: Paul H. Brookes Publishing Company, 1995.

Lennenberg, E. *The Biological Foundations of Lanugage.* New York: John Wiley and Sons, Inc. 1967.

Marschark, M, Lang, H., and Albertini, J. *Educating Deaf Students: From Research to Practice,* New York: Oxford University Press, 2002.

Traxler C. B. (2000). Measuring up to performance standards in reading and mathematics: Achievement of selected deaf and hard-of-hearing students in the national norming of the 9th Edition Stanford Achievement Test. *Journal of Deaf Studies and Deaf Education, 5*, 337–348.

APPENDIX 12A
MEASURING ADEQUATE YEARLY PROGRESS FOR DEAF AND HARD OF HEARING STUDENTS

PRINCIPLES

- Deaf students are not hearing students who cannot hear; that is, the effect of hearing loss is far reaching in terms of language acquisition, social, emotional and cultural development, all of which directly and profoundly influence academic achievement.

- English is a second language for many deaf students. Moreover, the second language is one that is not heard completely or, in many cases, not heard at all.

- For deaf students whose first language is English, the acquisition of English still may present barriers to academic achievement.

- Testing can play an important role in educational accountability, but test performance alone should not be seen as the ultimate goal of education.

- The most important role of testing should be to provide information that supports and improves instruction.

- Valid measures of Adequate Yearly Progress (AYP) should and can be developed for deaf students.

- Measurement of the academic progress of deaf students that is done through statewide tests alone, especially those that were developed for hearing students, is inappropriate for numerous reasons; instead, valid multiple measures should be used.

- Because of differences in language functioning, language delays, and the great variation in the development of language and academic skills among deaf students, a grade-level-based approach to the measurement of progress may not be appropriate for this population.

STATEWIDE TESTING

- The current statewide testing motivated by the requirements of NCLB by and large does not appear to serve the purpose of supporting or improving instruction for most deaf students.
- Deaf students' access to communication must be taken into account when using results of statewide, high-stakes tests. A position paper by the National Association of the Deaf is a good resource.
- The nature and extent of the accommodations necessary for deaf students to equitably participate in statewide testing programs are such that they are more likely test modifications rather than accommodations.
- The small number of deaf students tested—especially at particular grade levels—makes the use of existing statewide tests and associated performance levels of questionable validity because of the small sample size.
- Further disaggregation and analysis of the performance of deaf students as a subgroup on statewide tests must be completed for there to be any meaningful use of these measures.
- A concern exists about the degree to which statewide tests have been studied to ascertain whether or not items, formats, and test content might contain biases that adversely affect the performance of deaf students on those tests (test validity).
- An analysis of subtests should be conducted to determine which subtests are most difficult for deaf students and whether or not particular subtests might have item, format, or content bias.
- The only existing, widely used, standardized test with valid norms for deaf students is the Stanford Achievement Test.
- To date, there is no apparent statistical relationship between scores on statewide tests and the Stanford Achievement Test. The relationship, if one exists, of these two instruments, should be empirically demonstrated.
- "Out-of-level" testing, based on the student's instructional level, should be considered for deaf students.

RECOMMENDATIONS FOR MEASURING ADEQUATE YEARLY PROGRESS

- Measurement of deaf students' academic progress must be based on multiple measures.
- The possibility of using scaled scores on the Stanford Achievement Test over a minimum of 2 years as part of a system of measuring AYP should be investigated. (The Gallaudet Research Institute, which developed the Stanford-9 norms for deaf and hard of hearing students, recommends that the Stanford Achievement Test be given at 2-year intervals.)
- Performance standards developed for the Stanford-9 (Traxler, 2000), which are named similarly to performance levels on many statewide tests (e.g., advanced, proficient, basic, and below basic), should be further investigated to determine whether they are appropriate for the measurement of deaf students' academic performance.
- Statewide test scores could be used as one of several multiple measures of progress in a coordinated system such as the value-added assessment systems. The Stanford-10 could also be incorporated as one of the multiple measures as part of a comprehensive assessment system.
- Statewide test scores should be not only reported directly back to schools and programs serving deaf children but also reported to their home districts. Individual school or program scores should not be published until validity issues have been resolved.
- Use of the current NCLB "safe harbor" principles should be considered as a more appropriate measure of progress within a program or school for deaf students rather than the current fixed percentage goals for specific performance levels.

13
The Effect of No Child Left Behind at the Maryland School for the Deaf and Nationwide

Richard C. Steffan, Jr.

For many years, schools for the deaf used the Stanford Achievement Test—a norm-referenced test with out-of-grade-level options—to assess the academic strengths and weaknesses of their deaf students. The schools used individual student scores and technical manuals with norms for deaf students as sources of information that were helpful when making instructional and placement decisions in Individualized Education Program (IEP) meetings.

With the enactment of the No Child Left Behind Act (NCLB) of 2001, however, deaf children were required to be tested with the same criterion-referenced, statewide tests as hearing children, presumably to provide information concerning the adequacy of instruction in schools. The law implied that there was little leeway for excuses when the performance of students at a school was considered too far below standards. Because of NCLB's insistence on universally high standards for *all* students, what should have been a readily accepted law, considering its name, has become instead one of the most hotly disputed laws in the history of the United States, especially among special educators. The goal that *all* children in *all* grades will be reading at grade level by third grade is an admirable one, but doubt remains in the minds of most special educators that it is fully achievable, particularly given the short amount of time allowed for full implementation of the law by 2014.

A UNIQUE POPULATION

Of the 814 requirements in NCLB, not one addresses the unique needs of deaf children. For centuries, deaf children were recognized as a group with such distinct needs that they were usually separated not only from the general population of students but also from other disabled children. Not until the advent of Public Law 94-142 (the Education for All Handicapped Children Act of 1975) were deaf children lumped into the larger category of "special education" and pushed as much as possible into the mainstream. When that law was written, no mention was made of the unique communication and instructional needs of deaf children. That oversight has been promulgated for more than 30 years, in spite of the hue and cry for recognition of these students' needs from educators of deaf students. NCLB has compounded that problem a hundredfold.

Because deafness is a low-incidence disability, it is easy to ignore deaf students' educational needs on a national and state level. According to Moores (2005), approximately 50,000 deaf children receive special education services, which is less than 1% of approximately 7 million children in the United States who receive special education services. Deaf students make up one-tenth of 1%, or 1 in 1,000, of 50 million children in American schools.

DILEMMAS IN REACHING ADEQUATE YEARLY PROGRESS

When Maryland School for the Deaf (MSD) staff members first learned that the state of Maryland was developing an assessment required by NCLB, they made repeated requests for expert consideration of deaf children in the development of the assessments. Because of the rigid requirements of NCLB, however, Maryland State Department of Education staff members were unable to address adequately the requested special consideration of deaf students.

Under NCLB, states are required to develop assessments in reading, mathematics, and science to be administered annually to *all* children in the public schools and phased in over a 4-year period. The assessments must be based on "rigorous" state content standards that will result in determining what students know and what they are able to do. By 2014, 100% of students in the United States *must* show proficiency in reading, mathematics, and science. The law requires that *all* children read at a third-grade level by third grade.

Schools are held accountable for assessment results that are measured by Adequate Yearly Progress (AYP). AYP standards must be met by all required subgroups for a school to meet AYP. The subgroups are Indian/Alaskan, Native American, Asian/Pacific Islander, African American, Hispanic, White (not of Hispanic origin), Free/Reduced Meals, Special Education, and Limited English Proficient. Deaf students may be included in all categories *except* Limited English Proficient. When one subgroup does not meet AYP in a subject area, then the whole group does not make AYP.

AYP can vary widely from year to year, especially in a school for the deaf that has small numbers of students. Another concern is that the bar is raised annually, thus increasing the Annual Measurable Objectives from year to year so it becomes even more difficult for a school to meet AYP depending on the numbers of students achieving proficiency in the various categories.

Deaf children who take the Maryland State Assessment with accommodations face a particular dilemma. If a student has accommodations in verbatim reading of the test items or extended time beyond the testing protocol (or both accommodations), the state will not give that student a proficiency score above the basic level. For a school to meet AYP, students must be at the proficient or advanced levels of proficiency on the Maryland State Assessment. Because all deaf children will need accommodations of some kind on this assessment, it will be difficult for schools with deaf students to meet AYP.

One provision in the law allows parents to remove a child from a school that fails to make AYP within 2 years. This provision could have serious consequences for schools for the deaf that fail to make AYP. Sadly, some parents will not understand that the state assessments are not the best indicators of a deaf child's achievement. If a parent removes a deaf child from the school for the deaf, there is no way to make a comparison between the child's subsequent achievement in a public school and that child's potential achievement had he or she remained in the school for the deaf. One reason for this limitation is that the majority of local school systems that serve deaf children do not have a critical mass of deaf students that would increase the likelihood of their getting the special attention they need. Additionally, because of federal laws on inclusion, deaf students in most public school systems are dispersed among different schools throughout the school system.

However, in some instances, where a special effort is made to bring together at a public school deaf students within a geographic area, a reverse phenomenon occurs. In those instances, the critical mass of deaf students could affect the school's AYP, so when a deaf child fails in the public school, he or she is often referred to the school for the deaf. In that way, the public school will have a better chance of meeting AYP.

NCLB has strict requirements for reading programs. The programs must be scientifically based for kindergarten through Grade 3. Five required components of the reading program are phonemic awareness, phonics, fluency, vocabulary, and comprehension. Statewide assessments must be based on these five components. The reading assessments present a serious problem for deaf children, particularly in the areas of phonetics and phonemic awareness. Accommodations may be made for students with disabilities; however, because the tests require an understanding of phonetics and an awareness of phonemes—an awareness dependent on sensory experiences unavailable to deaf students—it seems particularly unfair that deaf children rarely, if at all, receive accommodations in those areas.[1] Such requirements make it almost impossible for deaf children to achieve proficiency in all areas on the reading assessments.

EARLY INITIATIVES BY THE MARYLAND SCHOOL FOR THE DEAF

Embracing a Public School Curriculum

Eight years before the enactment of NCLB, MSD (Frederick and Columbia campuses) was already focusing on improving education and raising standards for deaf children. At that time, MSD implemented a public school curriculum in the

---

1. In 2005, Maryland made a significant concession to the cries of MSD administration with respect to the scoring of "sound" and "sound-related" questions on the Maryland State Assessment. It was decided that although MSD students taking the Maryland State Assessment must answer such questions, the responses would not be included in the final score for the individual student's test results. This concession was a positive step forward in recognizing the unique dilemma presented by questions related to phonetics.

form of a bilingual program that used (a) American Sign Language (ASL) for most instruction and discussion and (b) English taught through various visually accessible ways to support learning to read printed materials and to write. By 1993, the School Improvement Team had been meeting for 2 years about many issues facing the school. One of these issues was the outdated curriculum that was in use at the time—a curriculum that basically no one used. MSD staff members and administrators believed that adoption of a public school curriculum would be the best way to effect curricular change.

MSD negotiated with the Frederick County Public Schools to adopt its curriculum, which was well-known as one of the best comprehensive curricula in Maryland. The move to a public school curriculum predated the 1997 reauthorization of the Individuals With Disabilities Education Act (IDEA; formerly Public Law 94-142), which required that all disabled children have access to a public school curriculum. Thus, MSD had already complied with that provision before it was even enacted.

For more than 100 years, schools for the deaf traditionally developed their own curricula or used curricula developed specifically for deaf children. When MSD decided to adopt a public school curriculum, fellow educators of deaf students said that MSD's move was bold and impossible to achieve. Today, the tide has turned and many other schools for the deaf have adopted or are considering adopting a public school curriculum.

The intent of MSD in implementing a public school curriculum was to adopt the curriculum fully, not to adapt it or water it down. MSD has been steadfast in maintaining that goal. However, MSD has added to the curriculum in areas where there was no comparable curriculum in the public schools. Added areas include the following: life-based education, enhanced learning programs, ASL, multicultural and Deaf studies, international studies, learning strategies, computer education, telecommunications, and spoken English.

The public school curriculum did not include an early learning component. Because MSD has a strong Family Education/Early Intervention program, the department spent more than a year developing the MSD Essential Curriculum for Early Learning (ECEL). The focus of the ECEL is that each child's linguistic, cognitive, social, and physical development is an ongoing process, guided by the shared responsibility and support of home, school, and community. The objectives for the curriculum are cognition, literacy (ASL and English-in-print), psychomotor, self-concept, social skills, and spoken English.

MSD used the ECEL as written for its special needs students for 11 years. However, it was determined that the ECEL needed to be adapted for use with multiply disabled students. The goals and objectives of the ECEL remain the same, but are reduced in number so multiply disabled students can more reasonably achieve the objectives established during their IEPs.

MSD developed a life-based education curriculum for students who are below the functioning level of the ECEL. It follows the format and principles of the MSD ECEL. These students take the Alternate Maryland State Assessment.

When Maryland introduced the Voluntary State Curriculum (VSC) in 2003, it was already closely aligned with Frederick County's curriculum. Therefore, MSD continued to base its curriculum on Frederick County's curriculum. Students taking the Alternate Maryland State Assessment must follow objectives of the VSC.

Embracing a Bilingual ASL/English Policy

In 1989, a document based on linguistic research at Gallaudet University, called *Unlocking the Curriculum: Principles for Achieving Access in Deaf Education* (Johnson, Liddell, & Erting, 1989) indicated that deaf students taught in ASL could make significantly better academic gains than those taught using Total Communication, a philosophy and method developed in the 1960s and 1970s that combined signs with speech. The problem with Total Communication was that the signs were often not true ASL signs. Some were ASL signs modified in an effort to represent English visually; others were completely invented to represent English words. The effort, called "Sign Supported Speech" by Johnson et al., was described as ineffective for numerous linguistic reasons, including the important fact that ASL syntax is completely different from English syntax and that there was no conclusive evidence that forcing sign language to be produced in English word order was effective in teaching deaf students how to read or write. MSD administrators, well aware of the difficulties deaf students had understanding Total Communication, decided that students would be better able to learn in ASL.

Overcoming Resistance to Change

In July 1992, the MSD Board of Trustees hired a deaf superintendent who supported both the new curriculum and a bilingual ASL/English policy. Within a year, the board had also approved both of these initiatives.

Implementation of a public school curriculum at a school for the deaf was difficult for a number of reasons. Resistance to change was the number one reason. Although everyone realized that curriculum change was needed, many teachers felt that deaf students could not meet the rigorous demands of a public school curriculum. A new curriculum, coupled with the adoption of a bilingual policy, meant overcoming seemingly insurmountable odds. MSD realized early on that the only way to make this effort succeed was to provide strong professional staff development. A massive effort was launched to re-educate teachers in areas including pedagogy, educational principles and practices, and the assessment of students.

Part of the success of the adoption of a public school curriculum was the close working relationship that developed between MSD staff members and a curriculum consultant hired by MSD from the Frederick County Public School system. With the assistance of the highly qualified curriculum specialist, MSD was able to develop a strong training program for teachers. Teachers soon realized that the ECEL not only consists of goals and objectives but also includes myriad associated activities such as keeping student portfolios, teaching across the curriculum, using content standards, and following benchmarks.

A phase-in process was used to adopt the curriculum over several years. First, the staff members were trained in language arts and mathematics curricula. Implementation of those subjects began during that first year. In the second phase, staff members were trained in the science and social studies curricula. During the third year, MSD fully implemented the new curricula in language arts, mathematics, science, and social studies with assessment in all grades. Training was then given in curricula for applied academics, including physical education, career and technology education, and art. These subject areas were the last to be implemented.

MSD staff members attended summer workshops for the first three implementation summers, which were provided by and at the Frederick public school system. Those workshops not only set the tone for successful implementation but also provided MSD staff members with the ability to partner with public school teachers. After the first 3 years, summer workshops were provided on campus every year for all teachers who could participate. The teachers recommended the workshops and received a stipend for the number of hours they worked during the 2-week sessions.

The first summer workshop in 1993 was the most intense. Everyone had to erase from memory everything they were used to in the old curriculum and instructional practice and start with a clean slate. Teachers and administrators had to discard the old method of *teach, test, grade, then go on.* The new Essential Curriculum supported a mastery learning approach to teaching and learning that used the method of *teach, test, adjust, re-teach, enrich, retest, grade, then go on.* Teachers learned the following basic principles:

- Curriculum = THE PLAN
- Teaching = THE WORK
- Testing = THE MEASUREMENT

The ECEL included five learner behaviors: (1) effective communication, (2) problem solving and critical thinking, (3) social cooperation and self-discipline, (4) responsible citizenship in community and environment, and (5) lifelong learning. Those discipline goals and course objectives were reinforced through instruction and were evaluated by formative assessments that included testing, adjusting, re-teaching, and retesting. The final outcome was evidenced in the summative assessment, which indicated that learning had occurred and the student had mastered the subject matter.

Reforming Curricula and Developing a Criterion-Referenced Evaluation System

The core of curricular reform at MSD was the introduction of an assessment system adopted from the Frederick County Public Schools curriculum. Without a doubt, this assessment system was the most difficult part of the curriculum to implement. The adopted assessment system was called the Criterion-Referenced Evaluation System (CRES) and was performance based. It had two parts: formative assessment and summative assessment. Formative assessments occurred as part of the teaching and learning process. Formative assessments were generally teacher made and included quizzes, chapter tests, expressive communications, homework, classroom discussions, demonstrated behaviors, projects, presentations, and book reports. Summative assessments occurred at the end of instruction and included school-made final examinations as well as projects, presentations, book reports, expressive communications, term papers, and demonstrated behaviors. On completion of summative assessments, a student could move on to the next level of the subject area. Depending on the subject area, assessments could be given on the student's instructional level or grade level.

The main purpose of assessment was to adjust instruction to improve learning. The CRES system used specific criteria to test students. Once test results showed student mastery of a subject area, the student could move on to the next level of instruction. If test results showed the student had not mastered the subject area, then he or she received further instruction in areas of weakness.

A rubric system was used to score a student's performance. A rubric is a descriptive scoring guide for each performance assessment. Anchor papers were developed by the students, which could be scored by them, by the teacher, or both. A score from 1 to 4 was given to each anchor paper. A score of 4 was exemplary and contained all the required components; 3 was proficient, but not perfect; 2 was approaching proficiency, but lacking some essential elements; and 1 showed no evidence of attempt. Once scored, students made revisions to their papers based on areas of need identified in the rubric score. Once again, mastery of the material was essential for student learning to occur. CRES helped both the students and their teachers know where the students were in the learning process at any given time in the curriculum.

The Curriculum Core Committee (CCC), which reported to the school's Instructional Leadership Team (ILT), was established to monitor MSD's ECEL. All curriculum matters had to go through the CCC, which met quarterly. For a number of years, the CCC has monitored the MSD ECEL action plans. Action plans outline goals and strategies for curriculum, set benchmarks, and ensure completion of goals in a timely manner. The CCC submits all requests for new curricular areas to the ILT for review and approval. The CCC also monitors all academic testing at MSD.

Accrediting a Radically Changed Program

In 1994, at about the same time MSD was making significant changes in curriculum and pedagogy, the school was preparing for accreditation by two bodies: the Middle States Association of Colleges and Schools and the Conference of Educational Administrators of Schools and Programs for the Deaf (CEASD). The accreditation process included a self-study using materials provided by these two organizations. Then, a site visit was conducted. The visiting committee met with staff members, students, and parents during the site visit. At the conclusion of the site visit, the visiting committee offered recommendations and commendations to the school. Later, a full written report was received to which the school was required to respond.

During the visit, there were many questions from the visiting committee with respect to the adoption of a public school curriculum. The Middle States Association group expressed many positive comments about MSD's efforts at curriculum reform. The CEASD group, however, expressed many doubts about the adoption of a public school curriculum in a school for the deaf. MSD stood firm in its belief that adoption, not adaptation, of a public school curriculum would go forth.

In 2003, the Middle States Association re-accreditation process began with a school self-study. The protocol for the self-study resulted in the development of goals and objectives set by the school. Objectives focused on student achievement and school accountability in reading, mathematics, and instructional technology. Action plans that were to be continuously monitored by the school were developed for each area. As part of the process, the CCC continued to monitor the reading and mathematics action plans. The next level of monitoring occurred through the ILT.

MSD's goals and objectives were fully accepted by the Middle States Association before it sent a committee to visit in November 2004. The visiting committee overwhelmingly endorsed MSD's plans and recommended full accreditation in 2005. This recommendation was fully endorsed by the Middle States Association by giving MSD full accreditation for the usual 7-year period. In 2007, the Middle States Association sent a member of the original visiting team during the third year of implementation to review progress on action plans. The reviewer was very impressed with the implementation of the action plans in both campuses.

Parents were enthusiastic about both the change in curriculum and the language of instruction. The deaf community also embraced the changes, especially the use of ASL in the classroom.

ACCOUNTABILITY AND THE MARYLAND STATE ASSESSMENT

Before NCLB, Maryland required students to take assessments that were used to judge school performance, not student achievement. The Maryland School Performance Assessment Program (MSPAP) was administered annually by the state in all schools in Maryland with the exception of MSD. MSD at that time was exempt from the MSPAP because the assessment program was geared specifically toward school improvement and, as in most states, the idea of using student achievement on standards-based tests to determine the effectiveness of instruction at a school for the deaf did not yet seem appropriate or necessary to state officials. With the advent of NCLB, however, the focus changed quickly. MSD was swept into the same accountability system as other schools across the state. MSD students were required to participate annually in the Maryland State Assessments, and their performance on these tests became the basis for evaluating the performance of teachers and administrators. The trouble with this sudden change, of course, was that when those assessments were developed, little to no consideration was given to deaf children's unique needs, especially those with additional disabilities, probably because of the low incidence of deafness,. On the plus side, the CRES experience at MSD had helped prepare students for the rigorous Maryland State Assessments.

MSD stopped administering the Stanford Achievement Test when the ECEL was adopted. It was felt that the Stanford did not meet the needs of the school in identifying student achievement. However, because the Maryland State Assessments are closely related to the Stanford, MSD has re-introduced that assessment as a pretest for the students.

In addition to CRES, which is administered for classroom testing in kindergarten through Grade 12, MSD uses a variety of assessment tools to determine student achievement. Students who are in kindergarten are assessed using the Maryland Model for School Readiness checklist. Students in prekindergarten, first, and second grades are assessed using the state's Work Sampling System. MSD also assesses students below second grade in the Early Childhood Education Benchmarks/Intervention checklists that were developed by Frederick County Public Schools.

The Stanford Achievement Test–1 and the Gates-MacGinitie Reading Test are used to measure students' performance and academic achievement. Stanford tests are administered at the student's instructional level whereas the Gates-MacGinitie Test is administered at the student's grade level. As mentioned earlier, the Stanford is also used as a pretest for the Maryland State Assessment. The Gates-MacGinitie Reading Test is administered as a part of the student's admission process. It is also given annually before the IEP meeting at an appropriate age or grade level. The test results of both the Stanford and Gates-MacGinitie assist in deciding whether a student will take the Maryland State Assessment or the Alternate Maryland State Assessment.

The Maryland State Assessment includes multiple-choice questions and questions requiring written responses. It measures basic and higher-level skills and involves 4 days of testing that include approximately 90 minutes each day for each test (2 days for reading and 2 days for math). Parents receive a home report with scores for all tests. These scores indicate how well students learned the reading and mathematics skills in the Maryland *Voluntary State Curriculum* and how children performed compared with other students across the nation.

ALTERNATE ASSESSMENTS

Although NCLB requires testing for all children, IDEA requires an alternate assessment for children with disabilities who could not pass the regular tests. The students must have significant cognitive difficulties, even with accommodations that would prevent them from taking the regular assessments. The Alternate Maryland State Assessment is a comprehensive assessment that includes an extensive set of activities to show what students learned, including test results, videotapes of their performance, and portfolios. A rule under NCLB allows only 1% of students to take the Alternate Maryland State Assessment. This rule places an uncomfortable constraint on schools with large numbers of multiply disabled deaf children.

In May 2005, the U.S. Department of Education released an announcement of a new policy on assessing students with disabilities. According to Secretary Margaret Spellings, "The new guidelines reflect the latest scientific research that shows students with disabilities—approximately 2% of all students—can make progress toward grade-level standards when they receive high-quality instruction and are assessed with alternate assessments based on modified achievement standards" (USDOE, 2005, p. 1). In April, 2007, the U.S. Department of Education issued further directives with respect to modified assessments. This development will assist MSD in making AYP for students enrolled in the special needs department at Columbia Campus and the high school Life-Based Education program at Frederick Campus. The Maryland State Department of Education is currently working on test development for the Modified Maryland State Assessment. In the meantime, the Maryland State Department of Education allows an appeal for students who would be eligible for this modified assessment. MSD, however, is exempt from the state's school improvement process; therefore, appeals for the modified assessment are not necessary.

RESEARCH FINDINGS

At the CEASD national conference in April 2005, Stephanie Cawthon of Walden University (now University of Texas, Austin—see Cawthon, this volume) presented research findings on the effect of NCLB on deaf children. She compared deaf students in schools for the deaf with those in mainstream programs across the United States. From this study, several emerging issues were identified: (a) the availability or lack thereof of appropriate alternate assessments for deaf students; (b) the availability or lack thereof of effective instructional materials to use in test preparation; and (c) the still undecided role of sign language in assessment practices. Cawthon questioned the adequacy of determining student proficiency in the NCLB framework. She also indicated concern about assessment practices for deaf and hard of hearing students in relation to NCLB policies. The most common accommodations used with deaf children that Cawthon identified were extended time, use of an interpreter for directions, allowing signed questions and signed responses, and testing in a separate setting. Although signed questions and responses may be accepted in some states, they are not accepted in Maryland.

ADVOCACY AND FAIRNESS ISSUES

Advocacy groups for deaf people, including the CEASD, have worked diligently to help the federal government understand the unique needs of deaf children. A group of administrators and advocates met in fall 2005 to address assessment and accountability issues facing schools and programs for the deaf. The forum's goal is to develop a CEASD policy on these issues that will be brought to the U.S. Department of Education. The proposal is for a "growth model" that recognizes when progress is being made toward meeting AYP, even when that progress is not occurring at the rate typically required by NCLB. For example, the growth model would recognize that students who are reading below grade level are making progress at a steady rate. Maryland does not recognize a growth model at this time (for more on use of the growth model, see Raimondo, this volume).

Without appropriate accommodations and consideration of the needs of deaf students, full access to a state's assessment program is not possible. Deaf students will continue to fall behind their hearing peers as long as federal and state governments require deaf students to pass tests that are unfair to them. The federal government has not paid attention to the cries of educators of the deaf who advocate that deaf children have communication needs that differ from those of hearing children. ASL, a language recognized by linguists as a complete language to which deaf students have full sensory access and through which much of the state's curriculum can be fully communicated, is not yet recognized by the U.S. Department of Education as a language worthy even of being included in the Limited English Proficient category of state assessments. With these strikes against the deaf child, state assessments become an even more unacceptable form of assessing deaf children's reading ability.

There is ongoing debate in the education field about "teaching to the test." NCLB leaves no doubt that teaching to the test is necessary to pass state assessments. Creativity in the classroom is lacking when the pressure on teachers is to prepare the students to take tests and pass them. Test taking requires a minimum of two skills: (a) learning *how* to take a test and (b) taking the test. For deaf children, especially those with special needs, learning how to take the test is as important, if not more so, than taking the test.

It is difficult to make a comparison of assessment results across the nation, not only for deaf children but also for all children, when every state develops its own assessments. This kind of comparison is especially difficult when it involves measurements of deaf children's success on the assessments. What one state might consider AYP for a student may not be the same in another state. Comparisons are almost impossible when there is no consistency among assessment programs. It would seem that using the Stanford Achievement Test would be a better measure of deaf students' abilities across the nation. Deaf educators may have to rally the federal government to allow states to assess deaf students with a national test. Using the Stanford test for a national assessment of deaf children would seem to be the reasonable approach, but it is not likely to happen because of the restrictions of NCLB.

There is a striking conflict between NCLB and IDEA. IDEA requires that *all* special education students *must* have an IEP that meets their *individual* needs in learning and related services. NCLB, however, raises concern about the lack of individualization it requires. Surely, no reasonable person expects that *all* children will be able to read at the third-grade level by the third grade. As admirable a goal as it is, this goal is unattainable. There are too many variables that come into play for all children to be at the same place educationally at the same time—which is especially true for children with disabilities.

The National Association of State Directors of Special Education has developed a document indicating that "the intersection of the laws (NCLB and IDEA) is not at all clear." It further notes that former Assistant Secretary of the U.S. Department of Education's Office of Special Education and Rehabilitative Services, Robert Pasternack, said that "[d]etermining exactly how AYP for special-ed students is defined will be one of the most burdensome obstacles [of NCLB]" (2002, p. 4). He further suggested that states could help by designing universal assessments to provide fair testing to all students. Pasternack's comments highlighted the idea that NCLB is unfair in testing special education students. Unfortunately, Pasternack's reasoned opinions were left unheard, and he soon left the federal government.

Assessing deaf students' full abilities is an extremely difficult task. A multitude of factors influence how deaf children learn. Early intervention has helped tremendously in improving deaf children's understanding of language. However, not all deaf children receive early intervention, often because they are not identified, because educational programming is inadequate, or both.

Without recognition of different learning styles and abilities, there can be no measure that is an adequate assessment for deaf children, even with accommodations. The federal government needs to recognize that "one size fits all" is an extremely faulty model. Requiring deaf students to answer "phonemic" questions is just one example of the government's lack of understanding of deaf children.

CEASD and other advocacy groups for deaf people must continue to pursue fairness and equity in assessments for deaf children. As previously mentioned, use of the Stanford Achievement Test could be a viable option if it were used in all schools and programs for the deaf. The test results would most likely give a better overall perspective on the achievement of deaf students both in the mainstream and in schools for the deaf.

There is no doubt that deaf students should be assessed to determine their achievement levels in core subject areas. However, fair and equitable standards should be applied to those assessments. Because of the low incidence of deafness, it is difficult for government agencies to recognize the needs of deaf students. However, that is no excuse for ignoring the repeated cries of educators of deaf students. Advocacy for appropriate assessments for deaf students should be ongoing and relentless until correctness in assessments for deaf students is achieved. Unfair testing of deaf students does not show what deaf students know and what they can do, yet such testing is happening nationwide, even though finding out what students know is one of the guiding principles of NCLB.

The NCLB legislation will come before Congress for reauthorization in 2009. With continued outcries from educators of deaf students working jointly with parents and other advocates, there is hope that significant changes could be made related to deaf students' needs.

REFERENCES

Education for All Handicapped Children Act of 1975 (Pub. L. No. 94-142), 20 U.S.C. §§1400–1485.

Individuals With Disabilities Education Act Amendments of 1997, Pub. L. No. 105-17, 20 U.S.C. § 1400 *et seq.*

Johnson, R. E., Liddell, S. K., & Erting, C. J. (1989). *Unlocking the curriculum: Principles for achieving access in deaf education* (Gallaudet Research Institute Working Paper No. 89-3). Washington, DC: Gallaudet Research Institute.

No Child Left Behind Act of 2001, Pub. L. No. 107-110, 115 Stat. 1425 (2002).

Pasternack, R. (2002, November). *No Child Left Behind: Closing the achievement gap in America's public schools.* PowerPoint presentation at the meeting of the International Dyslexia Association, Atlanta, GA.

U.S. Department of Education (USDOE). (2005). Spellings Announces New Special Education Guidelines, Details Workable, "Common-Sense" Policy to Help States Implement No Child Left Behind. Press release. Retrieved June 5, 2008, from http://www.ed.gov/news/pressreleases/2005/05/05102005.html.

14 The Potential Harm to Deaf Students of High-Stakes Testing in California

Pat Moore

The California School for the Deaf (CSD) has served students with distinction since 1860.* The school's faculty is supportive of and dedicated to the mission of raising standards and expectations for all CSD students, who are deaf, bilingual learners. Increasing academic, career, and technical education expectations and rigor to prepare students for postsecondary educational programs and employment is the heart of the CSD's instructional program. Denying a diploma to students who have worked hard and met the graduation requirements, however, is not in our vision, mission, or belief statements. The purpose of the educational system should be to reward students for their accomplishments, not to leave them empty-handed after years of study because they could not pass one test.

The California High School Exit Exam (CAHSEE) became a graduation requirement beginning with the class of 2008. This exam is being used to satisfy the high school testing requirement of the federal No Child Left Behind Act of 2001. California, like many other states, has decided that students who do not pass the exit exam will not receive a high school diploma, even though they may have studied diligently and passed their high school coursework.

WHAT IS THE EFFECT OF HIGH-STAKES TESTING ON DEAF STUDENTS?

Not receiving a diploma is a punitive lifetime sentence given to students who deserve to be recognized for their efforts. Because many companies require all employees to have high school diplomas, students will have fewer employment opportunities. It is challenging in the present system for deaf adults to obtain employment commensurate with their knowledge and skill level. The CSD Career Center contacted a number of resources attempting to find current employment information specific to deaf adults. The most recent statistics were from a 1988 research report from the U.S. Department of Education, Office of Special Education and Rehabilitative Services, the Eleventh Annual Report to Congress on the Implementation of the Handicapped Act, 1989. At that time 23.6% of deaf stu-

*The California School for the Deaf has campuses in Fremont and Riverside. This chapter focuses on the Fremont campus.

dents out of high school more than 1 year were employed full-time. The National Organization on Disability/Harris Survey of Americans with Disabilities 2004 poll showed that only 35% of Americans with disabilities reported being employed full- or part-time compared to 78% of Americans without disabilities. The Cornell University 2006 Disability Status Reports states that in 2006, the percentage of working-age people ages 21 to 64 with disabilities working full-time/full-year in the U.S. was 21.7%.

- In 2006, the percentage of working-age people without disabilities working full-time/full-year in the U.S. was 56.6%.
- The difference in the percentage working full-time/full-year between working-age people with and without disabilities was 34.9%.

This gap identified by both studies confirms that the great majority of disabled persons do not have paid employment.

CSD Career Center staff were informed that for the first time in history, the National Bureau of Labor Statistics and the U.S. Census plan to obtain statistics specific to deaf individuals' employment rates in 2008 and 2010 respectively so these comprehensive studies may make government agencies and the public more aware of this staggering problem. Many states and the U.S. Census Bureau have conducted research studies on the enormous high school dropout costs to the nation and to states. Students who do not have a high school diploma earn substantially less during their lifetimes (Bainbridge, 2006). Increasing the number of welfare recipients because students cannot pass one test will contribute to the state and federal deficit and will make the students feel they have nothing to contribute to society. CSD staff members have dedicated themselves to making the students feel proud of their Deaf identity, proud to be U.S. citizens, proud of their accomplishments, and proud of the contributions they can make in deaf and hearing communities.

The CSD staff members are concerned that students will become depressed and not value remaining in school if they have nothing to show for their work. They believe students deserve recognition for their efforts. The students' teachers feel defeated working in a system that values only an English and math test score, a system that insists that if teaching has been adequate, then 100% of students should be able to pass this exam. This insistence is not grounded in reality, and this system is simply too narrow in focus.

The reality of the high-stakes testing system is that it neither allows for individual differences nor values the individual. It is simplistic to believe that because students pass an English and math test they will be prepared for the future. Students come from different language and cultural backgrounds, have diverse interests and aptitudes, and grow up in families that value different careers and have different goals.

According to the 2000 U.S. Census, 25.9% of all adults ages 35 and older completed a bachelor's degree or higher (Bauman & Graf, 2000). This statistic indicates that the current high school and postsecondary educational programming is not addressing the career interests of 74% of the population. With the high-stakes testing movement addressing only English and math, more students are going to be turned off by the high school program offerings. Many students have a variety of desires and skills they want to develop and enhance in career and technical education areas, and these courses are usually highly motivating to them. They may want to become electricians, landscape designers, carpenters, automotive workers, chefs, graphic or Web page designers or prepare themselves for many other careers. The teach-to-the-test mentality is causing schools to close valuable educational programs that meet the needs and interests of the majority of students. It is critical for today's youth to feel a connectedness to the school program and to believe the program is relevant to their future. The educational system must have regard for individual talents and diverse interests, regard for students' backgrounds and goals, regard for students' abilities and disabilities, regard for the whole child, and regard for professions that require college degrees and for professions that do not.

The CSD faculty never dreamed they would be in a position to give students lists of all the companies at which they cannot work because one test has barred them from employment. The teachers have always believed in opening doors for students and have always encouraged them to pursue employment opportunities based on their knowledge and skills. A tiered-diploma system is needed so the majority of students who complete high school can have productive lives and be contributing members to society.

With high-stakes testing, more doors to employment are being closed. The CSD Career Center staff members contacted some companies to find out the effect of not having a high school diploma. Representatives from the following companies stated that their hiring policies would not allow them to hire adults who do not have a high school diploma: Alameda County Water District, LAM Research, Alaska Airlines, Microsoft Corporation, American Red Cross, NASA Ames, Bay Area Rapid Transit, Sears, Cisco Systems, Social Security Administration, Comcast, Sun Microsystems, Federal Bureau of Investigation, United Airlines, Federal Express, United Way, Fremont Unified School District, Waste Management, and Google.

The following companies require a high school diploma for all positions except entry level positions:

- Bank of America (tellers)
- Goodwill Industries (janitors, receptionists)
- Kaiser Permanente (janitors)
- Lawrence Livermore Lab (mailroom, janitors)
- New United Manufacturing (assembly line workers)

Deaf adults could easily perform a variety of jobs at all of these companies, but the barrier of not having a diploma will prevent them from being considered for the positions. At a meeting at CSD with a manager from Federal Express, comments were made about the majority of deaf workers being outstanding employees. This company pays well, has good benefits, provides round-the-clock interpreters for communication access, has high regard for deaf workers, and has promoted deaf workers to supervisor positions. But deaf students who do not have a high school diploma will not be able to work for this company.

Some students have transferred to schools in other states that have alternate assessments or tiered-diploma systems so they can receive a high school diploma. This strategy has caused emotional and financial hardships for families that have to send their children away from home and for students who do not want to leave their families and peers during their senior year. When students leave schools for this reason, their departure affects the morale of their peers and their teachers.

In fact, teacher and student morale will be at an all-time low because of the negative factors associated with one test controlling the curriculum. Students in particular will feel defeated, so there may be an increase in the dropout rate and an increase in the need for mental health counseling.

According to the Policy Information Center of the Educational Testing Service (Barton, 2005), the national high school completion rate has been falling. The rate dropped from 77.1% in 1969 to 69.9% in 2000. Almost one-third of the students in our nations' high schools are dropouts. By providing all students with options to earn a diploma, potential dropouts may find a more appealing educational plan that motivates them to remain in school. To motivate disengaged students, schools need programs that are meaningful and relevant to students' lives. Students must believe they will be rewarded after passing their high school courses.

WHAT IS CSD DOING TO TEACH THE STANDARDS, TO RAISE EXPECTATIONS, AND TO EQUITABLY ASSESS STUDENT LEARNING?

Even though CSD does not support the high-stakes testing movement, the faculty fully supports raising the standards, raising expectations for all students, focusing on the needs of the whole child, and developing systems to assess student learning and progress in an equitable manner. The teachers, many of whom are deaf, are highly qualified and enthusiastic about teaching. Deaf teachers, wanting our students to have better opportunities than were offered in the past, have an additional personal investment in improving the quality and raising the challenge level of the students' educational experiences. Historically, the curriculum offered to deaf students has not focused on state standards. This situation is no longer the case as teachers at CSD have embraced the state standards. The hallmark of the CSD staff is never being satisfied with the quality of programming offered. Visitors to the campus frequently state they can feel the pride of the students and the staff members, and they are impressed by our students' world knowledge as well as career and technical education skills.

CSD is a progressive school, and the faculty and support staff members pride themselves on offering a student-centered, rich curriculum to support a diverse student population. Table 14.1 illustrates the ethnic diversity of the student body.

Table 14.1. Number of CSD Prekindergarten–Twelfth-Grade Students by Ethnicity, 2005–2006

Ethnic Group	Percentage of CSD Students
African-American	14.3%
Asian	1.4%
Pacific Islander	5.6%
Filipino	4.6%
Hispanic	29.7%
American Indian	0.5%
White (not Hispanic)	40.1%
Multiple/No Response	3.9%

The sections that follow describe some of the activities that have been developed during the past 5 years to enhance the instructional programs. Nevertheless, despite all the efforts listed here, the fact remains that the possibility of *all* students passing the CAHSEE is not realistic.

Center for ASL/English Bilingual Education and Research (CAEBER) project. CSD joined the Center for ASL/English Bilingual Education and Research (CAEBER) project funded by the U.S. Department of Education. The mission of CAEBER is to provide an American Sign Language (ASL)-English bilingual professional development model that promotes effective bilingual instruction using ASL and English literacy for deaf students. The elementary and middle school departments were involved in an intensive 2-year staff development program to learn the following: (a) an overview of bilingualism-biculturalism, including the paradigm shift in viewing deaf learners as bilinguals; (b) instructional theories that are effective with deaf bilingual learners; (c) current applications and reflection practices; (d) assessment strategies; and (e) the integration of technology to promote visual learners. The high school departments will also participate in this research-based, data-driven project that is designed to increase literacy in both ASL and English.

Gallaudet University Language Planning and Leadership program. CSD administrators and teacher leaders participated in the Gallaudet University Language Planning and Leadership program. This project is designed to enhance the infusion of ASL-English language frameworks into every aspect of the school program through collaborative language planning.

Lessons based on the state standards. K–12 teachers designed lessons based on the state standards. Interested parents attended information sharing workshops about the standards, the K–8 standards-based report cards, and the high-stakes testing movement.

Professional development. Professional development activities were provided related to the state standards in all subjects; assessment of students' academic and career and technical education skills; reading, writing and math programs; the shared reading program; using books that match individual students' reading levels; teaching with a block schedule; integrating instruction; assessing mastery of standards and developing rubrics; project-based learning; backward design; instructional theory; student checklists and portfolios; student and teacher reflection; English-ASL instruction; working with students who have cochlear implants; speech instruction; and instructional strategies when working with students with learning problems. English, science, social studies, math, and physical education teachers have been given opportunities to attend statewide conferences that focus on state standards. Advanced ASL classes have been offered to instructional staff members to increase access to the curriculum.

Summer workshops. During summer workshops, teachers developed an Early Childhood Education ASL Checklist of Skills as well as programs to enhance reading, writing, career and technical education, health, and spoken English. They also identified K–12 technology benchmarks.

Assessment strategies and products. Assessment strategies have been expanded, and standards-based report cards were developed for K–8 to reflect the California standards. A schoolwide assessment plan was developed, and the faculty received training in administering tests and interpreting results.

Instructional supervision and mentoring. The instructional supervisors and teacher specialists attended professional development activities related to instructional supervision and mentoring. Mentors are provided to all new teachers and to teachers with identified needs. Teacher specialists consult with teachers to address the needs of students with learning problems.

Formal diversity services. A student diversity teacher specialist position has been added to work with families and students in an effort to close the achievement gap.

Focus on test-taking strategies and test content. CSD has always required that students take more English and math courses than mandated by the state. Summer school programs have been established to address the CAHSEE content and test-taking strategies.

Restructured high school programs. The High School Restructuring Team of teachers and administrators met repeatedly during the past 7 years to review graduation requirements, course offerings, and curricula. They analyzed the state standards, CAHSEE requirements, student achievement data, CSD's mission and values statement, the expected schoolwide learning results, the needs of adolescent learners, labor market statistics, graduate follow-up information, publications related to school reform, and feedback from the Department of Rehabilitation. New freshman, sophomore, and junior programs were designed and implemented, which were based on the Restructuring Team's study of the needs of the whole child. In addition, the new senior program began in fall 2007. This site-based high school reform initiative has brought all departments together to work for the greater good of all students. The course offerings and graduation requirements were redesigned to reflect an emphasis on meeting core curricular standards while also preparing students for employment.

Improved educational materials. Updated textbooks that support the state standards, reference materials, accelerated reader books, ASL dictionaries, captioned DVDs, library books, and books that match individual students' reading levels have been purchased. In addition, the school purchased multimedia workstations and SmartBoards for each classroom and hired technology resource staff to support teachers.

Recruiting expertise with bilingual-bicultural approaches. Recruiting efforts focused on hiring new teachers who attended bilingual-bicultural teacher training programs. The goal is to ensure that faculty have a shared vision regarding language and communication.

HOW ARE CSD STUDENTS FARING ON THE CAHSEE?

California state law mandated the CAHSEE to become effective with the class of 2006, and then extended the mandate to 2008 for special education students. The test was administered on a voluntary basis to the classes of 2004 and 2005. Students who passed both parts (math and English) with a score of 350 on each section received a certificate from the California Department of Education in addition to their diploma.

In the class of 2004, 11 seniors voluntarily took and passed both sections of the CAHSEE; 6 students passed one section. The high school principals estimated that if all seniors voluntarily took the test, probably 19 of the 44 students would have passed. Each graduating class is different, and this class had not only fewer students who had arrived in the United States from foreign countries without a background in ASL and English but also fewer students with learning problems. Had the CAHSEE been mandated at this time, 21 students would probably have left CSD without a diploma, even though they completed their high school coursework.

In the class of 2005, 19 seniors took the CAHSEE on a voluntary basis. Out of 43 seniors, 15 passed both parts of the exam (34.88%); 3 seniors passed one section (6.97%). Beginning with the class of 2005, the school decided to analyze what we consider to be a critical factor in the language development of a deaf child, so parents were asked when they began using ASL with their children (see Table 14.2). The following results will not surprise educators of deaf students: Children who had the benefit of acquiring native language competence in ASL at an early age achieve linguistic competence and milestones comparable with their hearing

Table 14.2. Ages at Which CSD Students in the Class of 2005 Began to Learn ASL

Number of Students	Parent Description	Age Beginning ASL
8 students	Deaf parents	ASL and English opportunities from birth on
5 students	Hearing parents	Began using sign language between the ages of 1 and 3
1 student	Hearing parents and a deaf sibling	Began using sign language by the age of 5 and made it their life's mission to provide their child with access to language
*1 student	Hearing parents	Began using sign language by the age of 5 but the parent was rarely present in this child's life

Note: * This student had a very unstable home life and was practically raised by the school.

counterparts As bilingual research also indicates, hearing English language learners who receive adequate first language support reach the 50th percentile in English reading in 4 to 7 years, while those who do not receive primary language support take 7 to 10 years to reach norms in English reading on standardized tests (Petitto, 2000; Johnson, Liddell, & Erting, 1989; Young, 1997). If deaf students do not have access to language at home, it will take them longer to acquire the ASL-English fluency necessary for academically-related language competence.

All of these students had access to a rich language environment at an early age and incidental learning opportunities throughout their lives. Also, they did not have learning problems.

Three additional students passed one section of the CAHSEE and almost passed the second section. One of the students had deaf parents, and the other two students had parents who began providing ASL development opportunities at the age of 1–3 years. One of these three students took the test very seriously, received consultation from the testing coordinator, studied very hard to prepare, made good grades throughout high school, but could not pass the math portion of the test. Even though this student was accepted into a university, the feeling of failure was evident. She viewed herself as a lesser person than her peers, and she was not by any stretch of the imagination a lesser person.

Beginning with the class of 2006, the seniors were legally mandated to take the CAHSEE and meet additional criteria established by the California Department of Education to receive a diploma. Ten out of 29 seniors passed both sections (32.25%); 9 seniors (29%) passed one section. Table 14.3 shows the information collected on sign language development among the 10 members of this class who passed both sections.

In the class of 2007, once again, the seniors were legally mandated to take the CAHSEE and meet additional criteria established by the California Department of Education to receive a diploma. Twenty out of 51 seniors passed both sections (39.2%), and 10 seniors (19.60%) passed one section. Table 14.4 shows the infor-

Table 14.3. Ages at Which CSD Students in the Class of 2006 Began to Learn ASL

Number of Students	Description of Parents	Age Beginning ASL
7 students	Deaf parents	ASL and English opportunities from birth on
1 student	Deaf and hearing parent who is a CODA (Child of Deaf Adults)	ASL and English opportunities from birth on
1 student	2 deaf siblings; parents use home signs and basic signs	Signed with siblings at age 6, after moving to the United States
1 student	Information unknown	Information unknown

mation collected on sign language development among the 20 members of this class who passed both sections.

Throughout the history of the CAHSEE, the legislature has not made timely decisions to postpone the exam for special education students. Students were not informed whether the CAHSEE would be a graduation requirement until the end of the school year. Because our students have the legal right to remain in school

Table 14.4. Ages at Which CSD Students in the Class of 2007 Began to Learn ASL

Number of Students	Description of Parents	Age Beginning ASL
11 students	Deaf parents	ASL and English opportunities from birth on
1 student	Deaf (native signer) and hearing parent	ASL and English opportunities from birth on
3 students	Hearing parents (fluent signers)	ASL and English opportunities from birth on
1 student	Hearing parents	Infant program used SEE signs; at age 3 years, began combining SEE with ASL; family currently signs and combines SEE with ASL
1 student	Hearing parents	Infant program used SEE signs; parents began learning ASL when student was age 12 years
3 students	Information unknown	Information unknown

until they are age 22, before the CAHSEE, many of our bilingual learners took advantage of the opportunity to advance their learning and employment preparation training by requesting 5- or 6-year individual education and individual transition plans. They participated in CSD's comprehensive academic and employment preparation programs. During the past 4 years (2004–2007), the collective fears of students (and their parents) that were related to not receiving a diploma influenced their decision to leave school at the end of 4 years. Taking the risk of remaining in school and possibly not receiving a diploma was too great. This trend resulted in many students returning to their hometowns unprepared to transition to employment or postsecondary education.

WHAT HAS CSD DONE TO ADDRESS TEST DISCRIMINATION ISSUES?

CSD has always prided itself on empowering our students to speak up when faced with social injustices. When the CAHSEE and other state-mandated achievement tests were administered, a few students reported that sound-based questions were on the exams. The students believed these questions to be discriminatory, so they informed their teachers of their concerns. The teachers are not allowed to see this test, so the students had to memorize the questions and then relay the information. As a result, the testing coordinator contacted the test publisher, and during the 2004–05 school year, the CSD high school instructional principal and the curriculum supervisor (one hearing and one deaf faculty member) attended the CAHSEE Guidelines for Bias & Sensitivity Review. They were not official committee members, but they were allowed to provide input. Four types of bias were reviewed: geographical, socioeconomic, religious, and gender. After the committee members and the CSD representatives reviewed the actual test questions, it was recommended that a disability bias category be added to address the number of questions that were sound-based and vision-based as well as those that discriminated against other disability groups. Even though some questions were not eliminated for the class of 2006, the school hopes that the test publishers will be cognizant of discriminatory types of questions. In 2006, information was also sent to the Assessment Division at the California Department of Education about test discrimination issues related to sound-based questions on the state-mandated achievement tests. The school has not received a response addressing our concerns.

This type of discrimination is prevalent with almost all achievement testing. The California Subject Examination for Teachers (CSET) multiple subjects test requires prospective elementary teachers who are deaf to pass a music section of the test. Candidates for the multiple subjects credential must demonstrate a basic fluency with the elements of music such as pitch, rhythm, and timbre, and music concepts including music notation. This requirement is blatant discrimination.

CSD's response to high-stakes testing during the past 4 years was to make presentations advocating for a tiered-diploma system. Parents and staff members made presentations on this issue to the school community, the parent and Deaf communities, the Community Advisory Council, the local business community by means of the Career/Technical Education Technical Advisory Committees, California Department of Education focus groups, the California Statewide Special Education Advisory Committee, and at the Gallaudet University 2002 High-Stakes Testing Conference. Parents met with legislative members and California Department of Education staff members. Despite our efforts, the California Department of Education does not support the tiered diploma concept. In 2008, all students in California will be required to pass the CAHSEE to be granted a high school diploma.

WHERE DO EMPLOYMENT PREPARATION AND TRANSITION FIT INTO HIGH SCHOOL?

CSD believes that in addition to providing students with the core academic courses, schools should also be responsible for preparing students for employment and community involvement. The Career Technical Education department offers the following employment preparation opportunities to students:

- Students can participate in an exploratory technical education program so they can sample a variety of classes to increase awareness of interests, aptitudes, and occupational awareness.
- Career/Technical Education classes in auto body technology, business office technology (including computer service repair and Web design), construction technology, graphic technology (including yearbook), food education and service training, health careers, horticulture and the environment, and woodworking technology. Six of the programs received program certification by the California Department of Education and were identified as programs of excellence. Funding is provided for updated equipment, technology, and instructional materials to ensure that students and programs meet current industry standards. Career/Technical Education checklists have been developed so students can show the skills they possess to prospective employers, Department of Rehabilitation counselors, community and junior colleges, job training programs, or trade schools.
- Student organizations have been created to promote citizenship and foster leadership opportunities, and these experiences are highly motivating to students. Students studying business office technology create and manage the CSD Web page; students studying food education and service manage the school's Mocha Café and perform catering activities; students studying graphic technology supervise the yearbook staff and create the school's annual yearbook; students studying horticulture and the environment participate in Future Farmers of America activities; and students studying woodworking and construction technology build the set for the annual spring play and work on special projects. The Academic Bowl, Robotics Club, and International Studies are other examples of student organizations. The high school principal visited Gallaudet University and encountered many of CSD's graduates who were in leadership positions after having developed a foundation in leadership during

their middle and high school years. The principal returned to CSD bursting with pride about the accomplishments of our students.

- The career exploration class, a graduation requirement for all students, promotes career awareness to increase students' knowledge of career requirements and work ethics. Students participate in field trips, informational interviews, and job interviews at companies. Also, they develop student portfolios. The portfolios highlight the students' educational and work experiences as well as technical skills. Letters of recommendation are included. Deaf guest speakers come to the class to explain how they overcame communication barriers at their worksites, how they faced and dealt with frustrations in their adult lives, and how they convinced employers to hire them.
- CTE Technical Advisory Committees are established to provide advice, support, and recommendations pertaining but not limited to instructional content, budget, facilities, safety standards, equipment and technology, current industry standards and expectations, and labor market demands. The committees are composed of representatives from business, industry, postsecondary programs, and other agencies. Students and parents also participate.
- An annual Career Technical Education competition is held so students can showcase their projects and display their skills. Judges from industry evaluate the projects and provide feedback to the students.
- Grants have been obtained to support career counseling and transition activities to assist students in increasing an awareness of their interests and aptitudes and to assist students in developing and implementing realistic high school and postsecondary transition plans.
- Work experiences are available for students. These progress in developmental stages. They include on-campus work experience, off-campus job placement or internships, and a Job Club Support Group.
- Students and families are guided to request services from the Department of Rehabilitation to support seniors in making postsecondary transition plans.
- A transition specialist position has been created to provide support to graduates for 2 years after graduation and to perform a graduate follow-up study.

CSD also has a comprehensive athletic program and a range of extracurricular activities. The purpose of this chapter is not to boast about the CSD program but to demonstrate that even though a school may have excellent programs and resources that focus on the development of the whole child, the reality is that not all deaf students will pass a high school exit exam.

ARE THE "LOW PERFORMING SCHOOL" DATA VALID?

CSD ranks in California's "low performing school" category based solely on state achievement test scores. No additional data are considered by the state related to the following:

- The number of students who take out-of-level achievement tests that cause the test scores to be invalid
- The number of sound-based or discriminatory questions on the tests
- The number of students who have IEPs that stipulate the student will not participate in the state achievement test process, a number that affects the school's Academic Performance Index score
- The number of students who did not have access to ASL or language development during their formative years
- The number of students who go home to families who do not communicate with them so language development opportunities and incidental learning opportunities do not occur[1]
- The number of students who enroll at CSD from other school districts during the middle or high school years and read at the first-, second-, or third-grade level on admission
- The number of students from foreign countries who are beginning to learn ASL
- The number of students who have additional disabilities or learning problems

And the list goes on and on and on.

Some readers will view the preceding list items as excuses. CSD staff members, however, view the items as factual information that should be shared with the public to ensure that an accurate assessment picture is painted. CSD staff members also view the items as challenges, and their belief that these children can be successful has produced some remarkable results because of the combined commitment and dedication of parents, teachers, staff members, and the Deaf and business communities.

CSD administrators and student outcomes teacher specialists spend a lot of their time explaining how the state's reported data are invalid and do not repre-

---

1. According to the 2004–2005 Gallaudet Research Institute Annual Survey of Deaf and Hard of Hearing Children and Youth, 69.3% of family members who live in the United States do not regularly sign to their children. Only 26.8% reported that they sign regularly to their children. (GRI, 2005). This lack of communication has a profound effect on the academic, cognitive, and social achievement of children. "Deaf children of hearing parents have not developed a sophisticated competence in any native language (signed or spoken) by the time they enter kindergarten. Because most deaf children are born into all-hearing families, they tend to be addressed in the home only in spoken English, a language and modality that may be almost totally inaccessible to them. Upon entering school they are consequently already well behind hearing age mates in both language development and cognitive and social development that comes from interacting with parents and peers using a natural language." (Johnson, Liddell, & Erting (1989). There is a widespread acceptance among linguists that there is a critical period for first-language acquisition and that children who are not exposed to any language before puberty, or perhaps sooner, are unable to fully acquire and use the principles of language. There also is evidence of similar critical periods for acquiring a second language (Cummins, 1980, 1981; Bavelier, Newport, & Supalla, 2003).

Table 14.5. Passing Rates of Special Education and English Language Learner (ELL) Students on the CAHSEE, 2004

	Special Education Students		ELL Students	
Subject	Number Tested	Number Passing (%)	Number Tested	Number Passing (%)
Math	35,167	10,441 (30%)	80,909	39,789 (49%)
English	38,494	11,732 (30%)	81,027	31,757 (39%)

sent an accurate assessment profile of deaf students. CSD faculty and staff members do not agree with the state's perception that CSD is a low-performing school. We are very proud of the accomplishments of our students. Are we completely satisfied with their academic achievement levels and the quality of their experiences at CSD? Never! The staff members are constantly on a mission to make the school's educational and extracurricular programs challenging and meaningful to our student population.

HOW ARE SPECIAL EDUCATION STUDENTS FARING ON THE CAHSEE IN CALIFORNIA AND ON THE STATE-MANDATED ACHIEVEMENT TESTS?

In March 2005, the California Department of Education published CAHSEE results that describe the passing rates of special education students and English language learners. Since deaf students are English language learners it is important to note the passing rate of this population (see Table 14.5).[2]

The California Department of Education State Special Schools Division distributed the results for deaf students on the state-mandated English Language Arts and Math achievement tests at the 2006 Cal-Ed conference, an annual deaf education statewide conference and they are posted on CSD's Web site in the School Accountability Report Card (SARC). Figures 14.1–4 were created by the California Department of Education, Special Education Division, Assessment, Evaluation and Support Unit.

Figures 14.1 and 14.2 illustrate that 871 (19.1%) hard of hearing students scored proficient or advanced on the ELA achievement test; 998 (24.7%) hard of hearing students scored at the basic level; and 2268 (56.2%) hard of hearing students performed below or far below basic.

2. Since this chapter was written, pass rates for special education and English language learner (ELL) students in California have fallen each year. In 2007, 12% of special education students passed the CAHSEE Math exam; 10% passed the English Language Arts exam. Also in 2007, 22% of ELL students passed the CAHSEE Math exam; 16% passed the English Language Arts exam.

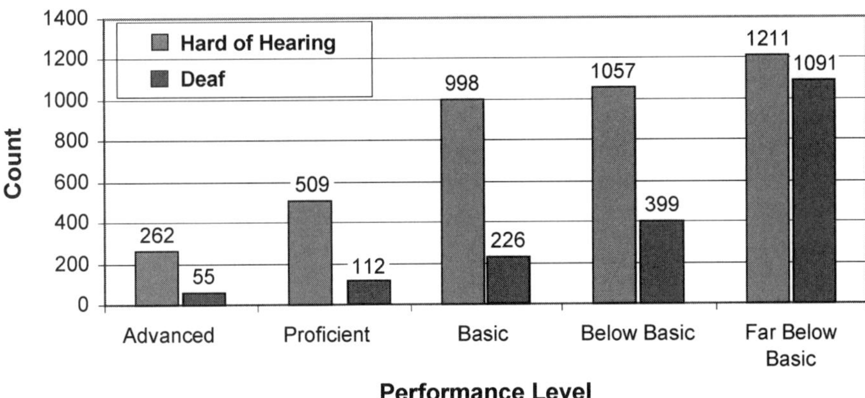

Figure 14.1. English Language Arts (ELA) 2005–2006 Number of Students at Performance Level.

One hundred sixty-seven (8.8%) deaf students scored proficient or advanced on the ELA achievement test; 226 (12%) deaf students scored at the basic level; and 1490 (79.1%) deaf students scored below or far below basic.

Figures 14.3 and 14.4 illustrate that 856 (21.3%) hard of hearing students scored proficient or advanced on the Math achievement test; 864 (21.5%) hard of hearing students scored at the basic level; and 2297 (57.2%) scored below or far below basic.

Two hundred thirty-one (11.9%) deaf students scored proficient or advanced on the Math achievement test; 294 (15.1%) deaf students scored at the basic level; and 1420 (73%) deaf students scored below or far below basic.

The results are not surprising to educators of deaf and hard of hearing students because they are consistent with how deaf and hard of hearing children have historically performed on standardized achievement tests. Despite these results for deaf and hard of hearing children throughout California, CSD staff members

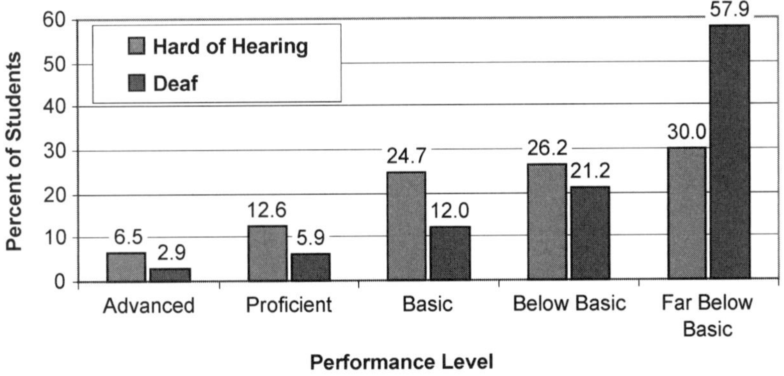

Figure 14.2. English Language Arts (ELA) 2005–06 Percentage of Students at Performance Levels

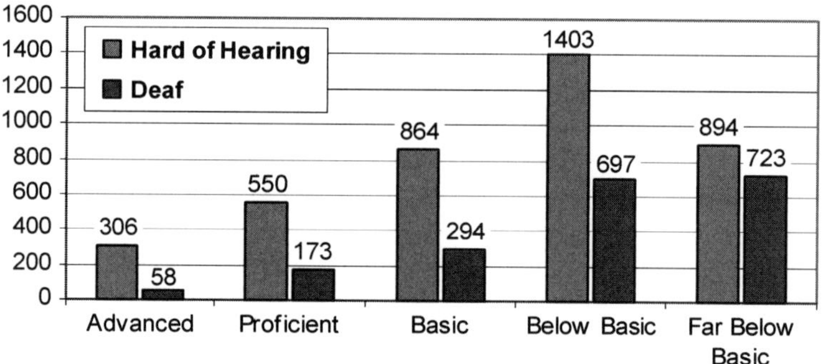

Figure 14.3. Math Skills 2005–06 2005–2006 Number of Students at Performance Levels.

believe that these scores do not accurately reflect deaf students' world knowledge or conceptual knowledge. For many of these students, using standardized tests in written English is not the most effective way to find out what they know. (Popham, 2001; Popham, 2005).

CSD staff members believe that the poor test performances of the majority of deaf and hard of hearing children throughout the state of California do not accurately reflect the conceptual knowledge deaf students possess, primarily because standardized achievement tests are English-based assessments. According to the California Department of Education's 2005–06 results, 8.9% of California's deaf students and 11.9% of the hard of hearing students achieved a score of Proficient or Advanced on the English-Language Arts California Standards Test. Deaf and hard of hearing students scored only slightly better in mathematics than they did in English language arts, largely because math test problems are increasingly posed in English sentences on tests. These statistics make it appear that deaf and hard of hearing students do not have knowledge about these subjects when, in fact, limitations in English literacy can mask students' content area knowledge. In the classroom for example, a group of students might use critical thinking skills to develop a PowerPoint presentation explaining how to design a Web page. Although they might reveal intricate conceptual understanding with a beautiful pre-

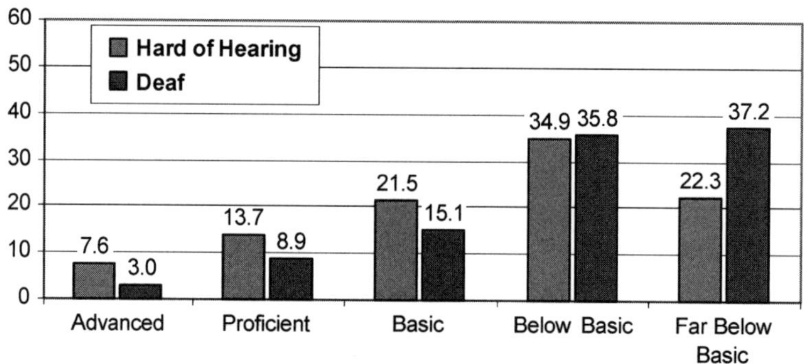

Figure 14.4. Math Skills 2005–06 Percentage of Students at Performance Levels

sentation to their class in ASL, they may struggle with the linguistic structure of the same concepts presented in English text.

Another assessment problem is obtaining achievement test data on all deaf and hard of hearing students in the state. There are 8,150 hard of hearing students and 4,337 deaf students enrolled in the California public school system; 4,037 out of 4,017 hard of hearing students and 1,883 out of 1,945 deaf students took the English-Language Arts/Mathematics California Standards Tests, respectively. Consequently, there are no results for approximately half of the deaf and hard of hearing students. It is possible the students either had parental waivers or took the California Alternate Performance Assessment, an achievement test for moderately to severely disabled students.

WHAT HIGH-STAKES TESTING LEGAL ACTION OR LEGISLATION HAS OCCURRED ON BEHALF OF SPECIAL EDUCATION STUDENTS IN CALIFORNIA?

In 2004, California bill SB 964 was passed by the California legislature. This bill required the superintendent of public instruction to contract with an independent consultant and select a committee to perform the following tasks:

- Identify options for assessments and graduation requirements for California students with disabilities.
- Identify options for assessments of California students with disabilities that are aligned with the academic content standards on CAHSEE and equivalent to CAHSEE.
- Identify equivalent alternatives to CAHSEE that would allow students to demonstrate their competency in the English language arts and math academic content standards assessed on CAHSEE and subsequently receive a high school diploma.
- Recommend options for graduation requirements and assessments, if any, for students with disabilities.
- Recommend alternatives to CAHSEE for enabling students with disabilities to demonstrate their competency in reading, writing, and mathematics and subsequently receive a high school diploma.
- Recommend an alternative diploma if the recommended options with respect to graduation requirements or assessments or alternatives to CAHSEE are not equivalent to the graduation requirements and assessments for nondisabled students.
- Provide a summary of alternative graduation requirements from other states that have a high-stakes examination as a condition of graduation.

The CSD high school instructional principal was selected to participate on the committee.

Per the SB 964 mandate, the recommendations that were developed focus only on students with disabilities. However, the Advisory Panel strongly expressed the concern that the full range of student populations be considered when implementing these recommendations. The recommendations fall into three broad topic areas: alternative assessment formats; graduation requirements; and diploma options.

ALTERNATIVE ASSESSMENT FORMATS

Recommendation 1: While several alternative assessment formats (with and without accommodations) hold promise as viable alternatives/supplements to CAHSEE, none has met sufficient technical or feasibility standards for full-scale implementation in California as an equivalent alternative to CAHSEE. Therefore none should be implemented until evidence is available that their implementation will meet standards of equivalence and have incremental validity relative to CAHSEE for students with disabilities.

Recommendation 2: Criteria for determining when alternative assessment formats are ready for statewide high-stakes implementation need to be specified.

Recommendation 3: The California Department of Education (CDE) should develop and implement a focused research agenda on the technical adequacy (e.g., reliability, validity, equivalence) and feasibility of promising alternative assessment approaches for students with disabilities.

Graduation Requirements Recommendation: Use successful student completion of coursework independently certified as equivalent to CAHSEE-level content as a substitute for passing all or part of CAHSEE. This recommendation cannot take effect until the development and implementation of all necessary infrastructure to support this option (e.g., professional development, monitoring, tracking/information systems).

DIPLOMA OPTIONS

Recommendation 1: Continue school and system accountability by collecting and reporting CAHSEE data for all students and subgroups, while delaying the graduation requirement of passing CAHSEE for students with disabilities for a period of up to two years. Award students with disabilities a standard high school high school diploma upon completion of all other non-CAHSEE requirements during this period.

Recommendation 2: If the CAHSEE graduation requirement is not delayed beyond the graduation class of 2005–2006, develop and implement a multiple-tiered diploma for students with disabilities in time for that graduation class.

Recommendation 3: Continue to offer the waiver process and certificates of completion for students with disabilities under current statute and regulations.

The classes of 2006 and 2007 were offered the waiver process. Beginning with the class of 2008, all students must pass the CAHSEE in order to receive a diploma.

In 2001, Disability Rights Advocates filed a class action lawsuit in Alameda County (*Chapman et al. v. California Dept. of Education et al.*). The suit contended that CDE failed to provide an alternate test or assessment for students with disabilities. The case was settled in 2005 with both parties reaching a temporary settlement that exempted pupils with disabilities in the class of 2006 and 2007 from the CAHSEE graduation requirement if they met the following criteria:

- The pupil has an IEP or a Section 504 plan on or before 2005.
- The student is on a diploma track for graduation in 2006 or 2007.
- The student has completed or will complete all state and local graduation requirements.
- The student has taken the exam at least twice beyond tenth grade, including at least once with the accommodations, modifications, or both during the student's senior year and did not receive a score of at least 350 on either part of the examination.
- The student or parent or guardian have acknowledged in writing that the student is entitled to receive a free, appropriate public education up to age 22 or until the student receives a diploma.

In addition, the ruling requires school districts to provide students with disabilities opportunities to participate in remedial courses or supplemental instruction designed to assist them in successfully passing the CAHSEE. A temporary settlement was reached on August 26, 2005, by both parties. Under the terms of the settlement, a procedure was established for certain students with disabilities in the class of 2006 to be excused from the requirement of passing the CAHSEE as a condition of receiving a high school diploma if legislation is signed to support the recommendations listed above. The governor of California vetoed legislation related to this agreement, so this court case will resume.

California bill SB 586 (Senator Romero) proposed to exempt pupils with disabilities in the classes of 2006 and 2007 from the CAHSEE in accordance with the terms in the Chapman case described above. The rationale was that (a) the number of special education students at risk of failing the CAHSEE and being denied a diploma is between 15,000 and 20,000 in the class of 2006, (b) the CAHSEE is not an appropriate assessment for these students to demonstrate their knowledge of concepts and standards, and (c) the California superintendent of public instruction needs to collect adequate data for evaluating the effect of the CAHSEE on the special education population. Until that task is accomplished, students with disabilities should not be denied a diploma. The governor vetoed SB 586.

WHAT WOULD BE THE MOST BENEFICIAL LEGISLATION TO SUPPORT DEAF STUDENTS?

If legislators were to pass truly beneficial legislation to support deaf students, it would include legislation to promote tiered diplomas so recognition is bestowed on all graduates. This system would reward all students who successfully complete a high school course of study with a diploma so they would not be barred from future employment opportunities. This plan would support disabled students (not including the moderately to severely disabled students who are participating in alternate curriculum programs) as well as other nondisabled students who have passed the required courses to earn a diploma, but who are unable to pass one test.

A tiered-diploma system is used in other states, including Arkansas, Delaware, New Mexico, and Virginia. The system could be designed so students who pass the high school course of study and pass the high school exit exam could receive a diploma with a seal of recognition on the diploma and a notation on the student's transcript indicating that the student graduated with honors. Students who pass the high school course of study but do not pass the high school exit exam could receive a diploma so they are not prevented from seeking employment at companies where they may have the opportunity for upward mobility.

Second, truly beneficial legislation would require parents of all deaf infants to learn ASL so these children will have a strong language foundation at an early age and incidental learning opportunities throughout their lives. Approximately 90% of deaf children have hearing parents (Rawlings, 1973; Karchmer, Trybus, & Paquin, 1978; GRI, 2005). Many deaf children are unable to acquire the naturally occurring spoken language of their homes because they do not hear it, and they are not exposed to sign language. This lack of language prevents them from fully participating in family member interactions that are crucial to their linguistic, cognitive, and social development. They do not develop a strong linguistic base with which to express themselves (Erting & Pfau, 1999). Generally, this group of deaf children enters school linguistically, cognitively, and experientially well behind their hearing peers who have had the benefit of acquiring native language competence within their home environments (Griffith, Johnson, & Dastoli, 1985). Exposure to sign language in the home reverses this effect as seen from the results reported by Ahlgren (1994), Mahshie (1995), Takala, Kuusela, and Pekka-Takala (2000), and Gibson, Small, and Mason (1997). Their research has shown that when deaf children with hearing parents are exposed to sign language at an early age, they do achieve linguistic competence and milestones comparable with their hearing counterparts.

The educational, societal, and political issues that schools face today are complex. Having one academic test determine whether or not students will receive a diploma is not a viable solution. This solution significantly reduces career opportunities and the quality of life for deaf students and other students in the state of California.

REFERENCES

Ahlgren, I. (1994). Bilingualism in deaf education: Proceedings of the International Conference on Bilingualism in Deaf Education, Stockholm, Sweden. Vol. 27, *International studies on sign language and communication of the deaf.* Hamburg, Germany: Signum-Verlag.

Bainbridge, W. L. (2006). High school dropouts cost nation billions in lost wages and taxes. *Florida Times.* April 15.

Barton, P. E. (2005). *One-third of a nation: Rising dropout rates and declining opportunities.* Princeton, NJ: Policy Information Center, Educational Testing Service.

Bauman, K. J., & Graf, N. L. (2003). *U.S. Census Bureau: Educational attainment: 2000.* Retrieved on June 6, 2008, from http://www.census.gov/prod/2003pubs/c2kbr-24.pdf.

Bavelier, D., Newport, E., Supalla, T. (2003). Children need natural languages, signed or spoken. *Cerebrum, 5,* 19–32.

Cornell University Rehabilitation Research and Training Center on Disability Demographic and Statistics. (2007). *2006 disability status report.* Ithaca, NY: Cornell University.

Cummins, J. (1980). The entry and exit fallacy in bilingual education. *NABE: The Journal for the National Association for Bilingual Education, 4* (3), 25–29.

Cummins, J. (1981). Age on arrival and immigrant second language learning in Canada. A reassessment. *Applied Linguistics, 2,* 132–149.

Erting, L., & Pfau, J. (1994). *Becoming bilingual: Facilitating English literacy development using ASL in preschool: Post-Milan ASL and English literacy: Issues, trends, & research.* Washington, DC: Gallaudet University College for Continuing Education.

Gallaudet Research Institute (GRI). (2005). *Regional and national summary report of data from the 2004–005 Annual Survey of Deaf and Hard of Hearing Children and Youth.* Washington, DC: GRI, Gallaudet University.

Gibson, H., Small, A., & Mason, D. (1997). Deaf bilingual bicultural education. In D. Corson & J. Cummins (Eds.), *Encyclopedia of language and education: Bilingual education,* Vol. 5 (pp.231–240). Dordrecht, The Netherlands: Kluwer Academic.

Griffith, P., Johnson, H., & Dastoli, S. (1985). If teaching is conversation, can conversation be taught? In D. Ripich & F. Spinelli (Eds.), *Discourse abilities in hearing impaired children: School discourse problems* (pp. 149–177). San Diego, CA: College-Hill Press.

Johnson, R. E., Liddell, S. E., & Erting, C. J. (1989). *Unlocking the curriculum: Principles for achieving access in deaf education.* Washington, DC: Gallaudet University.

Juleus Chapman et al. v. California Dept. of Education. (2001). No. C01-1780.

Karchmer, M., Trybus, R., Paquin, M. (1978). Early manual communication, parental hearing status, and the academic achievements of deaf students. Unpublished ms.

Mahshie, S. (1995). *Educating deaf children bilingually.* Washington, DC: Gallaudet University Pre-College Programs.

No Child Left Behind Act of 2001, Pub. L. No. 107-110, 115 Stat.1425 (2002).

Petitto, L. (2000). On the biological foundations of human language. In K. Emmorey & H. Lane (Eds.), *The signs of language revisited: An anthology in honour of Ursula Bellugi and Edward Klima* (pp. 447–471). Mahwah, NJ: Lawrence Erlbaum.

Popham, W. J. (2001). Standardized achievement tests: Misnamed and misleading. *Education Week.* September 19.

Popham, W. J. (2005). F for assessment–Standardized testing fails. *Edutopia.* April 2005.

Rabinowitz, S. N., Crane, E. W., Ananda, S., Vasudeva, A., Youtsey, D. K., Shimozato, C., & Schwager, M. (April 28, 2005). High school exit examination for pupils with disabilities (Senate Bill 964). San Francisco: West Ed.

Rawlings, B. (1973). Characteristics of hearing impaired students by hearing status: US 1970–71. Series D., No. 10. Washington, DC: Gallaudet College.

Takala, M., Kuusela, J., & Pekka-Takala, E. (2000). A good future for deaf children: A five-year sign language intervention project. *American Annals of the Deaf, 145* (4), 366–374.

U.S. Department of Commerce, Economics and Statistics Administration, U.S. Census Bureau, U.S. Census 2000: Educational Attainment: 2000 by Kurt J. Bauman and Nikki L. Graf.

U.S. Department of Education, Office of Special Education and Rehabilitative Services (1988 research report), the Eleventh Annual Report to Congress on the Implementation of the Handicapped Act, 1989.

Young, M. (1997). School effectiveness for language minority students, *CABE Newsletter 20* (6), 12–14.

Afterword

Ross E. Mitchell
and Robert C. Johnson

It is our sincere hope that this volume will serve to inform and enlighten readers about the many challenges that must be overcome to make a system of test-based accountability workable and beneficial for deaf students and their schools. We appreciate the fact that the No Child Left Behind Act is especially concerned with ensuring that groups of students historically educated outside the mainstream, as nearly all deaf students were until 1975, be given the best possible chance to attain proficiency in a general curriculum. At the same time, the expectation that deaf students (with the exception of those who are also severely cognitively impaired) must demonstrate their proficiency on English-based tests strikes us as problematic at best, considering the difficulties these students usually experience learning the printed code of a language they cannot hear.

One major reason politicians value testing is because externally imposed tests are supposed to eliminate an information asymmetry between the public (including policymakers) and schools (McDonnell, 2005). In other words, in the absence of testing, schools have monopoly control over such indicators of student learning as grades and, therefore, cannot be held accountable for how well or poorly students *really* are learning. But as Michael Jones (this volume) documents at length, politicians unfortunately rarely understand the complex on-the-ground reality of test-based accountability for deaf students. And with the exception of states like South Carolina (Foster, this volume), state departments of education have not fully explored and developed approaches to assessment that are standards-based, technically strong, and reflective of educational practices appropriate for this and other special populations.

There is no doubt that state and federal test-based accountability has transformed public schooling, including deaf education, over the last two decades. As several state, district, and school officials have noted, the general curriculum is no longer only for hearing students; deaf students are to receive instruction in the general curriculum and must be prepared for standards-based tests as well. Moreover, teachers are to identify "entry points" into the general curriculum for students with additional disabilities (Bello et al., this volume). Though not necessarily with the same quality or consistency from state to state, a tremendous effort has been and continues to be made to fit deaf education into state and federal accountability systems.

In other words, there has been tremendous progress within schools in creating the *opportunity to learn* the material that is supposed to be learned in a system of test-based accountability. However, as we address later, some significant opportunity to learn issues still loom large. Also, true accountability assumes that the *opportunity to demonstrate learning* is valid and reliable, but there are legitimate reasons to doubt that such inferences from test performance necessarily hold true in the case of deaf students. Also, for accountability to serve the development of improved curriculum and instruction, assessment needs to provide an *opportunity to diagnose and treat learning difficulties.* We shall close with a brief comment on how all systems of test-based accountability currently fail to provide this final opportunity and how this problem might be rectified.

The fit between deaf education and test-based accountability systems is still imperfect. The first major source of disjuncture we address is the testing itself, which, at its worst, fails to provide the opportunity to demonstrate learning, and, at its best, leaves considerable room for improved opportunities to demonstrate learning. The second disjuncture arises in the consideration of when and how to hold schools accountable for deaf students' learning; there are still important opportunity-to-learn issues in the delivery of special education to deaf students. The final disjuncture, which afflicts the entire system of accountability, regardless of deafness among students, is the information quality derived from accountability assessments. The information density provided by a student's responses to test items is too low to provide an adequate diagnosis of the student's learning difficulties, let alone to help determine how instruction should be modified to remedy the problem manifested by erroneous answers.

In the case of the testing itself, the assumptions underlying most standards-based and standardized tests simply do not hold true for deaf students. The most important failure is the assumption of comprehensibility. Tests are developed in English on the presumption that, even by the third grade, most students are reasonably fluent in the language and are able to associate written words with spoken words. In no case is there a state, district, or school that provides evidence for public accountability based on administering a direct assessment of deaf students in American Sign Language (ASL), the language in which the students who would take such a test ostensibly receive their instruction and through which they communicate their understanding. Instead, the best options offered to date (and not offered in most states), are when English language tests are carefully and uniformly translated into ASL and, when cognitively inaccessible or patently inappropriate items are present (e.g., asking deaf students to identify sounds typically heard at a beach), substitute items measuring the same construct are found or developed to overcome unmistakable biases.

Of course, English reading and writing fluency is a target outcome for deaf students as well as hearing students, but it is the fundamental lack of ready access to English, an inaccessibility more profound than that experienced by non-English-speaking immigrant children, that gives rise to this special education category. We wish to emphasize that in the absence of cognitive disabilities, it is not the capacity for abstract or sophisticated thought that is disabled by deafness but the opportunity to acquire English and all that is communicated through English with the same access and ease as those who can hear.

The absence of direct assessment in ASL is what gives rise to several of the test administration burdens and debates that surround deaf students' participation in accountability testing. Translation of an assessment instrument from its original source language to a target language (in this case, English to ASL) is guaranteed to introduce difficulties that may be avoided by developing both language versions simultaneously (see Tanzer, 2005). A parallel ASL assessment presented in a visual medium (e.g., videotape, DVD, or streaming video) would impose no additional preparation time for staff. Also, there would be no added threats to test security, no fear of incompetent or idiosyncratic signed interpretations, and no need for interpreter guidelines. Skilled personnel would not have to be reassigned to present the test. There would be no need for a bilingual dictionary or thesaurus. Extended time and other accommodations related to processing an English-based test would no longer be required, though an assessment in ASL might still require more time to administer. Finally, by developing ASL and English tests in parallel, ridiculous expectations about item equivalence between languages could be overcome. In particular, visual concepts like parallel lines and geometric shapes become recognizable as vocabulary rather than mathematics (e.g., "identify which shape is a triangle" is visual vocabulary; "identify which shape is a plane figure for which its interior angles sum to 180 degrees" is mathematics).

At the same time, a direct assessment in ASL does not eliminate all identified concerns. When it comes to tests of English language proficiency itself (e.g., reading comprehension), students who cannot respond in written English or identify the correct English word(s) or sentence(s) among a set of response choices find that they may require the assistance of a dictionary, thesaurus, interpreter, or scribe. Clearly, in cases such as these, getting at what these students know must happen in a manner that may differ substantially from any standardized assessment protocol. Often, the need for response supports at this level is viewed as modification that—even if the logistics of cost, personnel, equipment, space, and time were manageable—would invalidate test scores. This creates a peculiar and corrosive condition wherein getting the best access to what students know is not legitimate in the eyes of the state, while participating in an unmodified and state-approved testing condition can be a worthless assessment exercise (i.e., one that provides essentially no information about student learning) for students, teachers, and schools alike, not to mention parents and the greater public.

When and how to hold schools accountable for deaf students' learning remains a problem regardless of how test development and implementation issues are resolved. The emphasis on the unique needs and circumstances of the child receiving special education, formalized in the Individualized Education Program (IEP), creates an added layer of complexity for schools and programs serving deaf students. In particular, an agreed-upon plan that is purported to meet the needs of the deaf child may, in fact, be more strongly aligned with the interests of the child's parents, teachers, and school administrators than with an unbiased assessment of the child's needs.

Even allowing for substantial uncertainty in the best initial course of action, once it is recognized that the IEP has failed, the deaf child is as likely to be transferred to a new school capable of delivering an alternative program of instruction—often a state school for the deaf—as to have a substantial IEP revision enacted at the child's current school. When this move occurs, years of capitalized failure are transferred to the receiving school. The probability that the receiving school can overcome the early failure in a year is quite low. The likelihood that the receiving school will effectively bring the child up to a proficient level before reaching the maximum age allowable—assuming the student will persist rather than drop out or take a certificate of completion in lieu of a high school diploma—is unknown. In other words, school accountability for students in special education, especially if these students are mobile, should be considered very carefully. Attributing failure to a school or program can be a rather murky problem that is not justly handled by setting arbitrary timelines for transfer of responsibility for student performance. Just as it is not sensible to absolve the sending school of all responsibility and leave the receiving school alone to shoulder the blame for a student's poor performance, it is similarly not reasonable to perpetually hold the sending school responsible and leave the receiving school free of any formal accountability (see Bosso; Cawthon; Fischgrund; Jones; Steffan, this volume).

Finally, even if states were to create ways to get the results from summative assessments back to parents and teachers in time to inform instruction plans for the following year, the information density would be too low to facilitate effective planning. As M. David Miller (2007) has demonstrated, even the very best achievement tests ever developed would have to be doubled in length relative to current testing protocols to provide instructionally useful feedback. And given the fact that many accountability assessments are not of this premium quality (i.e., their reliability is still good, but not the very highest), these standards-based tests might have to be as much as ten times longer to provide such information.

In order to address the inadequacy of information in current accountability assessment systems for instructional purposes, we suggest that the secure test approach be abandoned in exchange for overwhelmingly large and public test item pools. That is, since it is very unlikely that any school or program will cover every possible spelling word, mathematics problem, novel, short story, science problem, or history topic in its state-adopted or state-approved curriculum materials, and since these words, problems, stories, topics, etc., should serve as legitimate items on standards-based tests, it should be similarly possible to create an overwhelmingly large pool from which to randomly select items for each year's assessment. Of course, there are technical challenges related to establishing reliability and comparable difficulty, especially in states that wish to have their own uniquely designed assessment systems (except for the largest states, it would be difficult to establish item parameters for such a large item pool), but there would be no doubt about what would possibly appear on the state test. Representative items could be used for assessment throughout the year, and the feedback from these intermediate results could be trusted to fairly correspond with the learning and performance requirements of the year-end summative accountability test. Though the idea of national tests does not appeal to most states, when it comes to special populations, especially low-incidence populations like deaf students, it is only at this scale that item characteristics can be examined to ensure that test validity and reliability hold true for *all* students who participate in statewide testing programs.

Other solutions to assessment dilemmas posed by special student populations will surely be proposed and experimented with as long as statewide or national assessments continue to be used to measure achievement levels in this age of accountability. Many chapters in this book contain hints of possible solutions to which we have added some in this afterword. But attention should also be given here to the importance of nurturing reciprocal rather than adversarial relationships between administrators of schools serving deaf students and staff in state departments of education.

In some states, individuals charged with implementing assessment programs appear to be driven by preconceptions that do not always square with the experience of educators familiar with special populations. A striking example of this was presented by Jon Levy at the 2002 Gallaudet University conference concerning high stakes testing and deaf students. Levy, principal of a regional program for deaf students at University High School in Orange County, California, said that during a workshop with representatives of California's State Department of Education he had informed the officials that students in his program were reading at fifth- to seventh-grade levels. This was significantly higher than national norms for deaf students, and he had reason to be proud of this statistic. He had then expressed concern that a new mandate requiring that all students in California pass tests in English and math at a tenth-grade level might prevent 80 to 85% of California's deaf students from receiving high school diplomas, greatly reducing their options for future employment or postsecondary education. Levy described the officials' reaction this way: "The response was clear, stark, and very upsetting. They said to me that it is you administrators and your teachers of the deaf who are at fault. If you simply raised your standards and had higher expectations for these deaf children, they would be reading at the twelfth-grade level and passing the High School Exit Exam" (Johnson, 2003, p. 7).

We concur with Pat Moore (this volume) and testing scholar Stuart Yeh (see, for example, Yeh, 2008) that some states, like California, need to adopt a tiered diploma system to provide proper recognition of and incentives for the highest academic achievements attainable by *all* students, including deaf students. As reviewed by Yeh, many standards-based high-stakes exit exams have little or no external validity; that is, much of their test content is irrelevant to the knowledge and training needs of employers who require a high school diploma for employment eligibility. More importantly, such exit exams do not play the incentive role policymakers intended. The quantum leap from minimum competency testing to world-class standards appears to have taken away the incentive for low achievers to meet the performance mark consistent with the social and economic meaning of the high school diploma in this country. All of the growth and leading success in employment and higher education among deaf students reported from the National Longitudinal Transition Study 2 (Wagner, Newman, Cameto, & Levine, 2005) may stall or reverse if current policies are left unchanged in several states.

Although some of our chapter authors, professionally involved in deaf education for decades, express deep frustrations with a lack of understanding among government officials in their state, this book contains signs of hope that assertive, persistent, well-meaning efforts by school personnel can lead to constructive working relationships with state departments of education, fostering collegial exchanges and joint efforts to make assessments of deaf students fairer and more valid (see especially Jones; Bosso; Bello, Costello, & Recane; Fischgrund; and Foster, this volume). We sincerely hope that state and federal officials will read this book and do their part to open a dialogue with experienced teachers and administrators in schools or programs for deaf students to learn what those who understand this student population's difficulties have to say about policies, procedures, and test forms that are not working well. We hope that astute readers can pick up many ideas here concerning work that is being carried out in some states that is helping make the curriculum and tests more accessible to deaf students—hence, fairer and more valid for measuring what deaf students do or do not know.

REFERENCES

Johnson, R. C. (2003). High stakes testing conference held at Gallaudet University. *Research at Gallaudet, 2003* (Fall), 1–11.

McDonnell, L. (2005). Assessment and accountability from the policymaker's perspective. In J. L. Herman & E. H. Haertel (Eds.), *Uses and misuses of data for educational accountability and improvement: The 104th yearbook of the National Society for the Study of Education,* Part 2 (pp. 35–54). Chicago: National Society for the Study of Education.

Miller, M. D. (2007, January). *School improvement and educational accountability.* Paper presented at the 2007 CRESST Conference: The Future of Test-based Educational Accountability, University of California, Los Angeles.

Tanzer, N. K. (2005). Developing tests for use in multiple languages and cultures: A plea for simultaneous development. In R. K. Hambleton, P. F. Merenda, & C. D. Spielberger (Eds.), *Adapting educational and psychological tests for cross-cultural assessment* (pp. 235–264). Mahwah, NJ: Lawrence Erlbaum.

Wagner, M., Newman, L., Cameto, R., & Levine, P. (2005). *Changes over time in the early postschool outcomes of youth with disabilities.* A report of findings from the National Longitudinal Transition Study (NLTS) and the National Longitudinal Transition Study-2 (NLTS2). Menlo Park, CA: SRI International.

Yeh, S. S. (2008, January 28). Raising the bar and reducing failure on state-mandated exit exams. (ID Number: 14939). *Teachers College Record.* Retrieved April 23, 2008, from http://www.tcrecord.org/PrintContent.asp?ContentID=14939.

Contributors

Michael J. Bello
Executive Director
The Learning Center for Deaf Children
Framingham, Massachusetts

Edward Bosso
Assistant Superintendent
Christina School District
Newark, Delaware

Elizabeth (Betsy) J. Case
Director
Special Needs Students Assessment–Students with Disabilities
WestEd
San Francisco, California

Stephanie W. Cawthon
Assistant Professor of School Psychology
College of Education
University of Texas
Austin, Texas

Patrick Costello
Middle School Director
The Learning Center for Deaf Children
Framingham, Massachusetts

Joseph E. Fischgrund
Headmaster
The Pennsylvania School for the Deaf
Philadelphia, Pennsylvania

Courtney J. Foster
Education Associate
Special Education Unit, Office of Assessment
South Carolina Department of Education
Columbia, South Carolina

Joseph "Jay" Innes
Interim Dean
College of Professional Studies and Outreach
Gallaudet University
Washington, DC

Robert C. Johnson
Research Editor (retired)
Gallaudet Research Institute and Graduate School and Professional Programs
Gallaudet University
Washington, DC

Christopher Johnstone
Research Associate
National Center on Educational Outcomes
University of Minnesota
Minneapolis, Minnesota

Michael (Mickey) Jones
Director (retired), Evaluation Center
Illinois School for the Deaf
Jacksonville, Illinois

Jana Lollis
Teacher
North Carolina School for the Deaf
Morganton, North Carolina

Ross E. Mitchell
Assistant Professor of Educational Administration
School of Education
University of Redlands
Redlands, California

Patricia Moore
Director of Instruction (retired)
California School for the Deaf
Fremont, California

Barbara Raimondo
Attorney
Law and Advocacy Center
National Association of the Deaf
Silver Spring, Maryland

Suzanne Recane
Curriculum Coordinator
The Learning Center for Deaf Children
Framingham, Massachusetts

Richard C. Steffan, Jr.
Deputy Superintendent (retired)
Maryland School for the Deaf
Columbia, Maryland

Sandra J. Thompson (deceased)
Research Associate
National Center on Educational Outcomes
University of Minnesota
Minneapolis, Minnesota

Martha L. Thurlow
Director
National Center on Educational Outcomes
University of Minnesota
Minneapolis, Minnesota

Elizabeth Towles-Reeves
Research Coordinator
National Alternate Assessment Center
University of Kentucky
Lexington, Kentucky

Index

Page numbers in italics denote figures or tables.